THE SECRET DIARIES OF TWO AULD GRANNIES

A Tale of Two Farmer's Wives 1882-1944

Mary Holmes

Marion Orr

Edited by
Jo Johnson

THE SECRET DIARIES OF TWO AULD GRANNIES

A Tale of Two Farmer's Wives 1882-1944

by
Mary Holmes and Marion Orr

edited by
Jo Johnson

Published by Rosebine Press

www.rosebinepress.com

Mary Holmes Diary, Copyright © 2022 Mary Holmes (deceased)

Marion Orr's Diaries, Copyright © 2022 Marion Orr (deceased)

Preface and notes, Copyright © 2022 Jo Johnson

Photographs copyright © Jo Johnson 2022

All rights reserved. No part of this publication may be reproduced in any form or by any means, electronic or mechanical, including Photocopy, recording or any information storage and retrieval system, without permission in writing from the publisher.

A catalogue record for this book is available from the British Library.

Cover by Jo Johnson www.jojohnson.uk

ISBN: 978-1-7397443-0-4

Paperback First Edition

PREFACE

THREE MONTHS BEFORE I was born, on 14th November 1956, my paternal grandmother, Janet Johnson, died at 33a Newton Street Greenock, the house where she and my father and uncle had lived. She was 73. My father, John Holmes Johnson, found three old notebooks among her stuff. They contained the handwritten diary entries of two of his maternal ancestors—a mother and her daughter. The first notebook belonged to his great grandmother, Mrs Mary Holmes, and the other two belonged to his grandmother, Mrs Marion Orr. (My great, great grandmother, and my great grandmother, respectively!)

Each of these ladies lived on farm steadings in the Kilmalcolm area of the West of Scotland. Dad's great-grandmother Mary Holmes (nee Spiers), married a farmer named Robert Holmes. They lived at the Wraes farm near Bridge of Weir. His grandmother Marion King Orr (nee Holmes), married a farmer named William Orr. (Not to be confused with their son William Orr, known to our family as 'Dad's Uncle Willie'.) Most of her life after she married, was lived at Gateside farm, near Kilmacolm.

Latterly Granny Orr divided her time between Gateside Farm and her daughter Janet's house at 33a Newton Street where my father, his brother Joe and their mother Janet lived following the death in 1930, of her husband Joseph William Johnson (my paternal grandfather). Granny Orr's son Robert Orr (Janet's brother), had taken over the running of Gateside Farm after his father William Orr senior died, on 9th January 1928.

Granny Orr records frequent bouts of what she calls *'bile'*, a debilitating stomach condition caused by reflux[1].

Both Granny Holmes and Granny Orr frequently mention a mode of transport which they call a 'machin'. I can only surmise that this was an early motor car, similar to the ones in the photograph below.

Motorcade, Glasgow International Exhibition, 1901. (T & R Annan & Sons Ltd.) Image, courtesy of Douglas Annan.

Granny Holmes and Granny Orr each recorded in their diaries, events and things of interest and significance to them in their daily lives, over a period of sixty-two years, spanning the late 19th century, and the early to mid 20th century, between 1882 and 1944.

Between the end of Granny Holmes diary and the beginning of Granny Orr's diary, there is a gap of four years, with no diary entries.

Both women used their diaries intermittently, only making an entry when they had something of importance to record. As such, they left a record, not only of their families lives over several generations, but of the times in which they lived.

Written from the perspective of two West of Scotland farmer's wives, their diaries give a fascinating insight into the transition from the Victorian to the modern era. They show how, even when cataclysmic world events such as the First and Second World Wars were playing out on the world stage, rural life continued in much the same way as it had done for centuries. Historians and sociologists will find much of interest in the records left behind by these two strong women, whose lives were typical of Scottish farming women in the years before the industrialisation of agriculture, when much of the work was done by hand.

The Christian faith of both women and their connection with the Church of Scotland, was an integral part of their lives as the frequent references to "our sacrament" or "our communion" testify.

Another diary entry reveals the spiritual interests of Granny Orr —in December 1940, she notes that she gave to a Mrs Whyte, a book entitled *"The cross in Modern Life"* by J.G. Greenhough, M.A.[2] This was a book of sermons which presumably, she considered to be of some spiritual value. Her daughter Mary who was my father's aunt, (known to many as 'Granny Black'), left the Church of Scotland to be added to the Church of God in Greenock. Some time later, Dad's mother Janet, also withdrew from the Church of Scotland and followed her sister, because she wasn't happy with the less than scriptural preaching from the minister. She was added to the Church of God in Greenock, which is how my family's connection with the Churches of God began.

Granny Orr however, remained faithful to the Church of Scotland, although her diary entries show that she broke ranks on one or two occasions, to attend meetings being held by evangelists John Miller and Norman Miller! (Despite the common surname, neither of these men were related to each other.) Of John Miller's preaching in 1939, she wrote "A good earnest speaker!"

Great Granny Holmes' diary 1882 - 1898

Preface

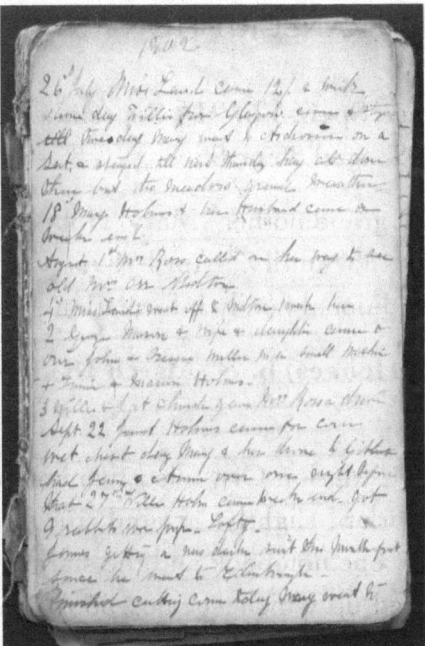

Granny Orr's Diary - 1st notebook, 1902 - 1924

Granny Orr's Diary - 2nd Notebook 1925 - 1944

AUTHORSHIP, TRANSCRIPTION AND PUBLICATION

Mary Holmes (nee Speirs) b. 21st September c 1813 or 14. d. 29th October 1899, aged 85 or 86.

My father's great grandmother, Mary Holmes, kept her diary from 12th October 1882 until 7th April 1896, with some incidental notes recording additional family information until 1898.

Marion Orr (nee Holmes) b. 7th March 1853 — d. 15th August 1945 aged 92.

Dad's grandmother, Marion Orr, filled two notebooks with diary entries. They overlap slightly around the transition period between the end of one notebook and the start of the other. (Perhaps she just picked up whichever notebook was to hand at the time!) The first diary, has entries between 23rd February 1901 and 6th January 1926, and the second, between 25th October 1925 and 4th September 1944.

In addition to those two notebooks, Marion Orr also set down on paper in another notebook (unfortunately, the original handwritten version has gone missing since my father transcribed it). She titled it: *"What I know of the family of Holmes to which I belong"* — a record of who was who on the Holmes side of her family. I have placed this at the beginning of this book, under the heading *'The Holmes Genealogy'*, so that readers can reference the identity of the people named in the diaries.

For years, Dad kept these precious artefacts in a brown manilla envelope at the back of a drawer in his grey metal filing cabinet. When he retired, he wrote his autobiography *"The Jone Cratur"*, which I published for him at the turn of last century, in the year 2000 when he was 82. After he'd written his own story, he turned his attention to the mammoth task of transcribing the handwritten diaries his Granny and Great-Granny had left behind. He laboured over them off and on for several years, whenever he had a spare moment between his not insignificant church commitments, painstakingly deciphering the ancient handwriting and typing up the entries on his computer. Where he wasn't sure of a word, he put a question mark in brackets, thus: (?) He also added his own notes here and there, which I have placed inside square brackets with his initials *[JHJ]*, to differentiate them from the original text. I have done the same with the few supplemental notes which I have added.

In 1930 and 1931 Granny Orr recorded two tragic family events. At the end of June 1930, she records the early death of my grandfather, Joseph Johnson (aged 50), from stomach cancer. Just over a year later, on 24th July 1931, she records the murder of her twenty-two year old grandson, Donald Black (my father's older cousin), as he returned from visiting his fiancé at a nearby farm. At the end of the book, I have devoted a short appendix to the details surrounding this shocking event.

It is my privilege to complete the work my father began, by publishing the diaries of his Granny and Great Granny. The original diary entries were not always written in chronological order. Sometimes, as an afterthought, both women added an entry dated earlier in the month, after some later entries. In the few places where this occurs, I have taken the liberty of rearranging the entries in their correct date order, so that the reading experience flows smoothly. I have also imposed a consistent format for the day of each month, for ease of reference. Otherwise, the content is exactly as it was written, including the sometimes-quirky spelling! The sampled photographs of selected diary pages show how the handwritten originals were composed.

My father's immediate family and the extended families represented in the diary entries, owe him a great debt of gratitude for his labour of love in transcribing the diaries and for the precious heritage of family information that he brought to light.

In typesetting and publishing the content of these venerable manuscripts, I have two purposes.

Firstly, for the benefit of future generations, to preserve as much information as can be found, about who was who among my father's forebears, before any more knowledge of this branch of our family tree is lost.

Secondly, I hope it will provide readers with an appreciation of the important place these two venerable women held within their families, of their strong personalities and sense of humour, and of the values they transmitted all unconsciously, through writing about the simple things of everyday life as well as their valuable first-hand impressions of the significant historical events through which they lived.

Jo Johnson, April 2022

---

1. **Bile:** Probably bile reflux, which occurs when the digestive liquid produced in your liver comes back up into the stomach. This can sometimes occur alongside the reflux of stomach acid and can lead to a chronic condition called GERD, (gastroesophageal reflux disease). Symptoms include severe abdominal pain, heartburn, nausea and vomiting up bilious yellow fluid and weight loss. Nowadays, the condition can be alleviated with medication or surgery.
2. **'The Cross in Modern Life':** can be read online at this Internet Archive address: https://archive.org/details/crossinmodernlif00gree/page/n3/mode/2up

Map of Renfrewshire and Kilmacolm area

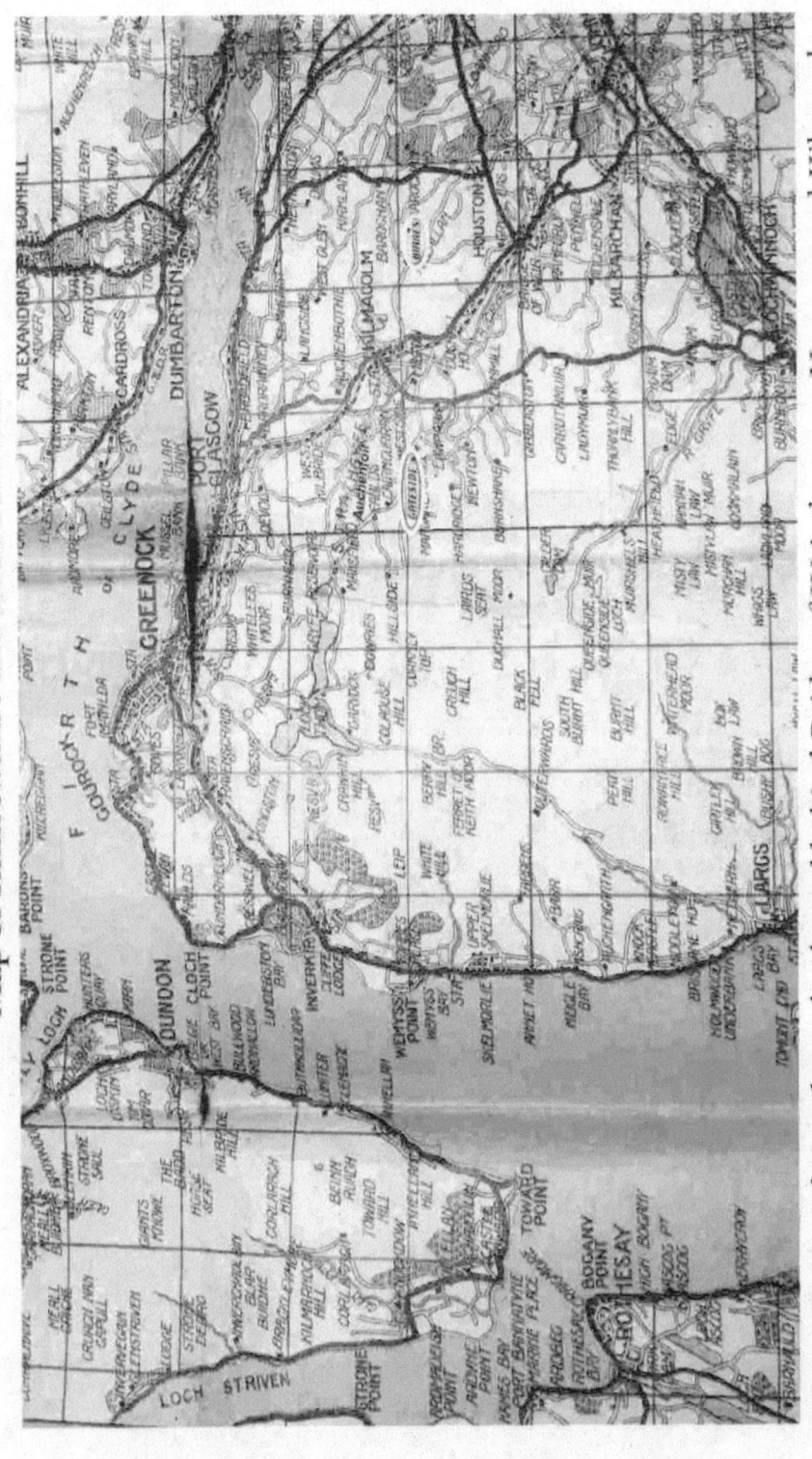

Wraes Farm, is located on a back road behind Bridge of Weir, between Houston and Kilmacolm. Gateside Farm, is situated between Margaret's Mill and Westside, on the road between Kilmalcolm and Greenock. (Their locations are circled on the map.)

The Holmes Genealogy

November 1926

I, MARION HOLMES OR ORR, do write what I know of the family of Holmes to which I belong. I don't know the exact dates when they first came into Kilmalcolm or the vicinity. It might be fifty or a hundred years before 1690 as that is the first date on the tombstone in the old kirkyard. My father with a twinkle in his eyes said they were banished from the Borders for stealing sheep - it might be true as in those days it was the good old rule, the simple plan, that let them take wha had the power and let them keep wha can.

We first hear of them in Birkhill and Barochan and from there a son went to Castlehill and a son to Nittinshill where Quarriers Orphan Homes are now. My great grandfather was in Nittingshill and had a large family.

A daughter of his (or a generation before that) married a Mr Scott in Chapel Farm. He owned it then sold it and went to Glenmill and were the progenitors of Scotts the shipbuilders.

Another daughter of his, Helen, married Lang of Planetreeyetts and one, Mary married Lang of Priestside whose descendant is Lang in Cresswell Farm, now farmed by the Buntains of Stepends. On their mother's side they *[presumably the Buntains — JHJ]* were descended from Lang Planetreeyetts.

Another daughter, Margaret married Blair of Pomillan.

Another, Elizabeth married Gibb of (?) Airtmaks (?) and one married a Mr Robertson in Paisley.

Of the three sons only my grandfather John married. Sandy and James were in Nittingsill till Quarrier bought it. They died in the farm of Midton, near Johnstone.

John was my grandfather. He married Marion King of Houston. Her father and brothers were builders there. It was a son of one of them, Walter, who contracted to take the water from Loch Thom to Greenock. He lost a lot of money over it. They also built the railway bridge across the Gryffe at Bridge of Weir.

Walter built for himself and family Woodend House Houston and John his brother built for himself Houston Cottage. His granddaughter is in it yet. Miss Galloway & her brother Mr Galloway live in High Tor, Kilmacolm.

My grandfather, John Holmes, took his wife to Barmofplet (?) [or Burninflet (?) or Barmufflock (?)] a farm above Bridge of Weir.

(The following entry was separated from its proper place and I have had to guess that it refers to the above John Holmes — JHJ):

"Who before he (?) was married took a tack (?) of the Wraes Farm but had to build a steading on it and so had John Thomson of Denniston as the laird (Porterfield of Ducal) was not going to build any more. He was the last Porterfield and at his death the estate passed to Sir Michael Shaw Stewart of Ardgowan and Blackhall."

My grandmother had 3 of a family, my father Robert, Walter and Mary. Walter died young. Mary married Robert Scott of Greenside. They went to Greenock where he joined his brother Sandy Scott, the sugar refiner. The latter made a big fortune and rented for five years Barochan House [North of the village of Houston beside Barochan Farm — Ed].

Robert Scott had four of a family - Jessie died young, Sandy married a Miss (?) got a chill and never worked after he was married. He left a family of one son and 3 daughters,

Marion (married) Malcolm Currie and had eight of a family. John who married Miss Haloway and had one daughter. Robert who died aged 14, Archie who went to sea as an engineer and made his fortune. Allic, a sugar refiner in Hong Kong. Malcolm a banker who went to the Great War and got his hand shattered and could not settle in the Bank took up hen farming(?) at Banks Farm Inverkip. Walter who died a young man, and Mary Jessie who married John MacNab and had three sons and Chrissie who married John Riddick, a banker, (was) some time in Inverness and from there to Bearsden.

My father, Robert Holmes, Wraes, married Mary Speirs, Burngill. They had five of a family,

Janet Lyle who married John Miller and had five of a family - Mary Speirs, Robert Holmes. William Speirs, Janet & Bessie Marion

Mary married a chemist named McKay and went to South Africa and had one daughter named (?) Robert died at 8 months. Willie went to the Boer War and did not come back for 2 years. When he came a visit but went back again to South Africa.

Janet Married George Tainsh, employed in MacSymons (Grocers) Greenock. Had two of a family, a girl and a boy.

Bessie married Mr Meason, a highland man. They stay in Glasgow.

John Holmes *[Granny Orrs brother—JHJ]* went out to America with James King and through time made his fortune. When he came back and retired took lodgings in Bridge of Weir. After his mother died he latterly lived at Mount Clare, Rothesay.

William Speirs Holmes married Christina Black (Teeny) of Auchenfoyle and took her to Glasgow where he had a business as a flesher. They had 8 of a family. One boy died in infancy. The mother died when she was 41 years old. There was Mary Speirs, Janet Blair, Teeny, Lizzie, Marion, Robert and William.

Mary married Charlie Stevenson (?) whose grandfather on his father's side was Simson of Barnbeth (?) and on his mother's side Charlie Caldwell of the Threeplay.

Janet married Willie Stewart. Teeny died aged 24. Marion married William Forbes. Lizzie was third wife to John Campbell. Robert married Annie Menzie. Willie married and had two boys & 2 (?) girls. Agnes Black had 3 boys and 3 girls, two of them twins.

Marion King Holmes married in 1876 William Orr of Gateside and had five of a family, Mary Speirs, James, Janet, Robert and William.

Mary was married to John Black of Auchenfoil and had eight of a family besides twin girls - one died at birth, the other lived a year (Maggy) and a son stillborn. Their names were Marion, Janet, Donald, Mary, Willie, John, James, Hugh besides twin girls and a son stillborn

James married (?) Polly Ward of 43 Gibson Street Glasgow. They went to stay in Edinburgh. He had got into the Registrar House there. They had four of a family, William Leslie, John Ward, Jean Clarke, and Marion King Holmes. James died when he was 41. His widow continued to stay in the same house they went to at first, 22 Glendevon Place, Murrayfield Edinburgh. The boys were taken into the John Watson School, the girls in a private school.

Janet Orr married Joseph Johnson and had three sons, William Orr, John Holmes and Joseph Robert. William died young and Mr Johnson died aged 50 on 29th June 1930.

Robert Orr was farmer in Gateside

Willie started business in Greenock as a Cabinet Maker at 9 Terrace Road. Bought the place.

Robert Holmes, Wraes was traveller for MacSymons of Greenock. He died suddenly aged about 44 unmarried.

These are the descendants of my father and mother, Mr and Mrs Robert Holmes, Wraes - There had been Holmes in the Wraes for many hundreds of years but a different Holmes from my father, after my father farmed it, it was joined into the South Branchal. My father when he died was 81, my mother 85.

My grandfather after he left Burninflet (?) was in Killochwraes Farm Kilmacolm and after Willie Orr's grandfather in Mathernock had bought Killochwraes, Cauldside and Gateside he put his son John in Killochwraes and John Holmes removed and went to Darndaff Farm above Greenock and from there he removed to Preistside in Kilmacolm and died there aged 85 years. His widow (his second wife)

Note found with photo: 'My grandfather James Orr, died Killochwraes in 98th year. Robin's great-great grandfather'.

Holmes
(Birkhill & Barochan)

Son (Castlehill) — **Son (Nittingshill - Taken over by Quarriers Homes)**

Son (Nittingshill) branch:

- **Daughter** m Scott, Chapel Farm (Went to Glenmill) Progenitors of Scott Shibuilders
- **Helen H** m Lang, Planetreeyetts, later farmed by the Buntains, Stepends
- **Mary H** m Lang, Priestside — Ancestor of Lang Cresswell Farm Near Inverkip
- **Margaret H** m Blair Pomillan
- **Elizabeth H** m Gibb Airtmaks (?)
- **Daughter** m Mr Robertson Paisley
- **John Holmes** m Marion King Barmoflet (?) Farm, Bridge of Weir — The Kings were Builders in Houston
- **Sandy H** unmarried (Nittingshill)
- **James H** unmarried (Nittingshill)

Both moved out after Quarriers bought Nittingshill. They died at Midton Farm, Johnstone

Children of John Holmes & Marion King:

- Robert Holmes, Wraes Farm m **Mary Speirs (Gt. Granny Holmes)** (Of Burngill)
- **Mary Holmes** m Robert Scott Greenside (?) — Went to Greenock. Robert joined his bro. Sandy Scott Sugar Refiner. Rented Barochan House, Houston
- Walter Holmes contracted to bring the water from Loch Thom to Greenock. Built Woodend House, Houston died young.

Children of Robert Holmes & Mary Speirs:

- Robert unmarried died aged 44
- **Marion King Holmes (Granny Orr)** m **William Orr (Gateside)**
- William unmarried founder of 'Orrs House Furnishers' Greenock

Children of Mary Holmes & Robert Scott:

- Jessie
- Sandy
- Marion m Malcolm Currie
- John m Miss Halloway

Children of Marion King Holmes & William Orr:

- Janet Lyle m John Miller
- John unmarried — Made fortune in America. Retired to Mt Clare Ho. Rothesay
- William Speirs m Christina Black of Auchenfoyle They lived in Glasgow
- Mary m John Black Auchenfoil
- Robert m Rebecca (Ruby) Dale

Next generation:

- James m Polly Ward
- **Janet** m **Joe Johnson**
- **John Holmes** *Editors father*
- Joseph Robert *Played for Glasgow Rangers!*

William Orr died, 3 yrs 8 mnths

Granny Orr's Maternal Ancestry

Sir [...] Miles married [?]
|
Cath. Miles m **Stewart** (Schoolmaster)
|
Catherine Stewart m **Lyle** (of Tor Farm)
|
Janet Lyle m Wm **Speirs** (Burngill, Bridge of Weir)
|
Mary Speirs (**great Granny Holmes**) m Robert **Holmes** (Wraes)
|
Marion King Holmes (**Granny Orr**) m William **Orr** (Gateside)

Grandfather Orr's Ancestry

Robin **Lang** (Mathernock) m Agnes Crawford (Youngston)
|
Janet Lang m James **Orr** (Faulds)-son of Orr, Dippany
|
William **Orr** (Gateside)-Grandfather Orr m Marion Holmes (Wraes)-**Granny Orr**

James	Mary	**Janet**	William	William Orr
m	m	m	unmarried	died, 3 yrs 8 mnths
Polly Ward	John Black Auchenfoil	Joe Johnson	*founder of 'Orrs House Furnishers' Greenock*	

Sub-branch under Janet m Joe Johnson:
- Joseph Robert *Played for Glasgow Rangers!*
- **John Holmes** *Editors father*

Janet Speirs, nee Lyle mother of Great Granny Mary Holmes

Granny Orr's Paternal Ancestry

John Holmes (Killochwries)
m
Marion King
|
Robert Holmes (Wraes)
m
Mary Speirs (**Great Granny Holmes**)

Great Granny Holmes' Diary (1882-1897)

The Diary of Mrs Mary Holmes,
The Wraes farm, Bridge of Weir. Written 1882 to 1897

Mrs Mary Holmes, née Speirs

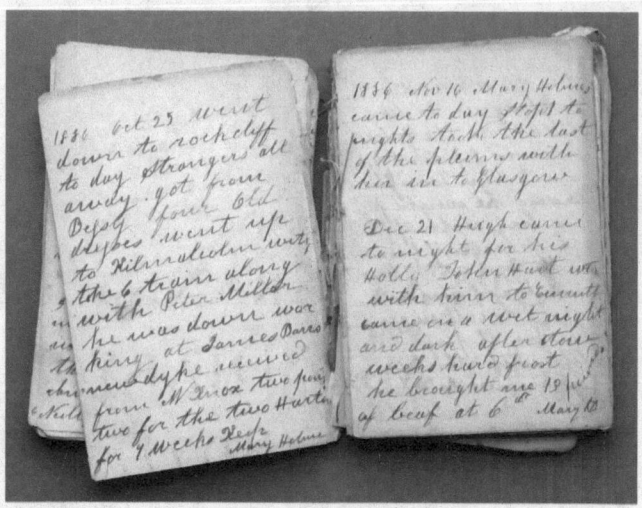

Pages from Mary Holmes diary

Editors note: In his transcription, my father noted that most spellings of the Wraes appear as "Wreas" in the diary.

1882

newspaper cutting on first page:

"Orr - At Bridge of Weir, on 11th inst., aged 88, James Orr, late farmer, Barngill"

29th August Mrs Holmes. Over (?) there Aunts and Miss Barr came from Rockcliffe Aunt Smillie Aunt...(?) Stopt all night went next day to Gateside had a splendid drive.

3rd October Mr Kirkwood commenced to pull down inside (?) Gibbliston on the 3 day of October 1882.

12th October Oct 12 1882 Two joiners came to Wraes to lodge 6 Nov to do the Joiner work. They stopt with me till 25 August the following year.

1883

10th January Marion and myself went into Glasgow on Tuesday 10 day of January to a Flesher Sorrie (?) Went up to James Barr next day. We went with him to see the Pantomime.

17th March Willie Miller born

18th April 1883 My son John left here on Wednesday the 18th day of April 1883 and sailed next day for America. Arrived all safe on May 1

28th August Janet and family left here August 28 after a stay of 8 weeks. John was working at the time at Bridge of Weir.

16th September 1883 I met Marion and Robert in (?) illiespark 16 September. We all went over and had lunch in Barnshake.

2nd October Hugh Black had all his corn in and stack second day of October 1883

3rd October Aunt Smillie, Aunt Rebecca Mrs MacDondal and Bessy Barr drove up here 3 October. Got a splendid day

10th October 1883 Marion[1] was delivered of a daughter Janet 10 day of October 1883. Janet came from Glasgow and stayed with her a fortnight at the time. Left here for Glasgow on the 27. Duncan went in with her.

12th November 1883 I went in to Glasgow 12th day of November to see Aunt. She was very bad at the time. She gave me her black Cashmer Clock with the lace.

December Aunt Smillie died on the 13th of December 1883. Uncle gave Janet Marion and me black dresses and me a ring finclock and Aunt's best Dolman[2]. Mrs Holmes

---

1. Marion was my grandmother Mrs Orr of Gateside. Janet was my mother —JHJ.

    Marion Orr's daughter Janet was my grandmother (Mrs Joseph Johnson, Greenock). She died in November 1956, just three months before I was born—JJ, editor.
2. **Dolman:** a woman's wrap with a loose, cape-like back and sleeves in one piece with the body of the garment.

1884

January This new year was very quiet. Janet came out from Glasgow on Saturday night. John came on Monday night. two MacNairs came on Nairday. Robert and Willie came about as usual. Did not go up to Kinlochs which they were greatly disappointed.

John Miller commenced business for himself.

7th April Received a letter from John his first from Dondlson Works. *[first had been stroked out—JHJ]*

17th April Janet came out from Glasgow the 17th of April and stopt a fortnight. Mary went in with her. She had stayed here from January.

16th May I went in to Glasgow 16 May 1884 to the General Post Office to receive my first present from John. Willie came with me. Went and stopt all night with Janet. Went next day to Uncle's and he gave me the furclock and Dolman and a good many other things. Came home well pleased.

10th June I went over to Gateside 10 June 1884. Went and saw Mrs Crawford Marion and two ladies that were staying in the house at the time. Came over to Wreas on the Saturday following. Willie brought them over in the cart

21st August I went down to Greenock Aug 21. Stayed all night with John Holmes. Sailed next day for Tignabruaich. Stayed three nights. Janet was staying here at the time. Went home 1 September. Left Mary.

2 September went over to Gateside to keep the house. Willie and Marion went to Gourock for a day's pleasure.

12th September Made 5 pounds of plum jam this morning. Going over today to take some to Mrs Black.

13th September Mrs Barr Miss Speir Bessie Barr our Robert myself went over to Gateside in a machin. Robert went home with them. Went to Kilbarchan Church next day and saw Grandmother's tombstone.

1st October Aunt Barr Rebecca Bessie Barr Miss Smillie came up yesterday. Came on a very stormy afternoon. John Barr had left Bridge of Weir 28 September for London. Going to sail from there to Melbourne.

2nd October John Holmes from Greenock was here today on a visit. Was Greenock fast day.

Hugh Black had all his corn stack today Greenock fast.

6th October Mr Fife was here today his annual visit.

28th October Went in to Glasgow with Tinnee and her 4 children. Robert was two months old. Mary Miller went home with us after a stay of 2 months.

1885

1885 This new year came and went as usual. Willie and Robert came about 8 at night. They all went up to Killochs the two Macnairs with them. Nelly Killoch was 14 years of age in May *[either 1880 or 1886 — JHJ]*

28th February John Miller left Glasgow today for Kilmalcolm to commence business for himself. He did not like Glasgow.

15th March Went to Rockcliffe to see Aunt Barr. She had been unwell for 4 months with a pain in her face. Was going in to Glasgow on the Monday to see one of the head doctors.

21st April Robert came here on Saturday night. We went to church next day. Met Marion. We all went up to Janets at midday. Beccy was there from Rockcliffe. Had come the night before. Aunt Barr and Janet was still in Glasgow. Had been in for 5 weeks under the doctor's care and no better

20th June Three doctors was at Aunt Barr today. Could do her no good. Doctors Cameron, Muir and Syme.

23 June John Barr and family drove up to here from Greenock in carriage and pair

13th July Went down to Rockcliffe. Aunt no better. Her face very bad swollen.

14th July Was at Greenock today. Got Duncans account. Brought Janet and baby home with me in Dunlops machin. Stopt 8 days. I was going over with her to Mrs Buntins to get the machin back. We met Bessy Barr on the road. I turned back with her. Millie Smith came after her. Had tea then we all went up to the round Hill.

18 July Glasgow Fair Saturday. Willie came with his two daughters Mary and Janet. Father him and I went on Monday to see Aunt Gibb at Aurtiochs (?) We got a splendid day. Willie went down to Greenock on Tuesday to see Robert.

5th August Went down to see Aunt. Did not see her. Was seeing no person. Her face very much altered.

7th August Father and I went to Gateside to see the foal. It was looking well.

15th August Was at Rockcliffe today. Miss Smillie and Mrs Fraser was there. Did not see Aunt. Her face getting worse and worse.

29th August Saturday Robert came up tonight. James Macnair Mrs Uire two boys from Glasgow was here. All stayed a fortnight except Robert. He went home on Sunday. Duncan and him went the length of Craigminen in the forenoon.

31st August Janet and I went to Greenock today. Went to Smithton about a little girl. Got tea in Mrs Curries. Bought 7 pounds of plums each.

5th September Janet and John came out today with Robert Dunlop. Went home on Monday. John came out for Father on Friday

7th September Was at Rockcliffe today. Her face worse than when I saw it last.

23rd September Small barrel of herring from James Barr Rockcliff

Beef from James Macnair my first order.

24th September Was at Paisley today. Called on old Mrs King. She was looking well. Came home by Kilmalcolm. Stoped in Janets all night. Brought Mary home with me next day.

25th September Received 10 stone sugar five pound tea 14 pound syrup and candle and fish.

1886

1st January This new year came in wet and stormy, the dullest ever I passed in the Wreas. Not a person till nine at night. Willie & Robert, Peter Millin then all went up to Killochs as usual. Came home at three in the morning. Robert went in to Glasgow with Willie

29th March Went to Kilbarchan. Paid Peter Barrs account and then went down to Johnstone. Came by Kilmalcolm. Came home next day

1st April April first Went over today to cast[1] Hugh Black's potatoes. Cut five bags in two days. All planted on the 28.

5th April Duncan Campbell left here for Gibbliston. Peter Logan went next day to Robert Orr Newton

own (?) there on shift

May Duncan left Gibbliston and went to Mrs Hunter Airdrie.

8th April This is Glasgow fast. Willie and family came today. Father and Willie went over to Blacks in the afternoon. He went home at night. Duncan and Hugh Macnaur went in to Kilmalcolm with him, the rest of them stopt till Sarurday. Black had no corn sown and no potatoes planted. Weather stormy.

29th April Went over today to Gateside. Their potatoes all planted.

30th April Went down to Rockcliff with Mary Orr. Uncle sent us home in a Machin along with Janet Barr and Becky

2nd May Sunday May 2 Janet came over today with Mary and Janet went home that night. Willie went home with them. He had stayed a month here.

27th July We went up to Hugh Gibbs today. He is failing very fast. Mary not so bad. Willie still with them. Have three cows

28th July Went down to Rockcliff. No stranger had plenty that week. Bessy going down to Kilcreggan.

13th July Miss Smillie Beccy and Bessie Donaldson came up here. It was very nice the forepart of the day. It came on a wet stormy night.

18th August Willie came today for his gooseberries. They were not ripe. Marion came over next day and pulled the last of them.

19th August Went to Greenock for Duncan's last account - three pounds 5/6 from M Boon

6th September The last of my summer boys went away today. Their names were Andrew Young, Neil Gourlay, John Rough

20th September Father and I went up and paid a visit to Aunt Gibb. Old Robert was in bed not very well. When we came home Maggie Harper and her sister-in-law was sitting at the fire. Stayed from Monday till Saturday. Mrs Harper came on Friday. They all went away next day.

28th September Mrs Alexander, Peggy Fleming came up today. A Machin came up for them at night. Mrs Alexander had not been up for nine year.

25th October Went down to Rockcliff today. Strangers all away. Got from Bessie four old dresses Went up to Kilmalcolm with the 6 train along with Peter Miller. He was down working at James Barrs new dyke. Received from M Knox two pounds two for the two Harts for 7 weeks keep Mary Holmes

16th November Mary Holmes came today. Stopt two nights. Took the last of the plums with her in to Glasgow.

17th December Went in to Glasgow today to call on the General. Received 8 pounds 4/6. I met John Laird Greenock. He said he would fill my bag with apples and oranges if I went to the Bazaar with him. I went as I was not going to call on any person. It passed the time. Left with the two train. Came to Kilmacolm had tea in Janet's. Home by 6

21st December Hugh came over tonight for his Holly. John Hart went with him to Carruth (?) Came on a wet night and dark after two weeks hard frost. He brought me 13 pounds of beef at 6 (?) Mary H.

---

1. **Cast:** Old Scots, meaning to sow (seed, corn, etc.). Now obsolete.

1887

1st January A very dull new year. John Miller and his son Willie came over in the forenoon. Other six came in. No other person till half past ten when Willie & Robert and Peter Logan came. (They) went up by as usual. Was down by one o'clock. Jamie Taylor came down with them. Had potato soup ready for them. Mary Holmes

18th January Mrs Walker and I went to Johnston today. Roads fearful bad. We had to hire a machin to take us home.

20th January Was down at Bridge Weir today. Called at the Bank and on Mrs Alexander. Janet Barr and Becky came from Glasgow the week before.

7th February Went down to Rockcliff today and staid with Becky all night. Next morning she went out to take the milk from the boy when she slippedd and fell and broke her arm at the wrist.

9th February John Barr died at Rangoon 9 Feb 1887 aged 39 years

6th March Our sacrament today. I was at church. The church well filled. Very good preacher, Alexander of Langbank.

9th March Went in to Glasgow today to be at Jamie Macnair's wedding at night. A very nice party. Was home at Willie's at half three.

10th March Went down to Greenock today. Called on Mrs Barr & Mrs Adam. Mrs Barr not so vexed as I thought she would have been. Miss Star(k) very bad.

18th April Went over to Blacks today to commence to cut the seed potatoes. Cut two full days with Mrs Bain

8th June Yesterday was our Cattle Show. Father was in. Came home at nine with the two Harts and Mary Holmes. I had Mrs Black over at tea that afternoon.

11th June Was over at Gateside. Came on a wet afternoon. Their crop was looking well and their foal.

17th June Father and I went up to Currithmure to see Hugh Gibb, first time since he came to it.

18th June Father and Peter Hart went over to Gateside to see their foal. They were thinning their turnips.

22nd June Was in at Glasgow today at General P.O. Called on James Macnair. Got tea and was taken to the station in a cab.

12th August Went down to Greenock today. Staid with Robert that night. Him and I went to Tignabruaich next day. He went home with the afternoon boat and I staid till Monday. He paid all expenses. Called on Mary MacCallum and Mrs Adam when down. *Mary Holmes.*

16th October Father, Robert and I went up to Lochwinnoch today to see old Aunt Gibbs. Robert ordered a machin from Kilmalcolm. Peter Miller driver. We got a splendid day. They were all glad to see us. Aunt was in bed not very well. Home at five. *Mary Holmes*

22ⁿᵈ October Was over at Gateside. They were finishing their potatoes. Went up and saw Mrs Crawford she had not been very well but was getting better.

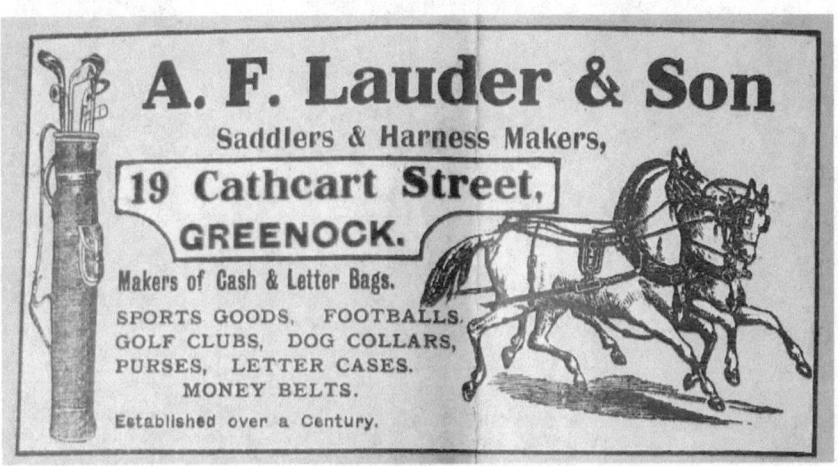

1888

2nd February Duncan Campbell & Peter Logan went from Wreas today and sailed next day for New York on their way to John

10th April I received my second letter from Duncan today.

11th April Finished the cutting of Blacks potatoes today. Fearful cold weather. Frost every morning.

17th April Went over today cut potatoes two days to Alex Taylor

12th June Willie Miller broke his arm today.

12th April Janet came here today with Willie and stayed two nights. Willie Donald and Mrs Donald came over on Saturday. John came out in a machin and drove them home. Janet and Mary had been here for three weeks.

6th June This is our Cattle Show. Father went in the night before. Hugh Macnair came home with him I met them in Buntins

10th August John Holmes left Wreas today. Going to sail in the afternoon for America. He was in good health and spirits.

13th August Went in today. Stopt with Willie that night. Robert came up to take me to Exhibition.[1] Willie came with us. Left with 5 train for Kilmalcolm. Took a machin out.

20th August Mrs Winning came today. Brought two cheeses one sweat (or sucut ?) at 6d half & half 4d per pound. They came to 1/12 Paid.

28th August Janet and two ladies who were staying with her at the time from Gourock came here for dinner and tea. Left here at 7 getting dark.

15th September Mr Chien (?) and John Miller came here today.

1st October I Was at Kilbarchan today. Called at Rockcliff. Saw Bessie banns (?) going to be married on the 17th

4th October Glasgow Holiday. Willie and his two daughters came. Willie was to meet Robert in Kilmalcolm at 7. Girls stayed till Sat.

---

1. **The Exhibition:** This may have been the Glasgow Exhibition of 1888, or it may have been a local exhibition of some kind.

1889

12th July This is Glasgow Fair. Willie and Robert came here on Saturday night. They went up to Craiganin next day. Willie Mitchell was with them. His mother has taken the wee room for a month. Mary and little Willie stayed a week. M.H.

12th August Willie came for gooseberries. Got none. All off the bushes by birds and thefts.

1st September Mrs Alexander Miss Flemings came up today. Mrs Miller met them here. Robert and John Laird came the night before. Went to (?) ookmalane (?) next day. Came home at five. Got tea and then took the road to Greenock. It was a beautiful day. All well pleased.

John Andrew and family came today.

21st September James Barr and Frank Brown came here today. Frank for the first time had tea and stayed to 8 o'clock

30th September Went down to Rockcliff today. Bec went up with me to see Bessie's baby, a nice smart child.

12th October Janet and family came out today Sat. John went home at night with Willie. Janet stayed till Tuesday forenoon. On Monday I went to Gateside. They were busy at their potatoes. Baby William 6 weeks old.

19th November Willie came here today about 3 o'clock. Came out at Bridge of Weir. He went up to RC to see how they were getting on. Frank and Bessie were there - had been from Saturday.

3rd December Was at Paisley today. Came with the 3 train to Kil. Went up to Janets. Hugh Macnair came with the 4 train and had a great many parcels. We came out in a machine and got them all out at once. He stayed all night. Went in with the 8 train next morning. Hard frost. M.H.

30th December Peter Hart went from here today for Greenock on his way to Galashiels. Not sure whether he will come back here or not. He is away his New Year holidays. We are sitting here very lonely tonight. The wind and rain blowing down the close at no wee rate. I wish I had a house in the village. It will come to it. Both failing.

1890

1890 Another year past. There were more young lads in with their bottles this year than last. Willie came himself at nine. He did not see Robert all day. Killoch was in when he came. Would not go away without him. John Miller was here. He went up with them. Home at 2 Hugh Macnair here too. Went off next morning

Peter Hart went from here Monday 30 Dec. Went to Mr Deas to get some cloths as he was going to Galashiels to pass Nerday. Deas told him his time was up and to stay when there. He did not come back. M.H.

1st February Janet came here on Thursday. Went home on Sat. Wet weather.

17th February Willie and John Laird came here today, a very cold day. Went away to catch the 8 train.

20th February Mrs Walker and myself went down to Gourock to a friend. Came home in a machin at nine.

6th March Went down to B of W. Stayed one night with Beck. Next day so stormy could not get home. Stayed with Peggy Fleming that night.

1st April Went over today to help Mrs Taylor to cut a few bags of potatoes - first day 4, next day 4...4 4day   16

11th April Went over today to cut the first of Blacks potatoes. 26 bags. He did not plant many this year.

27th April Two Miss Flemings came up today. Got a splendid night for going home.

3rd May Mrs Miller came out today. Went home Monday night.

29th May Went down to Rockcliff today. Stayed all night. They gave me a drive home next day.

June 2 I went in to Paisley today. Went down and saw Mrs King. Was looking very well but always in bed. Mary King was in helping Jean to guide her.

11th June This is our Cattle Show. Father did not go in. It has been a dull cold day. Nobody at home but ourselves. two. Janet Andrew in at Kilmalcolm helping our Janet a day or two.

17th June We both went in to the opening of the new Parke. Robin sent us home in a machin Peggy Fleming kept house.

18th June Was over at Gateside today. Came on a wet afternoon. All things looking well.

19th June 12 birds out today.

21st June Peter Miller drove up here in a machin today with his own wife. Our Janet and two ladies stayed to tea.

29th June I was at Paisley today. Went and asked for Mrs King. She was very low that day.

2nd July I was up seeing Hugh and Mary today. Both in good health. Not getting any richer by appearances

5th July Marion and Mrs Taylor were over here today. Came on a very wet afternoon.

8th July Marion and a lady came today. Got a fine day.

29th July I went in to Kilmalcolm to see the last of the fair folk away. Mary, Lizzie, Willie.

21st July This is Glasgow Fair a week back this year. Lizzie and wee Willie came on Thursday, Mary on Sat. Willie and Robert came Sat night at half 12 and Hugh Macnair, James Barr & Frank & Daniel Brown met them up at the old house. They all went to see the Brittian (?) Min next day Sunday.

7th August Mrs Miller came here today with Mary and Janet. Stayed till Tuesday 12th. Janet Barr & Bessie, 4 of James bairns, our Willie from Glasgow for his gooseberries all met and drank tea. Janet got him in their machain. Willie went home with the nine train. They were all in best of health M.H.

20th August James Barr and family, Frank and Bessie came tonight. Got tea.

24th August Sunday. Mrs Alexander, Miss Flemings came up today. Mrs Caldwell came up in her machin in the afternoon. They got home in it. M.H.

1st September Monday Miss Black and I went to Glasgow today. Got a drive down and up. Bought fine boots and slippers and other things M.H.

6th September Uncle Smillie drove up today. Had not been up for years. Mrs Barr, Misses Barr, Whyte, Speir. Our Robert came at night Saturday.

9th September Went in to Kil today about my money from Knox. Some mistake with the Clark Macnab.

10th September Janet Barr came up today to tell me they were going to see Aunt Maggie next day. It was a wet morning and I did not go. M.H.

18th September Was up at Currithmuir (?) today with Mary Miller

20th September Mrs Mitchell came here today. Stayed till Monday 29. Got a fearful day to go home. Bessie and Willie and Mr Andrew came with her.

13th October Was at Johnston today. Came by RCliff. Stayed all night. Mrs Miller kept house.

28th October Was at Paisley today. Mrs King very poorly. Did not see her. Went down and saw Mrs Donald - clean and always something to give you to your mind.

13th November Was at Rockcliff today. Beck over at Bessie. Janet all alone. Stayed all night.

1st December Our Willie came tonight about 7. Stayed all night. Had beef and greens ready for him.

13th December Saturday A letter from John today with a check for 10 pounds. I am to give Janet 2/10 (i.e. £2;10/-), Marion the same, 5 to myself.

17th December (Wednesday) Mr Gibson from America called here today.

19th December Janet Barr and Bessie came up today. One had a bottle of brandy, the other a pair of new boots from Bec - my Christmas present.

1891

1891 We both commenced this year in good health. Willie and Robert did not come here till after 10 with the two Bryces. All went up to Killoch except Robert. They came home at 4. Went to get the 8 morning train M.H.

9th February Went down to RCliff today. They were all in good health.

13th February Was at Kilmalcolm today. Had not been in for a long time. John plenty of work, weans had the cold.

15th February Janet got a daughter this morning Sunday. To be called Elisabeth.

17th February Mrs Alexander, Mrs Frame, Janet Barr, Mrs Frank Brown came up here today. Mary Holmes from Glasgow here at the same time.

5th March Willie and John Laird that was in Gibbelston came here today and stayed all night. Both well.

23rd March Went down to Rockcliff today. Stayed all night. Next day a fearful wet day. Home at 4.

31st March Went over today to commence to cut the seed potatoes. Very cold weather. M.H.

13th April This is Glasgow Holiday. Willie, Hugh and wee Jock came last night Sunday.

29th April Was at Gateside today.

2nd May Janet and family came today. Stayed 8 days. Bessie three months old.

10th May Daniel and Frank Brown came up today. Daniel told me about his marriage. Going to be next month.

26th May Was at Greenock today. Went up to Janets in the homecoming. Met Mrs Mitchell. She came home with me. Stayed three days.

2nd June Willie came here today. He brought my beef. He was looking well. He went away to catch the 9 train.

12th June John Miller and the weans came out today. All went at night. Home. Sunday

21st June (Sunday) Mrs Miller, Janet Blair and the weans came today. Stayed till Wed. Very warm at the time.

29th June I was at Paisley today.

18th July This is Glasgow Fair Sat. Mary and wee Willie came here at 6 o'clock. Her father went to the Isle of Man. Hugh came on Monday. No trip to Craigmin this year. Willie came here on Wed night. Went away next morning to be at the market. He did not get up to see Hugh Gibb.

2nd August James Barr and Mrs Barr came up today Sunday. Both looking well. Our Janet here at the time.

8th August Mrs Holmes came here today. Willie came Tuesday following. Gaff and him went up and saw Hugh and Mary. Came home at five. They left here to catch the 8 train.

20th August I went in to Glasgow today along with Marion and Bessie Black. Was drove out and in Black's machin.

23rd August (Sunday) Ellen came up from Rockcliff today. John Miller came out in the afternoon. Mary and Janet both here at the time.... stayed till Wed M.H.

29th August Uncle Smillie, Miss Smillie, Miss Speirs, Miss Barr came up today. All looking well.

22nd August Went down to Greenock today. Bought boots and slippers for myself. Mrs Miller kept house. Janet Blair came out on Sunday. They all went home at night. Wet night.

1st October Willie, Mary, Miss Blackwood came here today. Mary Orr came over in the afternoon.

12th October John Holmes arrived from America. Not going back again.

24th November Went over to Kilbarchan with other 3 ladies to see Miss Fleming. Stayed with Mrs Alexander that night.

1892

4th April Glasgow holiday. Willie, Hugh Parker and wee Jock came here on Sunday. John was not at home. Was away seeing Bogside races.

7th July I went up to see Mary today. Was too late. She had died on Sat at one o'clock. Buried in Kilmalcolm. Hugh very bad when I was there.

30th July I went down to B of W today. Called at the Bank.

24th July (Sunday) Jean Fleming and Miss J came up today. Mrs Miller and family were here. All went away at night.

7th August Robert and Marion came here in Mr Curnells machin. He drove Robert up from Greenock. They called at Gateside and brought Marion with them Sunday.

9th August Mrs Miller & Miss Thompson came here. John Miller came out at night.

14th June (Tuesday) Willie and Buce (?) came here today. A splendid day. John was over at Gateside. Came home before they went away.

15th June Mrs Orr and a Mrs Fullarton that was staying in their house. Got a very nasty wet day coming over.

27th July Went today to see Aunt Maggy along with James Barr Janet Barr (?) our John. It was a good day and we had a splendid drive. Found them all well. Aunt looking well for her age. She was born at Back o' the Hill at Johnston in 1815.

8th August Willie Holmes came here today. He stayed all night. Next day Father John and him went up and saw Hugh Gibb.

12th August This is old Jamie Killochs funeral today. He died on Monday 8th. I saw him come and I saw him go, the third I saw leave the Branchal

26th August Went down to Greenock today. Stayed all night in Roberts. Went next day to Tignabruaich. Stayed till Monday. Went up to Glasgow. Stayed 3 nights in Willies

3rd September (Sunday) Ellen came up today. Told me Beck, Bessie, Janet and some bairns was at Lamlash for a month.

6th September John Andrew and wife came today. Came by Bridge of Weir. Went by Kilmalcolm. No weans with them. They had no machin. M.H.

9th September Two Miss Tweeds and Mary Orr came over today Sept 9 Larry came today. Brought flour tea sugar ham soup soda.

28th September Miss Sm.... (?) came today. Stayed an hour. Going in to Kilmalcolm to call on Mrs Miller.

1st October Miss Tweed came over with Mary Orr and a Mr Chalmers today. John went home with them.

3rd October John left Wreas today for Glasgow to work for Mr Boyle Contractor M.H.

11th **October** I was over at Gateside today. Met Mrs Miller there. We went up and called on Mrs Crawford. They were busy taking in their corn. Willie Orr would get all his in next day Tuesday.

12th **October** James Laird that was in Gibbilston called on us today. He had not been very well but getting better. He told us he had plenty to live on without working very hard.

21st **October** Went down to Rockcliff today. Becky staying with Mrs Brown her knee very bad.

26th **October** Went to Johnston today. I stayed with Mary Lyle that night. Mrs Lyle came down and invited us up to tea. She had everything very nice. Jessie Laird was married that day.

5th **November** John and Robert came here tonight. Peter Miller drove them over. Next day was our sacrament.

We drove in in Lairds machin to church. John went down with Robert to Greenock at night. I came home in Blacks machin. It was a nice day. We got tea in Mrs Millers in the forenoon.

9th **December** Larry came tonight. Brought Roberts present of whisky and cakes, shortbread and oranges.

1893

14th February Went in to Kil today. Had not been in for some time. Got a very wet day coming home.

Robert came here tonight Sat. Had been up at Glasgow. Went home next day by Gateside.

5th March (Sunday) This is our communion. John and Robert came Sat night Went to church next day.

21st March (Tuesday) Went over to Blacks today to cut seed potatoes.

24th March Went in to Kil today with Mary Holmes. She was going to Gateside to stay all night.

8th April (Saturday) Mrs Mitchell came today. Stayed till Tuesday. Got splendid weather

12th April This is Jean Killoch's wedding day.

19th April I went in to Glasgow today. Stayed 8 days. Went and called on Mrs Duff and then on Uncle Smellie. They were all in good health. Mrs Miller kept house.

29th April (Saturday) John & Robert came tonight. Went over next day to Blacks and got plenty of curds and cream

23rd May Went down to B of W Stayed with Mrs Alex the night.

4th June Sunday Mrs Miller and family came over today with Janet Blair.

6th June Willie & Bryce came today. Got a very wet day. Got no flowers. all past. Everything 2 weeks earlier than last year.

14th June Our Cattle Show today. Our John and John Laird that was in Gibbliston was there. Got tea in Mrs Miller at night. No other person called.

15th June We got new potatoes today for the first time. Very good, 1/- per stone.

16th June Went over to Gateside today. Came home in Taylors cart. Were all well. House well let.

22nd June Mrs Orr & I went to Glasgow today. She bought a nice dolmin and dress and I a shirt.

12th July Was in at Kilmalcolm today. Wet.

14th August Jamie Fleming and Peggy came up today. Stayed in Mary Lyles that night.

15th August The last of Willies weans went from here today after a stay of 6th week

14th September Commenced my first gallon of Parafin.

9th September Ellen came up today. Looking well but getting very tired of R.Cliff. Mrs Miller and family were here. All went away that night. Bessie had been staying here for two weeks.

16th September Uncle Smellie, Miss Smellie, Becky came up today Sat. Stayed two hours.

17th September Sunday James Barr, Mrs Barr and family came up. They brought 4 pair Kippert herring with them. Made them tea and gave them 1 dozen eggs away with them.

28th September Larry came today. Brought flour, ham and a great many things.

7th October (Saturday) John Miller and family and his mother came here today in a machin. Peter Miller driver.

13th October Willie Orr brought today 3 bags beans (?) Mary Orr & Mary Currie came over in the forenoon. Home in the cart.

16th October Willie Holmes came here today. Father and him went up and saw Hugh Gibb. Came home by Gibbliston.

18th October John Holmes gave up his contract to Mr Boyle.

16th November Went down to B of Weir today. Called at the Bank. Went up to Rockcliff. Stayed with Bessie that night

13th November Janet came out today. Stayed till Sat. Bessie went home with her after a stay of 4 weeks.

20th December Hugh Macnair and another lad came tonight to get holly with berries to deck out his shop for Christmas. They went home that night.

21st December Larry came tonight with my order & presents.

1894

1st January This has been a very dull Nairday. Hugh Macnair came here Sat night. John and him went in to Glasgow Monday morning. Came back here at night at 9 with Robert & Robert Brown mains (?) Hugh & Mary Holms went over to Glenmill and finished up there. Both went home Wed early. It was hard frost four days.

11th February Hugh Nair came here this morning quarter past one with beef & tallow.

19th March John went in to Glasgow today to commence his new contract.

22nd March Went over to Gibbliston today to commence our cutting.

18th April All cut today.

16th May Mrs Miller came here today. They came all out on Sat. All went home next day. My back was very sore at the time. Had been for two weeks.

7th June Miss Speirs & Bessie Barr, Mrs Miller came today in a Machin. Our Willie came and stayed all night. Sorted up the summer seat.

14th June Hugh Macnair came tonight Sat. Went back next day by Kilmalcolm to get a bus from there to Paisley

24th June This is our Sacrament the first day of our new way. John and Robert came Sat night. John and I went to church. Robert stayed at home. He went in to Kil. Both went to Port Glasgow. John to get a train for Glasgow

26th June I went down to B of Weir today. Stayed all night with Mary Lyle. Came home next day. Mrs Miller kept house.

30th June Sunday Marion came over today and then Alex Taylor & wife and son. After they went away John Miller came with Mary & Janet & Willie - a splendid day.

2nd July Willies weans came today for their holiday.

13th July Mrs Harper came today her holidays. Stayed till Tuesday 17th.

14th July Glasgow Fair week John and Willie came tonight Sat. John went to Glasgow Mon. Willie went on Tuesday. Going to Largs to see Sandy Crawford. Home on Thursday.

30th July (Monday) Went to Paisley along with Marion. Got Blacks machin down & back, wee Hugh the driver.

14th August Weans went in to Glasgow today after a stay of 6 weeks.

15th August Robert was here today for his account. New order coming with the baker Saturday.

17th August Lizzie Holmes Left here today with Mary Miller. Both going to Glasgow tomorrow.

16th August Mrs Mitchell and Jessie Donald came here today. Got dinner and tea.

20th August Willie came out for his gooseberries today. Got very few. Stayed all night.

25th August Willie Donald and Mrs D. came today Sat.

2nd September John came today at five in a machin. Left at nine. Janet and all her family here that night. It was Sat. Ellen from Rockcliff came up today with Mrs Watt, John Watts wife.

13th September Janet Holmes came here today for rowans and a few things that was left from Glasgow Fair.

22nd September Sat John & Robert, Mrs Miller, John Miller and family was here today to get our faces taken. A man came from Kilmalcolm to do it. John too late in coming.

26th September This is Glasgow Holiday. Mary & Lizzie Holmes came here. James Barr and all his family came in a carriage and pair Sunday. They had 8 children with them, five sons and 3 daughters.

2 (?) September I went over to Gateside today. Corn all in and had commenced their potatoes that day. Home with Taylor.

9th October Mrs Black and I went down to RCliff today. Dined in Mrs Barrs the other ladies away but Becky in at Alex Donaldsons wedding.

11th October I went over today to see Mrs Mitchell. She has a nice house and a nice place.

14th October Sunday James Barr came up today. 3 Miss Barrs & Ned

15th October (Monday) Our Willie came here today. Stayed all night. Came for his share of the plums.

18th October Mrs Miller came for her share.

27th October Marion and Mary Currie came over today.

5th November John Laird came here tonight. Brought a great many apples & grapes - a long promise.

18th November Mrs Miller came out today and I went down to B of W. Stayed in Mary Lyles. Went to the Bank next day. Had a crack with Mrs Alexander. Left at 4. Mary & Mrs Lyle came home with me all the road.

Carriage & Pair - old book illustration, 1819

1895

1895 Another year gone. A very dull day. Got better at night. Had my 3 sons, Hugh Macnair, Mr Bryce. We all sat at the fire till half 4. Janet and I sat at the fire. Had their breakfast taken. All ready to go by 8 to catch the 9 train.

10th February Mary Holmes came here tonight. Mary Orr came next night. Both went away next morning early to catch 8 train.

Feb. My old Aunt Maggie died this month age 90

9th March John came tonight Sat. Went over next day to see Willie Orr. Had not been very well but better.

21st March Mrs Miller came here today. Stayed till Sat. Went home in a machin.

15th April Glasgow Holiday. Willie, Hugh wee Jock Janet and Lizzie Holmes came in the afternoon. Gaff very unwell. We were thinking it would be the last time he would see the garden sorted

19th April We finished the cutting today. Potatoes all in that night.

8th May John came here today along with James Barr Mrs Barr & Miss Speirs

27th May Mary Miller and I went up to Bankbica (?) for a Chany of eggs. John came home from his work with sore legs that same day.

12th June John Scott and wife and his mother Mrs Scott stayed 8 days.

18th June Lizzie Holmes came tonight with a suit of new clothes to John. They all went to the School trip next day.

22nd June John went in to Glasgow today to begin his work. Was 4 weeks at home with sore legs.

25th June Went down today B of W. Called at the Bank. Got Blacks machin.

14th August Robert here today. Got his account 1/8

24th August (Saturday) Your father died this morning at 7 o'clock after two days illness. He went away without pain (for) which we were all glad. He had many a sore time before that. *[Robert Holmes, aged 80. Mother's maiden name - King -PJJ]*

23rd September (Monday) I went in to Glas today to buy my mournings. Stayed two days.

10th October Willie & Bryce came today for their plums. Stayed all night. Robert came at 8. He went home that night. Left at 11

5th October James Blackwood and his sister came today Sat. Stayed till Monday morning. Got a great many plums Went home well pleased.

15th October Hugh Macnair and another young lad came today. Got plums.

17th October Mary Holmes and John Campbell came today. Campbell went away next day. Mary stayed till Sat.

23rd October Mrs John Barr and Miss Stark came today. Got dinner and tea. Brought plenty with them.

3rd November This is our Sacrament. My three sons came on Sat night. We drove in to church. Got tea in Janets. Drove home again. Robert left here at 7 for Greenock. Other two left next morning to get the 7 train .... Mary Holmes

---

This has been a poor year for me. Gaff death. Hens did not lay from August till 13 January

---

1896

1st January This has been the dullest New year ever I passed in the Wreas till night when they began to come in in pairs like Noah's Ark. Willie was the Cock o the walk, could dance and sing at the one time.

9th February Robert came tonight Sat. He got John in Kil. Came home together. Next day was such a wet stormy day he could not leave till Mond morning.

22nd February (Saturday) Maggy Harper came today. Stayed till Mond.

Marion, Mrs Orr, went in to Glas today to go through an operation. Came home 7 March. All right and well to appearance.

4th April John Campbell and Robert Holmes from Glas came here Sat night at one in the morning. Willie came next day with Mary & our Robert

22nd April Robert came for his Account 1/4

31st May Mrs Miller came here tonight. Stayed till Sunday.

3rd June John went today to Greenock to James Holmes wedding. Our Robert Best Man.

16th June Hugh Macnair & a young lad came at night. Were going next day for a suit but did not get for rain.

6th July John gave Mary Holmes and me a trip to Glendaruel. Was there many a time when young staying with grandmother. I had not seen it for 47 years and many a time I said I would like to see it and I got my wish at 82. Mary Holmes

10th August John Campbell and a young man came today

24th August Mrs Miller and Bessie came out today. Stayed till Tuesday. Mrs Alexander came up on a visit. She got home with her in her machin

29th August John away in today to see how Willies sore hand is getting on M.H.

28th August (Saturday) Maggy Harper today. Stayed till Mond

1st September Hugh Macnair came today Stayed one night.

21st September Janet and Marion came today along with James Orr and Janet Miller. It was my birthday. I entered in to my 83 that day Mary H.

24th October Robert came here tonight with John Laird and his wife. Stayed 2 nights

9th December This is Nelly Killochs wedding day to William Dunbar, a docker in Sheffield.

1897

8th January This year has commenced very quiet. Just two in with their bottles. A great many marriages here about last year.

13th February Maggy Harper came today. Went home same day.

18th February John went in to Glasgow today to a party in Willies.

9th March John went in to Glasgow with Lofty today. (Lofty was the name of the collie dog) Left him in Willies. We have got a young one, his name Dash (?)

18th March Mrs Walker & Mrs Galbreath & Mrs Orr was here today. Got dinner and tea. This was John Kerrs Plough Match at Overwood (?), the late James Holmes

27th March Mr Miller came here tonight. John and he had been at James Holmes roup at Netherwood. Hugh Black drove him here in his machin

6th April James Gibson came here today Not well. Stayed 2 weeks. Went home rather better but not cured.

1st May Maggy Harper came today Sat.

8th June Jamie Fleming and Peggy came here today. Stayed all night. Next day was Kilmalcolm Show day

28th June John, John Miller, Mrs Miller and I went away a sail today to Loch Lomond. Had our tea in Roberts when we came back, ham and eggs. All up to knocker.

19th July Mrs Harper came today with a Mrs Craig who had take(n) the wee room for a week.

24th July Tinnie & Marion went away today from here. Going to stay a week at Gateside.

25th July Sund Willie Mitchell and another lad called here today. Willie Miller too. 1897 July 26 Janet going in to Kilmalcolm today. Mary Miller going away her holiday

12th August Mr Black & Mrs B and I went to Auchenfoyle today.

11th August John Andrew and family were here today. This is old Mr Browns funeral day 13 August.

16th September I went in to Glasgow today Stayed 4 days. Was not very well all the time. Mary Holmes and two Miss Stevensons came home with me. Got better after I got home.

4th October Mrs Adam and Miss Adam came here today.

30th October (Saturday) Robert came here tonight. Stayed till Mond morning. Looking well and in good health.

The diary appears to end at this point.
After a few blank pages the following entries appear:

John Speirs Carrier Bridge of Weir who died 13 December 1869 aged 52 years

Aunt Smellie who died at Glasgow on 13 December 188 (?) aged 58

Aunt Barr who died at Rockcliff on Sat 31 October 1885 aged 64

And (?) Barr died at Bridge of Weir aged 70.

1898 Rebecca Speirs died at Rockcliff on 11th January in her 69th year.

Janet Andrew came to stay at Wreas Nov 1873.

Still here looking fresh and this is Jan 1893   M.H.

1894 April 16 Set a hen

Sept 27 Cart coals 11 shillings

1896 Set 2 hens today Apr 7 Eggs from Janet Lang Killochwreas

Mary Speirs Miller born February 17th 1881

William Speirs Miller.born March 17th 1883

Janet Holmes Miller born June 19th 1885

Robert Holmes Miller born 7th July 1887 Died of Hooping cough Feb 12th 1888

Newspaper cutting

> SPEIRS - At Ingleholm, Bridge of Weir, on the 11th inst., Rebecca, aged 69 years, daughter of the late William Speirs, Burngill. - Friends please accept this intimation

January 1898 Peter Hart went from Wraes to Galashiels Dec 30 1889

Willie Holmes and Tinnie Black married 28 Dec 1874

Newspaper cutting

HOLMES At 2 Albert Place, Caledonia Road, on the 29th inst, Christina Black, aged 40 years, beloved wife of William Holmes, flesher

Willie Orr and Marion Holmes was married at Wreas in December 1876.

Great Granny Mary Holmes, (nee Speirs), died at 5.30 am, at Wraes Farm, Kilmacolm, on Sunday 29th October 1899. Aged 85

Granny Orr's Diary
(1901~1922)

Granny Orr (Mrs Marion Orr, née Holmes), and Grandfather William Orr, on the occasion of their daughter Janet's wedding to Joseph Johnson, (the editor's grandfather.)

Editor's note: This is the first diary kept by Granny Orr, (Mrs Marion Orr). She was born and brought up at Wraes Farm,

Bridge of Weir. Following her marriage to farmer William Orr, she moved to Gateside Farm. This was her place of residence when she began keeping her diaries. This one covers the years 1901 to 1922. Marion Orr was my father's grandmother, daughter of Mary Holmes, his great-grandmother.

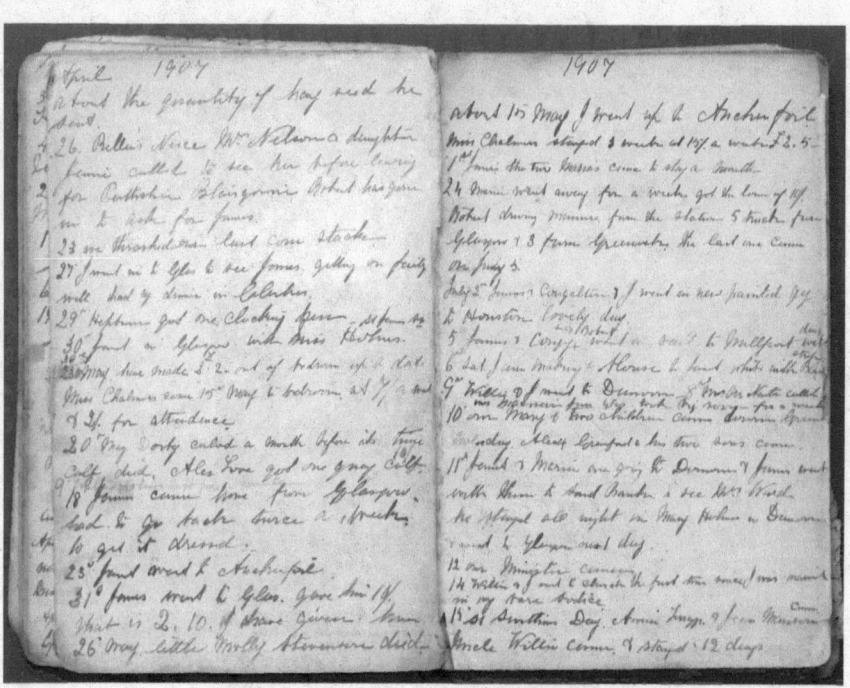

Two pages from Marion Orr's diary

1901

23rd February Hens laying 18 a day.

1st March John and Robert came. John went to Sacrament. Both went away on Monday morning

6th March Jenny Holmes came with Marion

12th March Mary went to Mathernock with Marion Holmes & Horsecraigs. Got 11 shillings for two dresses

13th March Maggie Caldwell came and stayed 2 nights.

15th March Lizzie Taylor called on her way to Cairncurran. JB called. Commenced to go every day with milk. Robert taking eggs to McMenimie.

16th March Robert harrowing the field at the Bridge. (?)

17th March Commenced set potatoes. Sh..ton (?) sent £1 due.

M. Chilsness (?) called with (?) of two (?)

29th March I went to Glenmill with Marion Holmes. Stayed all night. Had on new black silk blouse.

1st **April** James stayed at home.

5th **May** Robert ploughing himself in park at Hedges red land. Wasn't 3 months off 14 years. Father bad with cold.

6th **May** Mary Went in to Glasgow. Stayed two nights. Got a pair of boots for father 10/6. Robert ...me slippers. Mary shoes and slippers

27 **April** Our ... Mary Holmes came and stayed two nights. J went to ... with her. Willie Miller had been left home a week

9th **May** Brown (?) was kicked and two days after...... (?)

29th **May** Willie and I at Exhibition. Got my brim (?) capes.

1st **June** Mary at Greenock (?) Robert Orr very ill. Mrs McLaren took (?) a shock. Mary at milking at Mathernock got 4/-. I sorted cape and (?) 2/9

3 **June** Started to hoe potatoes. James set.

7th **June** Uncle Robert and Davy Miller came at night and Uncle John and Willie Miller came through the day. Willie going to South Africa. Mrs Orr Newton came.

5th **June** Mary Brown and John Kinloch married. James over at Killochwraes. 10 days before that gave her a present of mocassin with front lace cover and Mary a toilet set white lace sewed with yellow silk over yellow lining.

12th **June** Mrs McCowan came 8/- a week by Sun Got the (?) all taken up to (?) this week. She stayed one week.

16th **June** Willie Miller left (Sun) for South Africa.

21st **June** Greenock Show. James got no ticket for it

22nd **June** Children's trip to Barochan.

21st **June** Mary was at Greenock and Whitehill

John and Mary at Whitehill. Stayed all night. Aggie died that morning.

27th June Mrs Crawford of Dippany had her second son.

1st July Mrs Scott and family came £5 a month.

5th July The boy Matthew Scott fell off saiking machine and broke his leg. Chrissie Currie came for the weekend. Got the two (?) of hay cut between the midden and the Bridge.

7th July Robert Orr Lynedoch Street died Sun

10th July Willie was at his brother's funeral

11th July Mary at Greenock. "Some morning"

15th July Bridge of Weir (?) James (?) Janet (?) children all at Loch Tom. Grand hay weather.

19th July Will finish the hay today. Two women went to Horsecraigs. Hosie for a week.

July About the 14th John (or Josh) Miller underwent his second operation for a disease in the bones, his rib. Maggie H. Collville came Going to Archonon (?) the next week

21st July Our John came and stayed one night.

23rd July Willie went to Greenock and trysted some truck (?) of dung from James Holmes. It came two days after.

17th August Robert came last night. We went to waterworks next day. Maggie Collville came.

20th August Commenced our corn at Bridge. Willie just recovering from a severe attack of Asthma.

21st August Jenny Holmes came and helped with the corn. Splendid weather. The Scotts stayed five weeks, a week in August £6. 14th JB called... 22nd+ -

22nd August Maria came and stayed three weeks.

26th August J...y went home.

2nd September Uncle Willie came and stayed a night. Worked two days at the corn inputing and finishing 18 stacks. Had Wull Andrew for a week then he went to Mauls Mill for a week.

13th September Mary 24th birthday. JB came.

15th September Isa Archibald and Polly came and stayed Sunday night and went to see the Glasgow Exhibition[1] the next day.

Opening Parade 1901 Exhibition, Glasgow (T & R Annan & Sons Ltd). Image, courtesy of Douglas Annan, who provided this interesting background information: "The 1901 Exhibition opened in "half mourning" at the King's request due to the death of his mother Queen Victoria earlier in the year. He was supposed to have opened it as The Prince Of Wales but cancelled when he became King. Louise, Duchess of Fife unlocked the Grand Entrance with a golden key."

16th September Wull Andrew came back. Skaling dung on the braeface.

18th September Alex Crawford and his mother came in cab

20th September Mary and Willie went in to Glasgow to see the Exhibition with Willie Holmes on Sat afternoon. The boys came down with Mary Holmes on Sat night. She went in to meet her lad on Mon. When at dinner James Campbell and Mr Wilson came then when I had the tea out James Barr and family came. They had a cup of tea in good spirits. Gave Janet Andrew 4/6. Mary Holmes had her engagement ring, (?) opiel (?) Our Mary came at night. Mrs Colville went away on Mon morning

24th September Wull Andrew came and sorted dyke.

24th September I wrote to John.

28th September Willie and I went to Auchenleck and came by Mathernock.

2nd October Marion came. Father ill pleased. Were busy sacking potatoes. Mary James Janet and Father. Marion helped in house. She stayed a fortnight. Finished digging on 12th. Robert half through his first ploughed field on braeface.

14th October Father went to Greenock to pay Holmes for dung. Came home the worse of drink. Next day went a message to Kilmacolm. Got more drink. Fell off cart of coals which passed over both legs and a very sore shoulder.

17th October Mrs Orr Newton called. She had been at Blairs.

13th October Meeting at school. Annie Drylesde (?)

26th October Jenny Holmes and Miss McMillen called. Maggie Love called at night.

29th October Alex Love came up at night.

30th October Dubbs (?) got 4 bags potatoes. 4 got before I think.

3rd November Our John came.

5th November James in Edinburgh standing an examination. He was the best of 20. He went to stay in Edinburgh on the 9th December 1901 and lodged with Mrs Macles (?) for 13s a week. His hours are from 1/2 past 9 till 1/2 past 4.

6th December Martha Blair got married to her cousin. I was up and saw the Iraws (?) Gave her an album. Mrs Orr Newton gave her a large lamp. Janet a dozen of teaspoons. Jenny Baxter a small cruit and Jeanie Barr a brass kettle. About 30 at the marriage-a gay wet stormy night. I was in Glasgow on the 6th. Got James bag, father with me. Had a nice pie in Willie's. Bought James two pairs of drawers at 7/- a pair and gave him £3 away with him.

19th December Sent fro, on trial, father's Asthma cure. The week that James went away we took in and threshed 4 stacks, snow on ground. Snow continued on ground for 3 weeks till 31 Dec. Mary went in to Glasgow that day.

---

1. **The Glasgow Exhibition:** "The Glasgow International Exhibition was the second of 4 international exhibitions held in Glasgow, Scotland during the late 19th and early 20th centuries. It was held in Kelvingrove Park and ran between 2 May and 4 November 1901. It marked the opening of the city's Kelvingrove Art Gallery and Museum and also commemorated the fiftieth anniversary of the first world's fair held in the UK, doubling that attendance with 11.5 million visits." (Wikipedia)

1902

1ˢᵗ January New Year day. Never had a nicer. John Miller then Alex Crawford then another fellow from the Port then Uncle Robert then Tommy, a Mr Hyslop from Johnstone. Not much drink. Uncle Robert stayed all night. Next day I had bile. James Barr and wife came a bunch(?) of Haddows. I gave him 2 rabbits. On the Friday following they had a grand party at Rockcliffe, the girls first. A special train from Glasgow to take the guests home.

3rd January James Laird came to stop some months for his health at 15s a week. Got a small cheese from John as a Ne'er present. I sent him a pair of socks. But got no answer.

13th January Laird was gay dull this week.

14th January J.L. got dull again but not so bad. Still frost. No ploughing 3 weeks

4ᵗʰ February James came home - first time from Edinburgh, his 22nd birthday. Went back on the 6th. Came back in 4 weeks again. On the 13th I went to Glasgow and stayed a night with Mrs Holburn. We went and saw Mrs Scobie then next night I stayed in Willie's and went and saw Mrs Stevenson. Called in at Peter Miller's as I came home next night.

24th February Robert and father went up hill to plough first time. Gey wet.

25th February Very dark and dull.

A woman came to door. Maggie Love sent up. I bought from her a piece of cloth for a suit to Jennie and Mary Black and a piece of black dress cloth.

26th February Clear and dry. First droughty day. Mary went to Greenock with Willie. He got a new suit and new books. Janet new shoes for church - a concert in church, the Messiah.

27th February A little snow and sleety showers. Still ploughing every day. Few eggs. The grocers are giving 1/4 per dozen. I get about 10 eggs a day. Mrs Morrison takes 1 dz and Mrs Speirs 1 dz and Mrs Laird 1/2 dz in the week. About the 1st of Feb Mrs Barr had a parcel of clothes. Mary took hen on the 26th, a hen 2 dozen eggs a piece of comb honey.

Mary papering (?) room.

15th March Willie from Glasgow. Gave us a day's ploughing. M King Holmes was down at the March Sacrament.

31st March Glasgow Holiday Monday Lizzie and Marion Holmes came on Saturday night late. Janet and James went in to meet her. Our Mary was ill with bile that night and lay all next day. Lizzie and Janet went to Greenock and got J. Orr and Cuthbert Napier with them. Uncle Willie delved the garden. Our Willie went to Paisley and bought two cows £20 both stand (?) at the window.

7th April Willie went to Paisley and got another cow and that same week one of our own was choked bottling it.

26th April Willie and I in at the laying of the Memorial stone (Church).

28th April Ducal men at Hardridge sowing. Janet and Willie turning (?)

29th April Mary away to Paisley.

2nd May Janet went to Glasgow. Came back next night with Janet Holmes. I went in to Glasgow with her on Monday 5th and helped Mary Holmes pick her blankets and choose her furniture. I bought her china. They were 3 pounds. I gave her £2

8th May Menzies and the wife called. I took a bad cold quite hoarse for a week - cough and spit

23rd May Glasgow holiday. Lizzie Holmes came for 2,3 days. Mary went up with her.

24th May We had a picnic with Laird. Jane Manson and Annie (?) came

30th May James Laird went away. James came home for 3 days.

5th June I was down at .... Bell a visit.

26th June Mary Jessie came coronation day.

28th June McLean and wife and Jessie Henderson then Maggie Harper.

29th June John Miller and Mary and Bessie. We have old Malcolm these last 10 days. Willie owes paid

July Mrs Runcie came for a month but just stayed a fortnight - £2;8/-

26 July Miss Laird came 12/- a week. Same day Willie from Glasgow came and stayed till Tuesday. Mary went to Ardrossan on a Sat and stayed till next Thursday. Hay all done then but the meadow ground weather (?)

18th July Mary Holmes and her husband came a weekend.

1st August Mrs Ross called on her way to see old Mrs Orr Midton.

2nd August George Mason and wife and daughter came and our John and Bessie Miller in a small machin + Tinnie and Marion Holmes

3rd August Willie and I at church. Gave Mrs Ross a drive.

4th August Miss Laird went off to Midton. 1 week here

22nd September Janet Holmes came for corn. Met next day. Mary and her drove to Gibblaston. Had Jenny and Annie over one night before that

27th September Willie Holmes came weekend. Got 9 rabbits (?) ... Lofty. James getting a new dark suit this month - first since he went to Edinburgh. Finished cutting corn today. Mary went to Glasgow Saturday. Came back with machin. Willie on Monday put up one stack of corn. Not good.

26th September Mrs Ayre and her son came will (?) with Janet. Miss Mitchell and Robert came one day before that & John and wife in August

8th October I went to Greenock to nursery. Ordered fruit trees had seen in Baillie Adams.

10th October Julia McLean came. 18/- a week

27th October Mary and Janet went to G. and Glasgow and got J a jacket £1.3/- Uncle Willie came same day and howked the rest.

26th October Harvest thanksgiving.

November Got a cheese from Roger 78lb. Got a cask of butter 31/-

29th November Willie and I went to Glasgow. He went to MacElben (?) and I went to Mary Holmes. We met in Willie's. Robert met us with gig.

19th December I went over to Mrs Orr Newton - not in her new house yet.

We sold our potatoes to Muir and Howie (?) Muir and Howie lifted 12 tons of potatoes this week. "£2 the ton and the remainder for £2.2.6. Annabella Crawford and Hugh Laird are courting ...(?) ... (?) night. Heard John was going to get married.

Potato Howking, as it used to be done

1903

1st January Ne'erday No one all day but Willie Congalton & Willie Holmes came the day before.

5th January Our Mary came home from Glasgow. Mary Holmes and her husband came. Wet. Stayed two nights. Next day... Maggie Harper came stayed one night. Our Mary went with Mary Holmes to Wraes and Gibblaston. Janet went in with Maggie Harper in gig with Charlie, the horse

7th January Janet went in with Willie Holmes to Glasgow. Came home the following Monday with Daisy. First time Daisy had been at Holmes. Lizzie Holmes walked up from Greenock that night and next night we had Lizzie and Frank Blair.

18th January Willie and I at church. Maggie Collaton (?) came on Sat went away on Monday... our John came out that day to see us.

13th February Had Jim and Janet Tainsh. J. B. came that... (?) I am busy every day in the garden.

20th February Julia going away after being 19 weeks for which I got £17.2 Hens laying 11 eggs a day

6th March James came home. Mary Stevenson... two blouses for Mary to make.

8th March Our sacrament. John at it and came home with us for dinner. It has snowed more this February and since than it has done for a long time before.

14th March Mr Forbes McLeod came.

16th March Father Robert and James lifting potatoes at pit. Much griling (?) McLeod was 3 weeks £3

12th April Willie Holmes and his father from Glasgow came on Monday. Willie helped to sow corn and delve the garden. And a gentleman and lady called and engaged the big room for Tom Young so he and his mother came on Wed 15th April at £1 a week.

John sent a coat and vest but they are no use for wearing. I also got a ... jacket from Robert.

17th April Janet Holmes came for Marion who had been 3 days. Lizzie Blair came down for Mary to cut potatoes next day. She went but I don't want her to go any more as we have

April plenty to do ourselves. She paid Mary 6/- for two blouses and she got 6/- for Mary Stevenson.

18th April (Saturday) Janet and the rest lifting stones. Jenit Holmes away to Auchenfoyle. There has been severe frost this week. This is the church bazzaar. I sent in 2 doz eggs, 3 lb butter, 1 hen 9/-

8th October We have not got touching the corn for a week, rain every night and day. Maria going away today.

7th November Took in turnips but.......to boil for cows. 3 lately calved cows. James came home; is going to to try to pass an examination on 9th December when going down at ... (?)

I will finish our Invitation on 10th

9th November Lizzie Holmes came helped to finish the potatoes digging next day. Janet and she went up to Auchenfoil and Faulds. Donald came down the road with them. She went away next morning.

18th November Maggie Harper came and stayed the night. We took in our first stack <u>JB</u> and thrashed and also finished our turnips. Mary making a .... dress for Mrs Day...

Getting 7d the stone for a few stones of potatoes in Greenock.

23rd November Mary went to Glasgow and got a jacket for herself £1.15.6 Came home after two nights

27th November Father Janet and me went to Glasgow. Got a jacket and ..... £1.5/- and a grey...We went to Mrs Ferguson 16 Haldane Street got Julatus (?) pits all covered.

30th November A few days keen frost.

1st December Lofty not well. Thought he was going like Ben. (?) Willie 10 & 10 before (?)

Granny Orr in Gateside garden, with Lofty the sheepdog

9th December James tried an examination 10th JB

Father B...and Willie laying the dung in Carsin (?) field top side of the hedge at Bridge.

Sir Michael Shaw Stewart died.

Christmas John came and stayed from Friday till Monday morning.

31st December James came home and stayed till Monday

A Collie dog just like Lofty! (Photo by Chung Nguyen on Unsplash)

1904

2nd January Mary and James went to Greenock He got a pair of boots. Leim (?) Manson and Annie, Twigg came. She had left Tobermory

5th January Got word that James had passed the exam. Hugh Gibbs (?)

8th January Our tea meeting

9th January Janet and Daisy at Miss C (?) to tea. Mr and Mrs Smith got a currin bun from John at Neerday.

13th January One had the Congaltons and Lizzie (?) and Frank Blair to tea. Father and Robert bring (?) at Hardridge

14th January John came out from church. Stayed night. Peter Millers - old Mrs Miller ill.

27th January Mrs Miller… (?) & Mary M. came. Mary….them in in gig

28th January Mrs Bell and Miss Cseg and Mrs Black Auchenfoil to (?)

29th January James came home.

3rd February the con & Mary. Janet Robert and Willie going up to Blairs

4th February I was up and saw Mrs Crawford for the last time.

8th February Janet and Polly Laird, Janet and Robert Orr at night, Mrs Orr through the day. Wrote to John about C

9th February Lifted some lilies and snowdrops. Fine day.

13th February Blairs old cow went away to McKay.

16th February Old Mrs Crawford died. Our first cow calved 2nd from (?)

18th February Willie and me up at the coffining.

20th February I was up at Blairs. Got a washing bine 3/-

Funeral in Largs. Mrs Love called.

27th February James came home for 3 days. Going to start his new job on 1st March

1st March Janet and Janet Laird went in to Glasgow.

5th March Janet came home and Lizzie Holmes with her. Uncle John came for the Sacrament. Went away on Monday morning.

7th March Janet and Lizzie went up to Auchenfoil and Faulds. JB (came) at night.

9th March Robert and Willie and Janet went in to the church. I wrote to Maria.

4th April Glasgow Spring holiday. Mary went to Glasgow and Uncle Willie and John Campbell came. Marion Holmes came the 24th March. A lady "Miss Scott (?)" came to buy room at 30 of March for a month at 10/6 a week and give her coal and attention. I have asked for 20/- out (?) of the rooms this year. I will see if I get it.

7th April The rhododendron is flourishing.

8th April Old Bell died aged 85. Father at the funeral on the 11th

12th April We sowed park of corn "The Howme". Next day it poured. Set a hen 13 eggs.

13th April Nannie beeling foot.

25th April Uncle Willie came. We were thrashing our last stack. Next day he was to go to Hardridge but it was too wet. He helped me delve in garden and in the afternoon he drilled for potatoes and went home at night. Old Black has got his neck cut. Confined to bed. I sometimes get 40 eggs a day.

30th April John came the 2nd of May and stayed a night. 31st April Maria came with Tinna Holmes. Maria went home with Tinna. Got a drive in MacNab's gig.

5th May Janet and I went to Paisley for her hat and got my bonnet sorted (?). Saw Miss Cassmill.

6th May Went to Johnstone and saw about the Piano (?)

7th May went to Greenock and got £6.10/- and £1 extra. James has been home a week's holiday. The Cattle Show father at it, not (?) Allie Currie came. He went to church with us next day.

8th May Finished the harrowing at Hardridge.

16th May Got our Piano from Mr Thomson in Johnstone. Cost £13 & 7 shillings to bring it. James is getting a navy blue suit to cost £4. Two Marias goingaway tomorrow.

20th May Sent James £2.

17th May Miss Casswell came.

19th May James Barr and wife & May came

23rd May Victoria Day J Barr & family & Bessie and May wet day, had to turn on the way to Loch Tom. Sir Hugh and Lady Alice called - first time.

28th May Willie himself has been very ill all week, asthma bad cold had spit.

31st May Janet went to Paisley the weekend. Beautiful weather. Got stuff for a blouse & 3 window screens.

4th June Mr and Mrs Holmes came to see Miss Casswell Jenny Holmes & Miss duer came the weekend. The cow blair (?) has a beeling foot. 1st (?) my kitchen (?)

6th June Willie started to learn his trade with Laird.

11th June James came home. Spoke next night in school

12th June John Miller's men came to sort byre & stable & rones & plaster back of house.

16th June Mary Holmes and her guid mother went to Girvan for a fortnight.

15th June The trip to Port....Ettrick Bay. James at it. Wet day blowy

18th June Old Black's funeral day. 29 machins. Mrs Orr Newton our Willie's second pay 5/-

19th June Mr Martin at school

4th July Janet and I went to Lochgoilhead. I was sick coming back. Went up to M. Miller Jessie Donald, Mrs & Miss Needham were at Gateside. Met them in Millers. Bought a fucshia in Doeys

5th July Maria went away.

6th July Maggie Harper came stayed a week

7th July Miss Casswell went to Parish church.

8th July Mary went to Lochgoilhead and Janet came home. Daisy went with Mary.

12th July Maggie Harper & J went to Tighnabruich. A splendid day. Saw old Mrs Henderson 85. Took her a dozen eggs and a hen.

11th July Had a letter from Mary Holmes. Got a flower root from Mrs Henderson called The Rose of Sharon.

12th July The (?) Communion (?) day. James at it with Miss Casswell Mary and Daisy came home. Miss Bell not so well. Commenced to cut the hay up on the brae. Lost a swarm of bees. Mary and Daisy came home from Lochgoilhead. Willie got a fortnight's holidays. Went off to Lochgoilhead

13th July Robert got a suit from Jackson £2.15/-

19th July Uncle Willie came at night from Lochgoil. Next day helped to cut with scythe below garden. Came on wet. Next morning wet. Got 23 lb of strawberries & made 30 lb of jam.

20th July Bella went to Greenock & walked home - not tired. Saw Miss Derrick's (?)

21st July Maria and daughter came for a fortnight

22nd July Willie came back from Lochgoil

30th July John came and stayed 5 days. James came for a month's holidays - one week at home helping with hay. 2 weeks at Tighnabruich

1st August Charlie Bell got the fork through his leg. It healed up all right. One (?) of L's assistant. He stayed with us 3 weeks.

20th August James came from Tighnabruich and stayed another week at home.

27th August Chrissie Currie came a weekend with her lad, Mr Redick. She went to church with us next day.

29th August James went back to Edinburgh. Father and I went to Greenock to Walker to sign in papers. Mary Miller went with us. We went up to Meli (?) Willie had a steak pie.

30th August Mr Murray sorted the jumper.

31st August Got a cheque from Walker of Smillie's money for 318 pounds and he took £3.1 for his bother.

2nd September Mary and I went to Greenock. I lodged in the Clydesdale Bank 300 pounds. Called on Mrs Currie

3rd September We commenced to open our cornfield above Blairs. I gave Willie £15.

16th September Finished our corncutting. Jenny S... and our Mary went to Gibleston. Stayed all night. John was at the finish.

17th September Our James came home for weekend & Autumn holiday.

19th September He along with uncle John & Congalton helped to ... the corn on braeface.

20th September James went away. Father went into village and got drunk bruk (?) a 3/- whisky.

3rd October We commenced our potatoes & expect to finish in a fortnight. Had helping us Jock and Jenny, Jock and Lizzie & his brother & wife & 4 weans.

8th October James came back again the weekend. Had bought a watch £5.10

9th October Bella went off to Greenock. Came back with milk cart.

11th October Duncan MacDougal died aged 73

10th October Dr Wallace died. Our John gave half a day at howking potatoes

12th October Dr MacDougal called. Mary busy making whitesum.

11th October Robert started to go to Paisley Agriculture class.

15th October Janet and I in Glasgow. She got hat 10/-

14th October Finished our howking potatoes.

17th October Janet came back from Glasgow and Mary and she went down to Bells Janet and Jean Laird then 24 Janet and Daisy at Mathernock for tea then Mary was at Priestside Peggiemills (?)

27th October Mary at Dippany. Jenny ill so is Betty (?) ....

28th October JB at night. Mr and Mrs H. Gray came with 10 hens and a cock 16/6. It was paid for the 24th November

14th November Mary and J and Maggie Harper went to Glasgow to buy chrimes 2 gammars (?) I was out £8 besides gave him 16/10 (?)

15th November Miss Casswell went to Mount Blow after being here 6 months.

8th November Gave Willie 23 pounds

24th November Mary with her father and I met John Black at the Registrar's Office, Townhead, Kilmacolm and signed our names to their marriage ceremony, afterwards appearing before the Sheriff in Greenock (?) & getting leave to register it

6th December Gave Willie £10. He went and paid... (?) John was out. Janet went up to Auchenfoil at night

8th December I was up at Auchenfoil first time.

9th December Got a citation from the Court of Session

10th December Snow an inch thick

27th December Bob Con & Will worked 1 hour & a half. Next day both for an hour 73 quarters.

28th December Had 3 Blairs Lizzie Badly(?) ill. D. & W... father ...(?) went to ... (?)

30th December Willie for taxes £2.7.4 and £1.10.9 - £3.18.1 plus (?) 1/- = £3.19.1.

1905

27th January Janet up to Auchenfoil second time. Called in at Faulds

1st February I was up at Blairs Lizzie going to Walker...Home on the 3rd

4th February Got back £4

13th February Willie and I at Greenock to see Walker about going to Court of Session & went to Glasgow. Wet day.

17th February Janet in Glasgow getting her dress fitted on. (?) and she going to Edinburgh. They went about 11th March a weekend. James came home on 25th & Maria comes then to stay a month.

We cleaned our big room new .... end of April.

Cleaned the wee room for a lady but she did not come.

20th April The lady teacher came 7/6 a week for room and fire.

26th April I went to Greenock. Gave Mary Jessie 10/- from myself and 10/-from Mary. Called on Annie Twigg. Peter Miller

...(?)

4th **May** Mary Miller called on byke.

6th **May** Tinna Holmes & Daisy came. Tinnie and I went to church next day. Best brown cow dying supposed to be a ... (?) James came home weekend

8th **May** MacGregor called in about the account for park (?). Father better but had been ill a fortnight with asthma.

Cattle show on the 6th in new position.

1st **July** I was at Greenock with Mary. Called on Jean Laird (?)

6th **July** Lizzie Holmes went away.

8th **July** Willie Congalton came. April 8th Maria came stayed 4 weeks. Went back 29th April.

Came back 13th May stayed 4 weeks went back 10th June.

Came back 24th June went back 15th July & came back 1st August

22nd **July** Congalton went back to Glasgow for a week

23rd **July** Jney got hurt on gate.

24th **July** Hugh McNair came and stayed a week.

28th **July** Willie and I went to Millport - a beautiful day. Hugh McNair went away.

1st **August** James went to Burntisland. 2nd I went up to Auchenfoil

5th **August** Baxter helped us with his buggy.

6th **August** Bella has gone off this morning. Sunday Came back all right.

9th August I went to Greenock with Willie for his suit and Waterproof.

15th August I went back to Greenock to get my dress tried on. Navy blue.

14th August James went to Glasgow with Maria (?) ... Holmes stayed 2 nights

16th August Mrs McNeil came in Robins milk cart from Auchenfoil. I pruned the Gooseberry bushes.

1st September James got 3 weeks holidays, 1st week at Burtisland, 2nd at Gateside. Willie went back with him & saw the Mound (?) in Edinburgh. 3rd week at Dunbar.

5th September Marion Holmes Black went home, Mrs McNeil with her.

25th September Glasgow Holiday John Orr & wife, John and Archie Currie came. I went back to Auchenfoil for 3 nights then Marion came up.

29th September a visit from Mrs Daly

7th October Marion went home after being 10 days at Auchenfoil. Willie got a pair of boots from MacNab 9/6

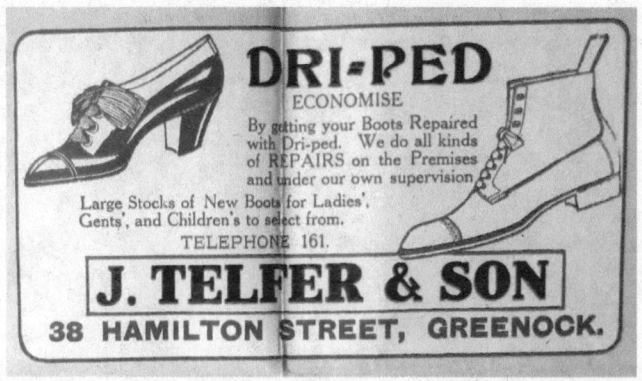

12th October Finished our potatoes howking. Robert ploughing a week since. Garden nice. No frost yet.

18th November James home week end

22nd November Willie and I in Glasgow Paid off McLean & McKellar bond £150.

25th December James home weekend

The garden at Gateside. Unidentified group.

1906

1st January James did not come as expected. Charlie Stevenson, Tina and Marion Holmes came on Saturday night fine quiet New Year.

Bella slipped away to Greenock on the morning before Christmas. Marion stayed a fortnight then went to Auchenfoil.

Jenny came the Saturday after Ne'erday Conference in Greenock. Auchenfoil at night, here on Sunday morning. Gibbleston from church.

15th January This is Parliamentary election time. John came out in good spirits. Promise (?) of a job.

12th January James came weekend no fatter.

16th January Mins (?) men came to lift potatoes in home field - first egg for 3 months.

9th January Robert commenced ploughing at hardridge.

22nd January Marion came down from Auchenfoil Stayed a week and went back again.

25th January I had a letter from Daisy. She was ill in Lochwinnoch. Matthew Armour's son got married this month.

5th February I went up to Auchenfoil. Janet went to Glasgow with Marion. Our Mary went up on the 3rd to see Mary Holmes.

12th February A good day but frosty. Robert carting out dung to hill park. Mrs A. Crawford came in a machine

10th February James came the weekend. Janet went up with Marion to Auchenfoil. Daisy in at Mrs Ross's in Greenock.

15th February I went to Glasgow saw Mary Holmes. Took her a dish of flowers in root (?) Called at Mount Blow coming home and asked up Miss Craig. She and Miss Stewart came next night and Miss McLaren and Maggie Sc... (?) Mrs James Black and Jean Laird did not come.

24th February Our John came out. We broke the thrashing beam this week.

26th February Got in a new beam today. Buchanan put it on. I am making a new blouse for myself.

25th February Got a disappoinment in the bogey not coming.

3rd March James a weekend. 5th Lizzie Holmes came for a week

5th March March Mary Holmes had a daughter.

7th March Mary came to spend the day.

8th March Janet and Lizzie went to Auchenfoil and Faulds.

Miss Bell died, buried on 12th. Robert at it.

9th March Father at Greenock. Got his insurance returned at Mauls Mill with white ... (?) Robert at Hardridge - snow storm.

11th March Our sacrament. Willie Janet and I at it. Cold and snowy.

4th May Mary called. I am papering the wee room and cleaning the traproom. J. sleeping in it. Got a chick from Walker for 17.3 and another from Brown for 5.15

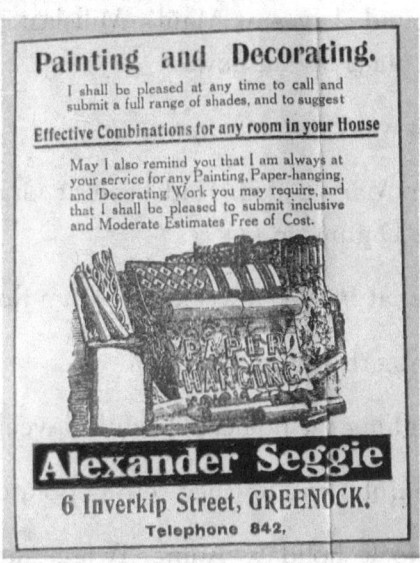

5th May Cattle show Father Robert and (?) at it. ... (?) there a whole day.

10th May Thrashed first half of last stack of corn.

7th May Blair's old cow had a quey calf. It could not go to the station to meet Stark's other ones

9th May Harrowing at hardridge all finished

10th May Got 2 ... (?) manure to put on hay field that faces above the bridge. We have a hay rick standing yet.

14th May Willie and I went to Greenock Got chicks. Lifted £50 out of Bank of Scotland. Got over £2 interest. Went to Johnstone and ... (?) to Glasgow

15th May Old B cow taken to Paisley.

12th March Lizzie Holmes went back to her place. Marion went home with her.

14th March Took in a stack and thrashed it. Two stacks...snow and frost on ground. I was at Maul's Mill last night. Mrs Ross there. Daisy at a place in Glasgow.

21st March John was out.

22nd March Our Mary called. Had been at Greenock getting a new dress. Made Digumson (?)

24th March Janet at Paisley a weekend - got a flower in hat

29th March Sowing the hill park corn.

31st March Ploughing the home. A beautiful week.

12th April Uncle John and finished setting potatoes.

9th April Greenock holiday. Annie Twigg and Mr and Mrs Orr...D Carson Mrs Crawford (Janet) came out with ... (?)

16th April Glasgow holiday. Jenny Holmes and her lad.

18th April Father and I at Greenock and Gourock

19th April Bella at Greenock by train.

20th April Janet at Greenock to meet the Maclarens. We have a few turnips yet. Thrashed half a stack and one out yet. Marget calved a quey calf. The dancing has commenced at Side school

23rd April Uncle Willie came, garden nearly all done. James came too for a week's holiday.

25th April Father and I Glasgow & Janet and I in Glasgow got her cloth for dress light tweed 28/- and white silk blouse 17/6etc 6/6 £2:12 for Janet altogether and dressmaking and boots make it £4.0.0

19th May James and Daisy came the weekend.

21st May Janet went with James to Edinburgh. Lizzie Holmes joined them next day and came home at night. J stayed in Glasgow a night.

24th May Thrashed our last corn. Maggie in Auchenfoil very ill this week.

20th May Janet had on her new dress made by Dysen.

28th May Hear that Maggie in Auchenfoil is a little better. Had an operation Yes - Willie Crawford very ill this last week and uncle John is at Harrowgate. Adam Byrkmire died last week.

June James came for a weekend sore throat.

5th July Mary came going by Mathernock. Last day of June the Miss Dennys came to my big room for a month at 17/6 a week.

6th July Miss Tierney came to wee room for a fortnight at 7/- a week.

16th July June John went to a job at Forth the Rosyth line of railway to finish.

26th July June Mrs Smith Slates Farm died aged 66.

14th July July James came a weekend. Keeping better

16th July Willie Crawford went into Glasgow to undergo an operation on the bowels.

28th July James came weekend.

1st August Maggie Colville came two days. Got (?) record at (?)

2nd August I went up to Blairs. Frank came and milked on Thursday and I got a black and white kitten for thanks.

4th August John came back from his work at Forth unwell.

9th August Father, Janet, Robert and I at Ardgowan Garden Party.

12th August A heavy day's rain

10th August Janet went away with Jenny Holmes by Gibbliston to Glasgow. Cutting burnsides.

3rd September Willie came to help us with corn.

8th September Daisy came a weekend. James was a weekend at Bradford.

10th September I saw Mrs Crawford about (?) Willie wanting (?) 3 night in the week. He is attending Classes in Glasgow.

10th September Old Crawford died.

21st September Willie went home. All the corn in today. Two cows... (?) the Bull picked calves this month one, two months the other 3 months from time. Willie's first week's lodging 2/6 entitles 3/4 1/2

22nd September James went to Glasgow weekend to Clarks. Stayed till Wenesday night.

26th September I went to Orphan Homes with Mrs Bell and Katie and Mrs McGlyn (?)

Got a photograph from Mary Holmes - she and Lizzie.

1st October James went back to his work on Monday night. Miss Russell came at 6/- a week for room.

6th October Miss Kerr came to see her and waited Saturday night. Finished digging potatoes.

8th October Robert at Smiddy with Jess. Getting cny (?) holes in it to be ready for ... (?)

18th October Sent a parcel to Mary Holmes, Polmont.

20th October Janet up at Auchenfoil. Miss Bessie Kerr came to see Miss Russell. Stayed the weekend.

12th October Janet and I at Greenock. Got her a hat - a green one. Called on Uncle John. He gave us a fish tea

14th October Our harvest thanksgiving. Father and I at it.

21st October No one at church.

22nd October Got a letter from Daisy.

23rd October Janet and Miss Russell at Newton - Blacks

24th October Thrashed.

27th October James came home. He has got a lass - Polly Ward.

29th October Miss Russell went away and Mrs Young came.

31st October Janet went to Glasgow for Halloween. Robert went with Miss Maclaren to Cauldside. Willie at his classes in Glasgow.

November Agnes Ross up to tell us Daisy was there and left her job.

9th November I went to Mary Holmes ....(?)

13th November We thrashed. Uncle John came out. He took ... (?) from the Mill. Got stockings from M. Orr.

14th November Mrs Young went away after being 3 weeks at 6/- a week.

20th November Anderson came. Robert at Smithy with two horses. Jess lame taking out dung and spreading it on corn stubble.

24th November James weekend. Late train.

26th November Mrs Orr at Blairs and called in. Cart came for her. Best cow ill at calving. Calf died..... very ill third day but getting better.

27th November Sale of work. Sent in flowers and one pound of butter, value 6/8. James and Robert and Miss Maclaren at night.

8th December Daisy came a weekend.

12th December I gave Willie £2.5/- to pay tax at Police Office.

15th December Mrs Ross came up.

18th December Got back £2.5/-

16th December Mary had her second daughter. Snow on ground on Sunday. I went up M. forenoon came back next. I went up in a week after.

1907

January New Years day was quiet. No one but Lizzie Holmes. Janet and her went to Newton on Ne'erday Liz stayed all night.

11th January Christmas tree Lady Alice at it. I got a hat in box.

18th January Miss Maclaren had her performance in the school.

30th January I was at Johnstone and Greenock.

2nd February James came weekend with train qr to 5

4th February I had a letter from Daisy. She had been ill in bed for a fortnight.

6th February Got my new teeth.

29th February Alex William Mans Wraes was married to Maggie MacPherson Branshlie (?)

18th February Another letter from Daisy saying she would like to come for a little.

19th February Daisy came. Cow Paisley calved as quey 10/- Stormy weather with snow showers.

Daisy stayed a fortnight

11th March Maggie Colville came for a week. Mary and baby were down last week.

28th March Sowed our corn at Bridge. James came home for a week. Lump on his throat. Not looking well.

1st April Glasgow holiday. No one came. Uncle Willie came next morning. Slept on hat rick. The teacher Miss Maclaren gets a week's holiday. Miss Holmes came from Paisley. 2 bedroom 6/- a week

4th April Sowed the corn on hill park. In the afternoon Uncle Willie and James went to the Wraes. Paisley B big ... (?) came the day before.

8th April Commenced to set potatoes in Hill park. Uncle Willie helping

9th April ... I wrote to Mrs Douglas about the Fainshie (?)

8th April James went away a bit better. Paisley holiday two ladies to see Miss Holmes. Miss Miller and M Macd (?)

Cold east wind. I got £1 from Willie for household expenses.

12th April James came back. Throat (a lump on side of his neck) far hotter, talking of getting it cut. Got a doctor's line to say that he is not fit to go back to work.

13th April Uncle Willie went away after being a fortnight

21st April (Sunday) Uncle John came out. He is working at Halfway House near Paisley. Sewage work 40 men to superintend. He saw Geordie there one day.

22nd April James went into Glasgow to see about his neck. Miss Clarke asked him to wait and on the 25th he got into a Home, "Elmbank" Elmbank Terrace.

23rd April We thrashed our last corn stack

26th April Ducal men are sorting the fence at park below the bridge. and Robert was harrowing the half of the hill for turnips.

26th April Bella's niece, Mrs Nelson and daughter Jennie called to see her before leaving for Perthshire, Blairgowrie. Robert has gone in to ask for James.

27th April Murray called yesterday and had a dispute about the quantity of hay seed he sent.

I went in to Glasgow to see James - getting on fairly well. Had my dinner in Clarke's.

29th April Hepburn got one clocking hen

30th April Janet in Glasgow with Miss Holmes.

May Have made £2.2/- out of bedroom up to date. Miss Chalmers came 15th May to bedroom at 7/- a week and 2/- for attendance.

20th May Dorby calved a month before its time. Calf died. Alex Love got one quey calf 10/-

9th May ... Holmes left for America

18th May James came home from Glasgow. Had to go back twice a week to get it dressed.

23rd May Janet went to Auchenfoil

31st May James went to Glasgow. Gave him 10/- That is £2.10/- I have given him.

26th May Little Molly Stevenson died.

About 15th May I went up to Auchenfoil. Miss Chalmers stayed 3 weeks at 15/- a week £2.5/-

1st June The two Marias came to stay a month.

24th June Maria went away for a week. Got the loan of 10/-. Robert driving manure from the station - 5 trucks from Glasgow and 3 from Greenock. The last one came on July 5th

2nd July James and Congalton and I went in new painted gig to Houston. Lovely day.

5th July James and Congalton and Robert went a sail to Millport. Wet day.

6th July Saturday I am making a blouse to Janet, white with black stripes

9th July Willie and I went to Dunoon. 8th Mrs Orr Newton called.

10th July Mrs MacNair from Glasgow took the big room for a month. Mary and her two children came down. Greenock holiday. Alex Crawford and his two sons came.

11th July Janet and Maria are going to Dunoon and James went with them to Sandbank to see Mrs Ward. He stayed all night in Mary Holmes in Dunoon and went to Glasgow next day.

12th July Our minister came.

14th July Willie and I went to church the first time since I was married in my bare (?) bodice.

15th July St Swithins Day. Annie Twigg and Jean Manson came. Uncle Willie came and stayed 12 days and helped with the hay. Good weather all the time.

18th July Jenny Holmes came and went up to Auchenfoil.

19th July Annie Twigg and Jean Manson came and went to Auchenfoil. Jenny came down next day and stayed a night with Jean Black and then went to Gibblaston.

24th July Janet and Maria went up to Auchenfoil

26th July Janet went a sail with Jessie Henderson to Brodick and James came home from Sandbank

10th August James went back to Edinburgh after being at home 4 months.

14th August I went to Newton and Killochwraes.

Marion Holmes Bardrainey was married to ... (?)

15th August Mary and John Black came down and went by Newton. Got tea there with our John. He came this way and talked about going the sail -

21st August I went with Uncle John and Maggie Colville to Glendaruel.

23rd August Uncle John and James Barr called in motor

24th August Jessie Donald came. Janet went up to Auchenfoil with her and Agnes Holmes and Mary MacDonald and Joan H ... to spend the afternoon.

James came home weekend.

25th August (Sunday) Wet day. Robert the only one at church.

26th August Letter from Mary Holmes.................... complication in the lung. I sold 1 lb of honey and a chicken to Miss Lennox. Another letter from Mary saying Baby was not so bad.

30 & 31st August .... Show. James came home to see it.

1st September Willie and I at church. Got Maggie Harper and Uncle John out to dinner. James went off on Monday. Morning wet.

4th September Maggie Harper and I went up to Auchenfoil and Uncle John was there. Drove home with us.

5th September Robert gave me £1 and I am to give him £1 and there is one lying so that is £3 I have of his towards paying his suit.

Maggie Harper went away I got my check from Smillie £5.18/- I went to Greenock. Got my blue ring... (?) Got from Smillie's Trust £5.15/- five pounds interest.

7th September Willie gave me 13/- to pay for his books .... Sold 4 chickens to Mr ... Got 7 shillings for them.

8th September Mary Holmes at Gibblaston with Charlie and baby

12th September Mary Holmes came here and stayed two nights.

14th September Our Mary and baby came down and saw M Holmes. Mrs ... and two girls came from Netherwood. (Minnie Kerr & Jim Binnie (?)

16th September Uncle Willie came and the Marias a train later to commence the corn next day. Jock and J ... (?) came on Sunday night but wet all day on Monday.

Sent to Anderson by James two chickens. Paid 4/2

19th September Finished our corn. James Barr, wife, Mary Lyle and a Mrs Brown came in motor. Jenny Orr Midton got 1 lb of honey. Not paid.

20th September 1 ½ stone of potatoes to Morrison & one before.

20th September Tremis (?) concert. Maggie ... (?) and Janet at it.

23rd September Janet and Maria went up to Horsecraigs.

24th September Maria went up to Auchenfoil. Stayed fully a week. John was ill with ... pleurisy.

25th September Sent £1 to James that leaves 19 nine (?)

26th September Put in a stack but after a few days had to take it down again it het so.

28th September Our John had gone to Paris ("It was a mistake" was written over this stroked out entry) James to Glasgow a week

29th September Willie and I at church.

3rd October Heard John Miller was not well - diarrhea. The doctor came to see Bella.

4th October 22nd Sept. Bella walked nearly into the village and was real done. Has kept her bed for over a week. Mrs Neilson came to see her yesterday Oct 3.

Getting very few eggs. More yesterday.

8th October Maria went home. Got 10/- from Mary 7/- from father. I went up to Auchenfoil. John worse. Went and came in milk cart.

9th October Bella not able to rise yet. Janet and Katie Bell are away to ... (?) Uncle Willie went away today after being 3 weeks. Wet weather. Not one stack up the first one had to be taken down. 11th Sent Willie a bag of potatoes.

15th October Uncle John came out. Macgregor and Katie Bell came down to help gather potatoes.

17th October Uncle John to come but he did not. Wet. Miss MacLaren at night. McGregor & K. Bell and Campbell. Got a letter from Jenny Holmes saying she is to be married next Friday.

18th October We thrashed. Two stacks up. I sent away 4 hens to Anderson 8/4. Willie Junior got a pair of trousers this week from

Holmes Kilbarchan for running. Not paid. Got a good suit beginning of September. Not paid.

30th October Got all our corn in.

31st October Janet went to Glasgow to hold Hallowe'en. Robert putting dung from corner midden on hill park. He has a boil on elbow.

4th November Willie went to Paisley and got a cow £17.10/-. It calved next morning afterwards was finesick (?) Got Buntain one visit. It got better. Had Buntain 3 visits to Nannie the week before. Sore frost.

5th November The Loves getting their potatoes digged at the Syde. (Chalmers their corn not all in.) I have a pretty red rose in bloom. Anderson owes me about £4.3/- never got aprons.

6th November Cow got worse and on the following Wednesday died.

9th November James came weekend.

11th November Janet to Greenock. Put £10 in Bank. Went to Johnstone. All well there.

15th November Daisy called. Janet went to Dippany with Miss Maclaren.

16th November John Miller's old man came to sort boiler and plaster the parlour roof. Arrived 20 past 8. Went away half past 2. 4hours and a 1/4.

26th November Janet and I went to Greenock. I put £4 in bank for Robert that leaves 1 I have for him & 3 before.

19th November John Black took ill second time, not so serious as the first time.

27th November Got from Willie £5 for Robert 7 £2 1/2 for Janet.

28th November I am making my navy blue blouse copying off Mary.

30th November James came weekend. Maggie Sinok (?) along with him. He did not go out on Sunday.

Janet Willie and he were at Maclarens and got pies. Mr Maclaren was buried that day week "previous". James left £1.10- I owe (?) Bella is able to sit at fireside 3 hours but feet badly swollen.

December Sale of work 17th I gave 2 lbs of butter scones 1/8. Janet and Robert at it and Katie Bell. I was at Greenock and got a bonnet and maral (?) church (?)

7th December Sent the blankets to Janet Holmes.

18th December Uncle John was at Newton and came over

19th December Robert went to Auchenfoil. Jenny a year old. Jean Laird at a hall at Largs. Janet and Donald at a party at Strone. Father had with Asthma this month. One hen laying. I owe Robert £5 except 14/- for book

30th December I gave Willie loan of £3. I got it back same day.

1908

1st January Ne'erday. James and the two Bells, Mary and Jessie, came from Edinburgh the night before. They walked about that day. At night we had Macgregor and Katie Bell and Lizzie Holmes came the night before. Tinnie came that day. Lizzie went home that night 10 train. Robert went to Paisley and Johnstone. Old Donald had been very ill. Had to sit 3 weeks in his chair. Could not lie. Tinnie Holmes went away the night after Ne'erday, her lad came from Greenock and went with her. James and the two ladies went that night too.

3rd January Xmas tree. Got a jewel box from Lady Alice. Jean Black & Jenny & John Orr came in at night & Miss Maclaren came up and Ada.

Mr & Mrs William and Marion Orr shaking hands with Sir Michael Hugh Shaw Stewart and his wife, Lady Alice. Date unknown.

9th January Went up to Auchenfoil with John's semit 4/3 not paid. Mrs Janners (?) 3 days ill. James cramp in stomach. James went up at Ne'erday. Willie off two weeks but going to his classes.

16th January To Clark 9 eggs 1/6 23rd 1 1/2 dozen at 1/11, 2/10 1/2

18th January James came home weekend.

19th January (Sunday) Bella felt pained at night. Next night worse. Both lungs sore. Got weaker and died on Thursday 28th aged 86.

22nd January Janet and Maclaren and Katie Bell went to Blacks Newton. John had gone to bed.

24th January Mrs Blair came down.

10th February (Monday) John came out. Went to the Loves (?)

14th February Party at Dippany Robert and Jenny at it. Mrs Orr Newton.........over

12th February Janet and Robert at a party at Glasgow. Uncle Willie not very nice. I got £2 from Willie for household expenses.

17th February Janet and Willie at Mrs Newton

22nd February Peggie calved a quey. Got 7/6 for it

25th February Church social - Minister a new robe & Mrs P a necklace.

26th February Plowing match at Knockmorton. 51 plows at it. Did not get enough to eat.

27th February The Orrs Newton over and Miss Mac up

First parcel to M.S.

28th February Ground covered with snow.

March Mrs Carson underwent an operation in Glasgow. Heard old Mrs Erskine of Law (Ann Speirs, Burngill) is dead lately. Willie stopped his classes in Glasgow. First class in Mathematics, the same in Building Construction and First Prize for most marks.

18th March Mary and Marion down.

17th March Uncle John out.

21st March James came. Was a fortnight since paid the doctor

22nd March I had bile. Had a letter from Congalton saying he was going to Rothesay

7th & 8th April Sowed the corn in little park at barn end and on half of the hill park next the road.

10th April Commenced to set potatoes on park below the road. Uncle John came out to help. John Laird, carter, fell out (of) his machine this week.

19th April Mr & Mrs McNair called. Was a few days at Kilmacolm.

20th April Glasgow Easter Holiday. Maggie .... (?)

23rd April Uncle Willie came worse of drink with Jimmie Crawford and Smith Slates. Last week our John had been a week at Paris and London.

24th April They are harrowing up at Hardridge but it is keen frost in the mornings. White cow next the byre door calved this week. Had to put a rope on it.

17th April Darby calved quey. Love has got 3 calves.

20th April James came late at night. Had been weekend at Glasgow.

25th April James and Janet went to Paisley and Johnstone. Getting a hat from Jessie 9/6, Japin (?) Johnstone 5/-

May Uncle Willie waited about a fortnight & went away the 5th of May.

We tried the kye to want (?) their dinner inside 7th May They did well. Took in our last haystack when Willie was here and haggd a lot of it

2nd May Janet up to Auchenfoil. Uncle Willie came at night and stayed 2 nights. I called in at Faulds. Gave Jean a ...... (?) present, a small table cover and tray.

I went over to see Jean Black and Mrs Orr.

8th May John and two bairns went to Bournemouth.

9th May James came home weekend. Left £4. I take one for Janet's bicycle. Janet's bicycle came today price £3.5/-. Katie Bell and her went up to Govan to see it. Willie has been two weeks with Walker Stepends 12/- a week.

23rd May Janet and Kate Bell & ... (?) Macgregor went to Orphan Homes and was late.

24th May Willie and I at church.

30th May Robert away seeing his lass over the hill. Came home late. James came weekend, very thin. Had been at Kilbarchan.

1st June John Black & Annie Brewsters Wedding. Dark and heavy rain at night. Fine weather fro 2 3 days

2nd June Bob Crawford Kilbride got married & Eliza Crawford Barnbeth got married & Miller Castlehill to Miss Sclors today.

3rd June Jean Laird Faulds got married to Tom Munn.

6th June Jessie Donald and Elsie Craig came. Father at the drains in Mid park. Robert cutting hay.

13th June James the weekend.

18th June Finished thinning our turnips

12th June Mary and family came home from England

22nd June Got £2 from Willie for Boges (?). I wrote to M. Holmes

23rd June Daisy and Clayston at Muirhouse (?)

24th June Janet went up to Auchenfoil.

30th June Bridge of Weir Show. Robert at it. Gave him 1/- the exam (?) Maria came and stayed 3 days. George Mason son and daughter came. Janet went on bike to Johnstone.

1st July I was at Congalton's wedding.

4th July James came weekend. & Miss Mitchell.

7th July I was up at Auchenfoil.

8th July Wee Ria came.

9th July I was at Maul's Mill

10th July Got the money back from ovenduke (?)

13th July Uncle Willie and Marion came. Marion went to Mary Holmes after staying 3 weeks. She had a son in August 1st. Marion went the 5th. James came home the 4th. Mrs Brown the next day at 15 shillings a week. Our John was to sail with Sandy Graham from Plymouth on Sunday 9th on a tour round the world.

11th August The Miss Macleishams came to big room at 17/6 a week two beds.

15th August Maggie Harper weekend.

12th August Uncle Willie, Willie and I went to Houston

13th August Janet went to Greenock to Agnes Barr.

18th August Maggie Collville came over for two days.

16th August Robert Holmes on bike from Kilbirnie. Father and I at church & Miss Maclacton

18th August Daisy called. I gave her a bunch of flowers.

20th August Father and I went to Rothesay. Mrs Miller (Maria) came. Mary had her first son.

22nd August Mr Brown went away. 2 in weeks and Miss Bell from Edinburgh came. Uncle Willie went away.

23rd August James Miss Maclaren and Jess (?) Bell went to Orphan Homes

24th August We commenced the hill park corn.

25th August James went to Glasgow to see P. Ward. Next day he went to .... (?)

28th August I went down with Jessie Bell to Sailors... (?) She went home. James came to the home with Willie Congalton and his wife to stay with me weekend. Finished the park on Friday.

22nd August Mary Holmes went to Rothesay for a fortnight. James and the Congys called on her. Uncle Willie there.

30th August (Sunday) James at church. Making him ...... (?) for James & the Congys & all.

31st August James went off to Edinburgh and Congy followed to Rothesay.

1st September Donald Maclachand came. The Marias went.

3rd September Janet went to Rothesay to stay a night.

5th September Received 4/- from Robert, that is 30/- I have for him.

4th September The motor came for me but I had too short notice.

9th September The wedding. I did not see the presents. 150 invited.

19th September James Barr called in a new motor. Our James came the Autumn holiday. He left £4.10/- We took the honey from the bees but they have made none since James.

16th October I went to Greenock. Put £2 in bank for Robert. He owes me 10/-

17th October Mr Orr went with Robert to Dumbarton.

19th October Uncle Willie came stayed a week. and went up to Auchenfoil.

20th October Mary came down for 2 nights with 3 children.

29th October Janet went to Edinburgh for 2 nights. James came with her.

31st October Lizzie Holmes came after family up at Restmuir (?) She stayed 12 days.

11th November Father and I went to James Orr. 98 Kirkcaldy Road and Uncle Willie. Had the Blairs down at night.

16th November Willie took bull to Paisley. Got £10.17.6 Home tight.

18th November Robert away to Tighnabruaich. Gave him 5/-. He owes me 15/- Robert got his pay. I gave him 5/- He gave me £1. I owe him £4 (December put £2 in bank leaves £2 with me.

30th November Janet went to Johnstone a night. Jean Black and Bob Dunlop were married in the Tontine Greenock.

14th December I was in Greenock in Provident Bank between James, Robert, Janet and myself £237. In 1910 £277

22nd December Thrashed our second last corn stack. Lizzie Holmes got a job in a baker's (?) shop.

23rd December Gave Robert £1 leaves one with me. Paisley cow calved - a quey calf. Keeping it

Rural Scene, old book illustration 1879

1909

1st January Willie, Robert went to Glasgow to the McNairs. Got James home at night with the 9 o'clock train. Marion and Tinnie Holmes and Alice MacKendric called on their way up to Faulds. I got two big cakes of shortbread from John.

2nd January Taking in a haystack at the school. 4th Got a quey calf off Paisley cow.

13th January Robert and me are clear. He gave me 10/- to myself. (About the 7th Uncle John came (?)

11th January Anna bella Crawford ran away with Hankinson the gamekeeper and got married next day.

13th January Janet (?) down at Maclarens.

14th January I wrote to Wm Martin & Mrs Congalton. Taking in a haystack. The thin cow got a chill not very bad. It got better.

19th January A bull calf off Blairs Lawpark cow. Keeping them both.

25th January Willie and I went to Greenock & Port Glasgow. A fule (?) errand.

26th January John Buntain put the... (?   ?   ?) the 8 going up to Blairs tonight. Robert went for cart of coals for Maclaren 2/-. James home the end of Jany. Left for (?) £6

10th February Surprise party at Barnshake.

11th February I went up to West Syde.

12th February I went up to Auchenfoil. Called at Chapel & Horsecraigs. Walked home.

13th February Went up to Blairs. Mrs Blair a sore leg. a hole at back of ingle

15th February I cleared traproom bed for Janet.

16th February A letter from Mary Holmes with a set of bed curtains. Gave father loan of £5. I got £1 back from father, leaves £4 he owes me. Getting about 17 eggs a day.

22nd February Janet Holmes, Mrs Stewart, had her first son. Mrs Dempster (?) Mathernock died.

24th February Janet and I at Glasgow.

25th February Polly Laird & Rachel Agnes and James Ross were in. Next Thursday Lizzie Blair & (?)

26th February Mary and 3 children came down and spent the day

2nd March A surprise party at Hardridge. 25 at it.

5th March Janet went to Paisley. Stayed a night.

7th March Snowing yesterday and today my 56th birthday. Our sacrament but just Robert and Miss Maclaren went down the road

8th March I got £3 back from Willie, 4 in all. Leaves £1. I wrote to Jessie Donald, (?) Maria and Maggie. Wee white cow got ... (?) on gate. Buntain... (?)

20th March I got the other £1 and two for myself.

16th March We had the Smiths, the Orrs and Maclaren.

24th March Lizzie Blair and Janet were at Auchenfoil.

25th March Jeny was at Newton.

28th March Willie & I at church. Gave Mac & Liz Crawford a chair

29th March Buntain was today that is five times anyway. Commenced to set potatoes at Barneuf (?) Park.

2nd April Setting pots in same park.

3rd April Robert rolled hill park ... (?) and wet days.

2nd April Had chickens out. Willie finished his classes this week.

5th April 14 chickens, out of two dozen.

6th April Uncle John out. Finished setting yesterday. Got two bedrooms cleaned.

8th April Janet went to Paisley and stayed a night.

10th April The Macfadzeans came - 3 rooms at £1 a week with attendance. Stayed a fortnight.

11th April Jean Manson came.

12th April Glasgow holiday Uncle Willie came and stayed a week. Marion went to Horsecraigs on the Saturday and went home on Tuesday. Aunt Lizzie went up to Glas on the Thursday & stayed a night & came home with Netta next day. She had gone up with Marion.

13th April James Orr, his son Douglas & ... (?) came. His wife could not get.

17th April Janet and James went to Tighnabruaich & Rothesay. Janet stayed the weekend at Tighnabruaich & James came back that night from Rothesay. Saw Bobby Congalton there.

19th April James went back after being his Easter week. Darby calved a bull little white ceros (?) side is getting better.

21st April Janet went in for her white hat with ostrich feathers.

23rd April I set a hen & am going to set another. Eggs from Hatrick

24th April Taking in rick of hay. Took in one a fortnight since.

26th April Willie Dunlop Knocknair went to New Zealand. Old hen died.

28th April The cows got their dinner (?) outside. All our hay in.

3rd May Katie Bell's birthday, the ...... at it & Maggie Sand & Carson. Janet did not go.

4th May Janet went up to Blairs. Will came home with her.

13th May Willie and I went to Greenock, Johnstone and Glasgow. Paid in to Mitchell £100

14th May Mrs Darroch came to wee room at 7/- a week. with attendance. Stayed two weeks.

22nd May The hay just a handful & a cow with sore side in the byre.

21st May The men to inspect the house came.

26th May I went to Greenock and saw Chrissie Curries train. Gave her 3 half sovereigns. Have to get 1 back from James & 1 from Mary.

28th May Gave Willie £5 for Robert

29th May Gave him £1 for Buntain. Heard Chrissie Holmes Bardrainey was married this week.

31st May Chrissie Currie got married to J. Riddick in the Tontine. James was at it.

6th June Willie and I at church.

7th June Robert cleaning ditch below old spring well. Willie twice was up on the 6th June having commenced his trade in 1904. Got work in Kilmacolm all the time. Was last summer with Harry Walker at Stepends. Harry has left there now and gone to America.

11th June Got £5 back from Willie. McGregor paid. The ... (?) ploughing.

26th June Sat Jean Manson & Annie Twigg came & the two Marias. Willie and I went to church and next day I had the bile. It continued 12 days before I had recovered.

1st July Mrs Thomson and two children came to backroom.

6th July Uncle John was out asked me to go a sail next day.

13th July 7 ricks up on hill park

5th & 6th August All our hay stacked & 3 ricks in byre loft. 6 stacks in all. Our Willie at home & Uncle Willie & two ladies in helping. Never got it up so quick. A letter from W. Congalton asking father and I & the boys to go and see him. Uncle John is at Harrowgate. Been away all month.

6th August A beautiful day. Got all our hay in. Daisy was up on sliding stone with children. Did not come in.

7th August I got £1 from Willie H. for self & £1 for tr... (?) watch less (?) 6 for hat (?)

11th **August** Father and I were at Rothesay. Had a nice day.

14th **August** Robert and Willie went to Rothesay to see the sports. Brought Willie Congalton with them the weekend. James here too. Got a lovely day on Sunday. Daisy pased (?) up but did not speak to any of us.

21st **August** Annie Bell had a daughter.

19th **August** Willie's birthday. Mr & Mrs John Kinloch & Tom Brown called & we are to go over.

21st **August** Jessie Dippany coming home tonight. Has been with the twins a fortnight in Islay. Yesterday and today in the Flower Show.

25th **August** Willie and I went to Killochwraes & Branchal & Wraes. Met Stewart Dunbar. Mary was down the day before.

27th **August** We cut a park of corn below the bridge.

28th **August** James came home for his holidays & Jennie Bell and Jessie came for a week.

31st **August** The third son born at Langs Barnshake. (James Scott Lang)

1st **September** James went to Devonport by boat to Ireland & the next week we cut corn.

4th **September** Bells went away & Tinnie Holmes came & stayed till yet the 14th helping to bunch. Will finish tomorrow. Janet and her going to Blackwater tonight. Were at Blairs last night.

14th **September** I gave George Scott (Miss Scott) 2/- for missionarys.

24th **September** Had the Orrs Newton & the Blairs & Macphail & Tinnie Holmes. She went away next day.

27th September Willie went to Paisley & got another cow. I got a cheque from Walker firm. Another divide of Uncle Smillie's money £43. I gave Willie £20 in present.

29th September Jean Black, the Blairs & Cissy (?) MacDougal called in & next day Mrs Currie and Mary Jessie called & little John McNab.

2nd October Robert and Willie are going into Glasgow with MacPhail to get their photos taken. I gave Robert 10/- to do for 10 weeks from 2 October including 11 December.

9th October We took all our corn in. It is not bad but it has rained for a fortnight and still pouring. Auchenfoil and others about (have) a lot out.

8th October Friday morning. Mrs Congalton got her first daughter. Robert went to Greenock sale & got 2 Leicester sheep - his first transaction in business.

11th October I got 2/6 from Robert & 2/- for Lairds account. He owes me £4.

19th October Uncle John came out. Went by Pomillan. Janet went to Mary.

23rd October James came home a weekend, had seen Polly.

John Carson died 17th October aged 94. Willie was at the funeral on Wednesday 21st.

18th October Mrs Martin, wife of Tom Clark died.

24th October None of us at church.

22nd October Janet and I at Greenock. Ordered my costume and got Janet jacket price 28/-.

21st October Mary was at Glasgow M... (?) and Byers for jacket.

22nd October Mrs Gault was taken to Greenock Infirmary. I loaned her a pair of blankets and got them back that night. My hens are not laying. 1/8 per dozen.

25th October Shawed the .... of turnips to give to kye and Robert went to Baxters to help with the corn as it was the first good day except Sun. The day before that had been for a long time. He was at Faulds at night, saying goodbye to MacKenzie who was sailing next day with Pollock and John Dunlop to New Zealand. Willie stay in Kilmacolm with Mrs Crawford, Tuesday and Wednesday night.

29th October Robert owing 4/6 for drawers & 1/- for braces.

1st November Janet went to Glasgow to a Hallowe'en party. Stayed two nights & Marion came down with her - party not up to much. Lizzie would not nor Willie contribute to it. Our Robert at school with MacPhail & Polly Laird & Rachel on the Saturday night. On Monday the 1st Willie and Robert dressed up with Robert Orr & MacPhail & went to Cauldside & Dippany. James came home on 30th October. Left £1.

4th November Robert and Willie & R. Orr and MacPhail went to Cauldside with partners, the teachers & Marion Holmes, P and A Laird.

7th November Our sacrament. M. Orr & J & Robert at it. My new house dress on first time. I shook hands with old Mrs John MacDougal.

8th November Father went to Paisley 1st Nov. with black cow. Got £14 for it. 5/6 came off for expenses beside his own. Gave me 10/-

Marion went up to Dippany. They are having a party on Friday night. MacPhail had been away a weekend & came in. We had ... (?)

9th November I have taken 1/3 from Robert, that leaves 4/3.

12th November Tinnie Holmes came to Dippany spree, a fine affair.

11th November I went to Johnstone.

13th November Marion came back from Gibblaston and Janet and her went to Auchenfoil. Tinnie met her lad on ... (?)

14th November Marion and Janet went to church & KIlmacolm at night.

15th November I went to Johnstone about Income Tax. Robert gave me 3/- which leaves 1/3 Got on all right at Johnstone. Heard that Fyfe had left James Barr's business to become a Government official. Willie, Robert Jenny and Marion Holmes & Jim Adam all went to Sailor Homes, a magic lantern. The boys went to Kilmacolm and had a great time at the Tally shop.

17th November Mary and Marion and Jenny came & Mary Holmes went up with them (Wed) & stayed till Sunday.

19th November Will Blair came down to see Mary. She was at Auchenfoil. 20th James came.

22nd November Monday night. John Blair called in & we had a pleasant game at cards.

23rd November Janet and Marion went to Smiths Slates and met Sandy Lyle Scort (?).

25th November (Thursday) We had the Smiths up & Peggy & Lizzie Crawford & had a lot of fun.

26th November Janet and Marion went to Newton & Robert met them. Tim (?) went home at weekend.

27th November I got a pc this morning from Marion saying her man had died at 9.30 the night before. Marion went home. Gave her Jeny's old blue petticoat.......woolly necklet (grey) & a blue flannel...

28th November (Sunday) A real snell day. Uncle John is ill with influenza. Robert and Willie are away to church & will ask for him. Heard that John Holmes Bardrainey fell down a stair in the Port & hurt his head last Monday. Still unconscious. Mrs Holmes was at Dumfries at Marion's who has got a son. Robert Dunlop called from Cardiff. The big brown cow is coming near her calving. Father says it will have to get a little warm meal. We have our last cart of turnip shaws in. The cows have eaten them well between meals and with straw. The straw is to be eaten first before we commence with the hay.

December The brown cow (Lawpark) calved again (?) Robert and John Orr came over with (?) Father went to Paisley today to pay back price of Paisley cow. It was returned. Got the account of Janet's cycle smash at B. of W. 15/6

5th December John Adam came the weekend. Paid for (?) up till today 2 bags of potatoes (?) yet. One of them useless (?) 6/2 & 6/4.

9th December The (?) came. A wet night. Janet went to Johnstone a weekend. Had toothache all week after & (?)

18th December James came home tonight (?) Sammie the horse took a bad turn. Had Buntain late at night.

19th December Robert at church. John Adam went away. Our minister said today that he was not going to accept the call to Edinburgh. I had the bile yesterday, the first time since the summer when I was last ill. (I paid MacNab for Robert 3/9)

21st December Robert owing for bin(?) 1/6

22nd December Sent off 3 hens to Jennies at 2/6 each. 11 for Curries (?) Janet and Maria went in with them.

23rd December Sandy Orr's son buried today, not a year old.

29th December Robert & Willie went to Edinburgh for one night. I got no present from Uncle John. He was ill from the effects of influenza.

This photograph of Emmy Soutar, with bicycle, was taken in the East Riding of Yorkshire, in the early 1900s. It illustrates the sort of bicycle Granny Orr's daughter Janet would have had when she had her expensive 'smash' on it in Bridge of Weir!

1910

1st January Quiet day. Andrew Smith was in at night.

3rd January John McGregor was in good form at Pit. Jim Adam went home on 31st December.

12th January Dusty (?) took a meal in either & picked ... (?)

14th January Our ones went up to Blairs & the Orrs, Newton were there. Frank Blair came down one night.

21st January Mrs Miller came back from Auchenfoil after being up a fortnight.

22nd January James Adam came back from Paisley. 3 weeks only getting about one egg a day. Jim Adam bought a woolen ... (?) light green.

18th January Jan Uncle John went to a Hydro at West Kilbride, Seamill. Not sleeping.

21st January The polling day at Kilmacolm for the parliamentary candidate. Mr Craig-l got in. 849 majority.

22nd January Jim came back. .... (?) the date for.

23rd January Willie and I went to church. Snowing. Very cold.

24th January Maria was very angry. This missing..................... (?) getting on to....who was.... (?)

25th January Janet went to Glasgow to a Burns concert.

26th January 5 inches snow on ground. The most severe frost I ever remember.

Mrs Lang Mount Blow had a party. 38 at it. Our Janet at one at Bells the night before. On the 25th she went to Glasgow & stayed two nights. Went to the circus & next night to McNairs. Got her photo with hat on.

28th January We had our children's party & next day the Marias went away after being here from 9th December.

30th January Robert at church.

31st January I wrote to James. Father and Robert lifting potatoes. Jim in the dumps, frightened for war. Uncle John came back from Largs Hydro.

4th February John Adam came and stayed weekend & Jim went off with him on Monday morning. Our James came the weekend.

8th February Janet went up to Auchenfoil.

9th February A letter from Maria saying she had got a house and Mary went to Greenock for cloth for a dress to ... (?) and asked Janet up today again. Mary called in coming back from Greenock & gave us haddies and sausages.

13th February Jim Adam, his mother Aunt & ... (?) came fro his clothing.

This was Mrs Peter Miller's funeral day. Uncle John was at it. Father bought a bull from Blair, some months old.

14th February Robert and James were at Slates - the Crawfords & Carruths at it.

17th February J. Blair called in late. Did not ask him.

Robert commenced ploughing at hardridge. I commenced to make a bed mat.

19th February James came a weekend. Had been seeing Polly & at Gibson Street.

20th February Janet and James at church.

22nd February Spree at Telfords. The Crawfords at it & told Janet not to go to Dippany. Old Blair in and got paid for bull calf. I gave father loan of £2. Got it back.

1st March Gave Robert £1.......................... (?) Janet and Robert were at Dippany party. two teachers, Smiths, Slates, Kate Bell & Dav Carson, James and Agnes Ross, Willie and John Crawford dancing. No Lairds at it. Heard Donald had got a moustache

4th March John Blair came in byke from Blackwater. Had a jolly game at cards. Father in bed.

6th March Janet in church with her velvet dress waited (?) in Millers for the last of Paterson's lectures.

7th March I commenced to sort garden and I am cleaning trap room.

8th March Paid Erskine 12/-

11th March Polly Laird & Rachel came & Katie Bell. James Baxter & Telfer outside.

12th March James came weekend.

13th March Father and I at church. Communion.

16th March Mary came alone.

18th March Mary sent word Mary Paton and J. Love (or Laird?) were coming but did not come because Polly & Rachel were at a dance in connection with their cooking classes.

19th March I wrote to Prentice about my account. Father and Janet were lifting potatoes in Barnend park. Had a letter from James. He had been best man at Mr Browns (the preacher) wedding. Robert got a new pair of wearing trousers last night.

Paid up the Baker 7/11 shortbread account.

28th March Easter was yesterday. Uncle Willie came today. Little Maria on Sat the weekend.

31st March Put in our seed potatoes - the Crawfords helping.

1st April Campbell Crawford helping to set today yet.

2nd April James came the weekend for a week. He helped to set the potatoes.

5th April Mary Paton called. Father owing me 3/- the 10th I loaned him. £1.10/- All paid.

30th April James home the weekend. - Mary Holmes the same.28th

28th April I was in & saw Mary Miller's .... (?) Gave her half a sovereign & so did James.

11th May Got Queen bee from London.

10th May Jenny Orr and Lizzie Baxter were over.

7th June Will Love got married to a servant girl in the Green & the following Tuesday Robert Taylor Branchal got married to a girl in Kinloch Branchal.

10th June Janet went to Johnstone Bought paper for Kitchen. Had on her sepher dress. John Carson got married to a servant in Chapel. Staying in Kilmacolm.

2nd June The minister and his wife were calling. Got tea and ham and eggs. Went up and saw the old sundial & the next week by Clarke's van I sent them a box of flower roots.

13th June Father and Robert are ploughing up the potatoes. The trip to Fairley is on the 15th. (The trip got a nice day)

16th June Janet started to thin turnips. I wrote Maria.

Young bees seen in strip for the first time since I got the queen bee a month since.

19th June Sunday Young Paterson brought me a book from his father Roman Catholic in Italy.

July Mr Paterson called on his way to Auchenfoil & thanked me for the flowers. Mr & Mrs Congalton came for 2 months. Commenced our hay 7th July. No rain for a week - a fellow in school helping us.

13th July Maggie and Lizzie Orr came and went by Killochwraes. I am papering kitchen.

15th July Annie Twigg & Mrs Twigg came by Mary. I am making jellies and jam. No word from Maria. James got his holidays today 16th.

18th July James came all the way from Edinburgh on his cycle. A letter from Mary Holmes saying she was not so well and one from Maria saying she was doing a little better & Uncle John is at Strathpeffer.

28th July James Barr died aged 66 past.

30th July He was buried in new cemetery. Willie & Uncle John & John were at it.

7th August Maggie Harper came in Baxter's gig on Sunday & stayed till Wed. Got a hey (?) of gooseberries. We stacked on the 5th and 6th Baxter helping. Put up 5, 6 altogether

1st Mary had a daughter. Name Mary Speirs Orr Black. The following Wed Mary Holmes came, not feeling very well. Nervous. James went away the end of Aug from his holidays & came back the next two weekends. Wee Ria came to stay & went up to Auchenfoil about the 23rd

26th August Mrs Congalton & James went to Auchenfoil. It came on rain & has rained for a week. Cannot get the corn cut. Little park at Barnend ripe.

A family name of Grant at school there two months 8 daughters Lethy, Meg, Elsie, Amy, Gwendoline, Gerty, Agnes & Joy & George.

21st August Maggie Brewster was married to Scott Mains. A few weeks before that two of her brothers went abroad. Sinclair along with Peter Douglas to Australia & John on account of a girl in B. of Weir.

28th August Made a blouse to Janet blue and white.

15th September Donald Laird was married to Jessie Lyle of Scart.

18th September Our James came this weekend.

20th September Edinburgh holiday James helped us in with the corn. I gave Robert the loan of £1 to pay Holmes taylor.

21st September We finished taking in our corn.

22nd September Had a letter from Mrs Currie saying Mary Jessie and her were coming next day.

23rd September They came. Good day. We went to old castle. I am knitting one white Shetland shawl.

28th September Janet and I went to Glasgow. Got her a costume green shade £2.18/-, hat 13/6, pins 1/6 = £3.13/- corset 2/- gloves 1/4, shirt 2/6 Vail 6d Total £3.19.4 blouse 1/6, shoes 8/6 Total £4.9.4

30th September John McGregor was married in a hotel in Glasgow. Fine day. The Bells and David Carson at it.

1st October Robert paid me 5/- for semit and 5/- for shirt. I gave Mr Orr the loan of 10/-. Got it back. Robert owes me £1 yet. Paid.

3rd October James went away being the weekend. He left £5 for bank.

29th October Uncle Willie came and helped with pot digging. Went away 4th Oct.

3rd October Mary came down with her 4 children.

5th October A young ladies sewing class at school. 3 from Dippany. Lizzie Crawford Craiglinshuch Bere (?) two from Faulds.

6th October Mary was at Paisley getting teeth pulled.

7th October Robert was at Greenock. We finished digging potatoes yesterday.

8th October (Saturday) Mr & Mrs MacPhail, son & daughter & Miss Martha Clarke called in motor.

13th October Mary called coming back from Paisley. I wrote Mary Holmes. Mather bank (?) burned top flat.

15th October James came the weekend. Called at Grants. Janet went in the weekend.

16th October Robert at church. Communion in Parish Church.

17th October May (or Meg) Grant was to go to a school at Quarriers Homes, Bridge of Weir. I loaned James this morning 10/- and W...8/6

18th October Maria went up to Glasgow for 12lbs butter 5/4

19th October Gave father for Scott 3/6

7th November Mrs Blair had a slight shock.

9th November I went to Johnstone.

10th November Robert Blair Craiglinsheuch fell down and died of heart disease, Aged 72 years.

12th November I have been at Blairs every day helping. Robert and Willie have gone to Glasgow & Janet to Monklands and Johnstone.

11th November Lecture and Ball in Kilmacolm teachers at it. MacLaren & Tarrell, the Orrs & Blairs have tickets but owing to the illness did not go.

19th November Denniston roup. I gave Willie £6. He got a cow.

22nd November I went to Greenock. I gave Willie 34 makes £40. I called and had tea with Mr & Mrs Paterson. Our John and the minister & Affleck went to W. Bunt... (?) Cold weather. Cows getting cut turnips.

26th November Janet went to Glasgow for 5 lbs of butter. Saw Maria. No coal inhouse. Lodger ill - a very blue doo. Uncle Willie tipsy. Marion bought a hat 4/11

29th November Eliza Blackwood died.

30th November Jumble sale at Kilmacolm.

2nd December Uncle John came out. 3rd James came the weekend.

10th December I was up at Auchenfoil seeing Marion who was not well. Polly and Rachel Laird were down on the 5th.

24th December James came home. Had a suppurating throat but was getting better. Stayed till the 28th.

27th December We took in our corn stack. James helped.

28th December A letter from Dolly Congalton & one from Willie. She is still in St Andrews home.

29th December Janet has gone to Greenock today last week & got the 4 large portraits, father, mother Willie and me.

31st December James came again & stayed till Tuesday.

1911

1st January Willie and I went to church. Old Jess will not drive us over the Ne'erday, I doubt.

2nd January Monday Held Neirday (?) Georgia Mason, Inna Holmes & her lad came & Marion she went up to Faulds & stayed with us the next night.

3rd January John Holmes and John Miller came out. John sent me a bun and shortbread.

4th January Lady Alice gave a xmas tree. Marion and Jenny Black & Aunt Maggie & Mary Paton were down. I did not go but Mr Macgregor brought up next day a small cruet stand.

6th January Willie Holmes got married to Agnes Caskie.

7th January Wee Ria went up to Auchenfoil. I wrote to Maria about M. Sh... (?) but she has not answered yet. I have made up last year's account tonight. Willie was out £185 and I was out £73.

'Wee Ria' feeding a lamb at Gateside.

[**Editor's note:** "Wee Ria" was brought up at Gateside. She married an Italian named Perpoli, who later died. My father wrote the following about her in his autobiography: "She used to boast that as long as she had 'these two hands' she did not need help from anyone. But the time came when she wasn't able and she was apparently not eligible for a pension - probably she had not paid sufficient insurance stamps. Uncle Willie asked his lawyer to take up her case and after a good while she was granted assistance. Uncle Willie often visited her when he was in Glasgow visiting furniture manufacturers or other suppliers.". *Extracted from 'The Jone Crater' by John Holmes Johnson.*]

12th January Got word Maria is engaged to M. Shim (?)

11th January A party at Muirhouse (?) Mary Campbell from Islay at it. Was on hire (?) PM went with her.

14th January Robert went to meet James to go to Curries & Amy Grant came to see us.

18th January Janet went up to Auchenfoil. Got a (?) cup (*or cap*) from Mary. I got a letter from Mary.

15th January James and Willie at church.

18th January Got a letter from Maria saying she is well pleased with being at M.Skimmer (?)

19th January Robert got price of his first sold sheep £2.4/-. I received back from William £20. Leaves 20 standing yet. Got cloth from M. Orr for James pyjamas 5 yds 2/6. Janet went to Glasgow to a family (?) of Holmes. Stayed two nights. Saw Daisy & Jeny Holmes.

23rd January Mrs Orr called on her way up to Blairs. In January I gave Robert the loan of 10/-. Got it back.

25th January Janet and Robert at a spree at Bells. Mrs Lang & son Auchenleck called in gig. I am making the pyjamas.

30th January Our John came out and told us that Miss Smellie died last week & I am to go to Glasgow on Wed with him to arrange to drop Walker

1st February We went. Saw Maria at Skinners. 2nd Party at school. Robert did not go.

3rd February Party at Carsons. Janet did not go but Robert did. I had bile.

6th February Marion Black went to school first time.

10th February Hardridge party Robert at it.

11th February Lelty & Meg eilne (?) with James went to church. at night with Janet. All went away in the (?)

20th February Church social. Janet at it.

15th February Party at West Side. Robert at it, a big party.

23rd February I had the bile for two days and not quite better for a week.

20th February Big brown cow Lawpark calved - a bull. Next day it could not rise. Got Buntain. He came three times. It got better.

24th February A valuable mare worth £70 or £80 died at Auchenfoil. Meg Duff & Mary Paton at Dippany. Robert did not go.

25th February Willie took a bad cold, went through him. Lay in bed for 3 days. Very wet weather.

27th February Mrs Bell's birthday. Party at Carseknowe & this morning Robert and Willie & Ria took in to station old darby cow. Buntain was taking it to Paisley. Paid £7 for it.

2nd March Willie just able to get up a little yesterday for the first time.

7th March My 58th birthday. John was out. A lovely day. He went up to Robert ploughing at the Hardridge. I am commencing to find the bees & to put in a hot fire (?)

9th March Mary was down with her 3 children & Marion came in from school at night. She went up to see Mrs Blair & took Jenny and Donald with her

11th March James came the weekend.

12th March Our sacrament. Robert, Janet and I at it. White pony. Janet & Bessie Miller came out in the afternoon & James went in to the church with them. I finished his pyjamas.

14th March Mrs James Black called in in the morning with the milk cart.

15th March Mrs Holborn came & we went up to Auchenfoil. Maria was to come in 3 weeks.

20th March Robert finished ploughing at Hardridge. Selling 1/2 ton of Longworthys (?) to Baxter & some to Chapel.

26th March None of us at church. James the weekend.

27th March John came out. Had been a weekend at Mary Holmes.

30th March Willie paid me what I gave him loan £6 allowed 4 for potatoes to Roger............. (?)

1st April Willie had an examination in Glasgow.

3rd April Word saying Uncle Willie was not coming too cold. Finished the Hithersings (?) at Hankinsons.

4th April Robert prepared the ground for pots and put out a little dung. First 2 lambs out of 4 sheep. Sold a sheep got 47/- Sold the tup on April 7th Got £1.15.6 Willie....... (?) he was at Exhibition.

8th April James came home for a week

10th April Finished our potato setting.

14th April I went to Greenock. Got a new bonnet & .... (?)

5th April M came and gave me 10/- the final payment of the loan.

17th April Maggie / Colville Harper came. Not well, lung affected. Went back on 20th - sore back. Got a note from Maggie saying she was not well.

20th April Going to thrash our last stack.

1st May Harrowing at Hardridge. 6th James came weekend. Left £2

9th May Our cows got dinner (?) outside below the Hedges and next day above the Hedges for first time.

Maggie came and gave me £1

10th May Blair cow at window calved a bull, a big one.

12th May I was up at Blairs. Go every fortnight. Janet and Maggie Colville going up tonight.

13th May The Cattle Show. Willie and Robert at it.

21st May Lady, Mrs Murray, came & took parlour and bedroom upstairs for £3.10/ a week

21st May Maggie's lad came Sunday. Mr Brown

22nd May A letter from Maria with 10/- leaves £3.8/-. Sent in July 10/- leaves £2.18/-

26th May Our Mary with Marion Janet and Donald and John called on their (?)

27th May Took ill & Maggie was sent for. She came back. She was better.

We finished putting in turnip (?)

31st May The minister called. Ham and eggs. Maggie Colville (?) Paisley Cattle Show. Robert did not get the weekend Currie not at service.

1st June Mr & Mrs Murray came to big room & bedroom upstairs for £3 a month & 10/- for washing dishes.

3rd June Robert went to Greenock & Willie to Glasgow to repair two bikes for selling end of May. I gave Robert £1

Maggie went the weekend, coming back Tuesday (?) 7th

6th June Lizzie Blair went to the Exhibition.

First week in June to Robert 1/-, second week 1/- 21st (?)

7th June Miss King and Miss Lochhead called.

8th June Maggie called. Came back & gave me another £1 & brought 9/- worth from polly (?) I wrote to Mrs Currie.

10th June James came the weekend.

11th June Janet and Bessie Miller came out (Sun).

13th June Father and I went to Glasgow. Got photos taken & went to the Exhibition. He bought a new suit. Paid for it 29/6.

17th June Janet went with Maggie the weekend (?) to Johnstone. Wet.

21st June Ria & Janet & Robert & father at turnips.

22nd June The coronation day. Very wet and stormy. The twins came up the road....with Ross & Mary with Macphail arms round them (?)

24th June Janet went to see Exhibition.

30th June The Ex..........Mary & Jenny came down. The Murrays left & McArthur came to big room and Mrs Paterson called. Got £3 from Murrays. Getting £2 from McA.

6th July ther 2 coming to bedroom upstairs, 6/- a week. Got 8/- 16/- in all.

7th July Ria went to Auchenfoil. Got dish of marmalade & some rhubarb.

8th July Mrs Paterson & Mr Paterson called. Bought some things for Ria. The rest out turning hay.

10th July Uncle Willie came and stayed weeks. Most of hay stacked before he went away.

19th July Mrs Blair died. Father and I at the coffining and burial on the 22nd.

13th July Lizzie Holmes came for a fortnight.

15th July Mrs Miller came for a week

13th July Miss Gray came & stayed a week & 2 days. 18/- for boarding

1st August Willie Congalton came. Went away with James & went to Exhibition on the 5th Hay all up. We called on … Mary and Janet Laird & Paton at Exhibition that day. & I got my photo taken at Woolworths.

6th August James and Janet went to church. 7th James went away for a fortnight.

11th August Mary Paton & Rachel Laird came. The boys did not go home with them.

12th August Lizzie Blair went to Largs for two days.

13th August (Sunday) Our corn will be ready for cutting this week & so will Blairs. James Blair called yesterday about a man wanting a room. Eggs are ¼ from Roger.

15th August Janet, Ria & Robert went up to Blairs to (?)

16th August A letter from Maria with PO 10/- leaves £2.8/-

19th August The Blairs down helping these two days. Agnes Robertson, James Lawson & James Broddick. In the afternoon Letty & Amy Grant came.

20th August None of us at church. Most beautiful weather.

15th August Maggie Colville and her cousin Thomson came a day. Got word Jeanie Bell was not coming & James did not come owing to strikes on the railway.

21st August Our ones at Blairs. Uncle John came out. Mr & Mrs Wilson brought John Shepherd aged 82 to stay a fortnight at 18/- a week. Ria went to Auchenfoil for a night.

26th August James Bell came for a week & Maggie Colville. James came with Jennie.

29th August Uncle John came & we put in a stack. Jennie helping.

2nd September Ria went a weekend to Auchenfoil.

4th September The school took up. Father went to Paisley with the bull. Got £12. Got two cows £26. Uncle John came out. Taking in corn. Keeping the quay calf.

11th September Gave Willie the loan of £5 for cows.

15th September Maggie Colville went away. Been a week fully. She means to work now. Had a grand summer.

9th September James came for his last fortnight holiday. A letter from Maria with enclosure. Mrs Robert Brown called with Jenny

13th September I was over at Killochwraes and Newton.

23rd September We have got a good week at potatoes. James helping. Nearly half done. James went up two nights to Glasgow and saw Polly. She is 29. I gave Jenny Lang a photo of myself and Willie.

22nd September Miss Holmes Paisley came. The holiday.

20th September Mr Affleck died and Mrs Duff has bought one of Laird's houses out Port road. Willie going to start his classes on 26th

21st September Uncle John was out.

26th September Marion Holmes came to help to gather potatoes. John Black is ill with cu... (?) of the bowels.

6th October Marion Holmes went away after being a fortnight helping to gather. All done.

7th October James came. I went up to Auchenfoil. He and Willie came for me at night.

9th October Uncle John out. Grand weather yet.

11th October Uncle Willie came to help cover potatoes. And he got Peter Douglas and went by Gibbleston

14th October I am sorting the garden every morning, putting in new earth off roadside and dung. Separating the lilies & crocuses & snowdrops. Denniston cow calved a bull. Keeping it. (10th Oct) that is two calves.

12th October Mary called in on her road to Blackwater. John was going on to Gibbleston. Hugh not well.

14th October Maggie Colville's lad sails today for S. Africa.

17th October Tuesday morning. Hugh Black committed suicide by cutting his throat.

21st October I went up to Blairs and asked Lizzie & Frank down. James came home weekend. C on P.

22nd October The minister made a touching reference to Hugh Black.

23rd October Miss Clayton called. The Blairs at the school.

24th October The Blairs at our house. Had cards with Uncle Willie.

26th October Uncle Willie went off at night. A stack in – the first. Just a few turnips to shaw. Did them next day. I am glad to get James ni (?)

28th October Sat Maggie Colville came for the day. Was at Muir House. Had on her new Navy blue costume quite bright in an easy situation as book keeper to a coalman in Johnstone.

11th November I went to Johnstone. Called on Flora in B of W.

13th November I sent James £1

22nd November I was at Greenock. Called on Mrs Currie, Mrs Orr, Mrs Crawford, Mrs McArthur. Lifted £30.

28th November Milton roup. Got a horse.

16th December The boys were over the hill.

18th December My big room papered by Campbell. Cost £1

19th December Letter from Congy.

23rd December James came home weekend. Brought shortbread. Willie gave £2 towards old Jess (?) I gave father £1 for the same purpose.

30th December James came home weekend.

Gateside garden

1912

1st January James Robert and Willie went to Glasgow. A quiet day. Maggie Colville came and big Maria was since Saturday. Went away on Tuesday.

6th January Maggie Orr & little Willie Orr came then Alex Crawford.

7th January James and Willie at church. One hen laying.

13th January James a weekend. Did not come back for a month & then took away the ring.

19th January Had a party. Agnes and Nellie Sands, Lizzie Carson….. Robertson good capp…. (?)

20th January I sent a pound £1 to James.

31st January Old Jess died & Maria left school & next day Jenny Black came to it. I went up to Auchenfoil a week since to see John Black who has been ill for some time with a sore hand cut about 6 times. I called in at Faulds going up.

The beginning of February the sewing class ball was.

10th February Janet was up at Blairs

12th February The teachers and Hankinsons were at Blairs. Janet & Lizzie Blair were at Hankinsons the week before.

10th February James came home weekend. Took away the ring.

11th February James father and I at church.

12th February Old Nannie took ill of paralisis & Buntain came that day. The next day when he went up & when he came down 2 and another visit, 4 altogether but just 3 he should charge for.

15th February Nannie was killed. A fortnight between Jess and her.

16th February Janet and I went up to Glasgow, came home & went back on the 19th & on the 20th she got lump cut away.

26th February I went and saw her. Spoke to Mr & Mrs Robertson.

24th February Robert met James and they went to Greenock (?) James is looking after a house & has found (?)

26th February I gave Willie (Young) loan of 5/-. Got it back quickly.

4th March Janet came home from Glasgow.

7th March I got £5 from Willie. My birthday. A shawl from Mary.

18th April Uncle Willie came and helped with the potatoes.

22nd April Mr Renfrew came, a boarder at 15/- weekly.

5th April James came for a fortnight's holidays. Had been a weekend a fortnight before that.

22nd April James went off. Left £8.

24th April George Mason came on bike. A clocking hen from Mary. 29 chickens out in March.

Mary a son in March 1912 called William.

30th April Mr Renfrew went away after being 10 days £1

1st May I set the second dozen from Congy 4 little black leghorns out of the first 33 chickens altogether & 3 hens set. (In April 2 … carts of hay to Frank Blair.)

4th May Janet and Ria got their costumes, grey and scarlet from Gilchrists, Janet's 26/6, Ria's 17/6. James came the weekend. Janet and Ria at church on the 5th. Ria's first time.

Lizzie Blair came down. I was over at Orrs Newton end of April. Cow went to John Buntain at Keithwood (?) & Peggie to Peace Muir about £21 the two.

8th May one cart to Roger. Commenced to drill for turnips. Potatoes ploughed up.

15th May Marion Holmes came for 12 days. Janet and her went to Faulds & Auchenfoil & Blairs Craiglinsheuch. Marion got a proposal from Mr Stewart in Canada.

29th May Maggie Colville & Mary Borland came.

27th May Set a hen. Duck eggs. Got 6 ducks.

1st June (Saturday) Robert 2/6 to do a month. M Colville & MB went away the 31st May. MC was coming back for a few days but the rain prevented her.

Janet and I went to Paisley. Got her a new lace blouse & scarf & one for myself. James came home weekend. Left £6

5th June Janet away to Greenock to see about her teeth. 12 Jessie Donald came for a week.

9th June Mare we got from Milton died – inflammation of the bowels.

14th June Poli (?) Currie's wedding. I sent her 10/-. Janet at the wedding with Jenny Miller. A man came to get my big room 12/- a week for 2 weeks. McDade.

26th June I was at Greenock. Mrs Kirkwood is coming for July at 15/- a week. Got our horse Dick end of June from Hendry, Kilmacolm.

28th June Mrs and Mr Congalton came at 10/- a week.

12th July Janet bought a dress in McGuesisies (?) for 25/-. **15th** We ricked the park of hay at B...end.

11th July Willie and Congalton went to Cooper Fife big show.

15th July Meg and Letty Grant called, in the hay field. The Murrays have the school for July.

16th July Robert and Willie going to Rothesay sports. I loaned Robert 10/-.

14th July I Willie and James were at church. James spoke to the minister.

19th July I went to Glasgow to see Miss Ward – gave her 4 sovereigns. Robert is owing me one & 10/- before that. Got 3 blouse lengths. Got Robert's back.

3rd August James's wedding. 53 at it, at the Douglas Hotel, Bath Street. They went north.

16th August Baxter helped two days & got all our hay in. A spate came a week since & took away all the Meadow & some quiles.

17th August Janet is going the weekend to Lizzie Holmes at Lochgilphead. Willie fell off cycle and hurt his arm. Jenny Orr and Lizzie Baxter came. Had a game at Whist with Mrs Congalton and M. Frances.

September No one in the house this month. I borrowed £15 from young Willie to give James 5 which I owed him to make up his £104.10

9th September Maria came for a fortnight and helped with the corn. Got it all cut & a lot in.

14th September James and wife came for the first time together a weekend. I had a sore finger and bile. Gave him his money & his grandfather's kist.

22nd September I gave Willie Senior £10 (the loan) to pay Cook & Blair.

23rd September Willie went to Paisley with the cow that we got from John Kerr……. Mains a week. Got barely £10 for it. Uncle John was out two 3 days helping to drive cutting machine.

Expenses in connection with bottled milk. Printing 5/-, after 1/-,

1st October Robert went first day to Port Glasgow with bottled milk, about 41/4 gallons. Ria went with him. He got it all away.

9th October to Port Glasgow 2/3, next day 6/-, Robert gave 3/6 Myself for stamps 6d… (?) ½, stamp 6d, tassel 5/- (Total) £1.1.5

21st October I wrote to Kate McLachlan.

22nd October Mr Muir came out at night.

23rd October Janet Blair & John Craig Monklands came in new gig. Our Mary and her family were down 2 weeks ago. Mary Donald & Willie.

26th October Robert & Willie paid a visit to James Orr & wife, 98 Kirkcaldy Road Maxwell Park Pollokshields (?)

31st October Robert and Willie with R. Orr Newton were over the hill. Halloween spree at Dippany. 8th in at Carsons. Janet at Lawpark the night before…(?) went to meet her & John Currie up the road a bit.

Denniston cow calved a bull calf. White one head of the byre a week. Got 17/6 for (?) before that. About 9 gallons now. Getting it away fine (?) in the huff. Ria went for a fortnight with milk cart. Frank Blair is insuring (?) himself. Carson is leaving Blacksholm. Had a roup not up to much.

4th November I wrote to Mrs A. Millar or Millin. Last week we commenced to shaw turnips to drive home and give to the cows.

13th November Robert at Glasgow paying Fleming £12. I gave him the loan of one. He went and saw Miss Findlay at Crookford (?)

15th November A spree at Faulds. Janet did not go thinking Willie would go instead but he had lessons & did not go……… Robert went. It was just the usual.

11th November I went to Johnstone. Met father at Paisley. Got the 2.20 train to Glasgow. Saw uncle Willie all right.   Father got a cow at Paisley. £17.15/-

23rd November Marion Holmes came the weekend.

25th November She got a drive in with father. He went to Paisley. Got a cow, black and white £19

26th November I went to Greenock. Paid the parks (?) Stormy day. Lifted £30. Lifted £66 before that.

27th November Robert got paid £10 & Janet £2.10/-

1913

January New year. The night before it Jennie and May Bell came. Robert met them with gig. Ne'erday night James and wife came. Father had some drink and went to bed but next night had singing round the fire. All went away the next day.

6th January We have 8 stacks out. Are giving the cows crushed grain (?) a bowlful each to the milk cows, 4 not long calved. Getting nearly 12 ½ gallons a day but not all sold Ne'er week.

4th January James' birthday. Heard that John Carruth died that night, a victim to asthma

6th January Got paid back £30. The cows get in the morning a basket (or bucket?) of cut turnips & the milk & the milk ones soft meet & turnips too, then at night the same. Milk foding (?) between.

11th January Robert emptied the midden up on the brae field nearest Horsewends (?)

6th January Katie Bell or Carson's son died of water in the head.

8th January Mary with Marion and Jenny went to see Jenny Holmes.

About the New Year time we heard that Willie Miller is still living. Uncle Willie Holmes confined to bed. On New Year's day Robert and Willie went to Telfers and Barnshake. Willie took 3 days at Ne'erday

23rd January .. (?) came with the gramophone (?)

24th January Janet went to Glasgow. Stayed all night. Lizzie came down with her. Uncle Willie keeping better.

30th January Robert and Willie, Janet and Lizzie Holmes went to Blairs big spate on Orr Newton there (?)

1st February Robert and Willie went to Edinburgh, first time since James got married. Mary Bell given up her lad Stanley going with Campbell.

9th February Feb Janet, Willie and I at church. I asked for Mrs Paterson. Every good morning Ly (?) Janet and father lifting potatoes in field above Carsons brae face.

10th February Janet and Ly were asked and went to Dippany misty (?) night.

11th February Bobby Erskine's wife died. Left 5.

12th February (Wednesday) Robert & ...(?) Went to Orrs Newton.

13th February They went to Monklands.

14th February They went to Blairs Lawpark & Robert went after them. Crawford in Shills died this week

16th February None of us at church. Most milk sold yet today.

17th February Janet and Ly & Robert went to church social. Ly went away next day.

19th February Blair cow calved a bull. I wrote to Congalton. Getting 9 eggs a day.1/6. This week took in hay. Lifting the last of the potatoes.

30th February Jan A new pailing at school. Dog Major got a pup since last holidays.

Laird 2 Balmoral Place, Langside, B (?) Crosshill, Glasgow.

7th March Joe came. His arm not better. I got £5 from Willie, junior, that is either £33.12.6 or altogether from him. I am getting about 30/- a week from cart & Willie.

8th March James and Polly and Jessie Donald came- they went in on Sun night. Willie drove them in milk cart. She went next day. She is making 6 shifts and 3 pairs of pillow slips & 3 bolster slips. Cost in all 1 guinea.

11th March Lizzie Blair came in at night for ticket for Cantata in village. Getting 15 eggs a day.

14th March Janet, L Blair, Robert and Willie at cantata.

15th March Ria at it.

16th March Ria at church. Sun and showers. No one else down the road. Duck laying every morning.

24th March Glasgow holiday. James Orr and wife 98 Kirkc…(?) Came. Robert drove them in at night.

27th March Joe and J at Glasgow. Bought a ring.

30th March He came up again (Sun). His arm to be sorted next day. Robert's sheep have two lambs each (6), one with broken leg on bottle. Hear Ria is leaving Holbourns.

31st March Father commenced to sow the corn. Got it all to do himself aged 73.

5th April Maria came a weekend. Has left Holburn. Quite happy. Mrs Maclaren Ada & two ladies at school.

6th April I was at church with Maria & Willie junior. Asked for Miss Lang.

22nd April James and wife came for a week.

21st April Uncle Willie came. Very weak.

26th April Archie Currie went away now at Miller................

(Next three lines indecipherable – written in pencil)

............he helped to.... last time he was at Glasgow with Janet he bought her a gold bangle and they visited his sister. He seems quite devoted.

27th April None of us at church..................Cold and wet. Half of potatoes to set yet.

28th April All went away. Uncle Willie felt it too cold. He might not be back again.

30th April 1 cow, 1 quey, 2 calves all went to Stirling £26. Willie gave me it.

1st May Cows got their .... (?) For the first time. Tatties not all set yet.

8th May Robert went to the Infirmary with scarlet fever.

10th May J Johnson came. He called on Robert next day.

13th May Uncle Willie came back to help.

14th May Uncle John came out to help but Bobby Baxter had finished for us the potatoes

11th May Maggie Love died to be ... (?) On the 15th. Aged 81.

15th May I was at Johnstone & visited Flora... (?) Went to Burnhill. It is sadly changed. Never care to go back. Robert has been a week in the Infirmary, making nothing of it but...(?)

22nd May (?) I was at Greenock. Saw Robert. He is ...(?) & sick. Not much better.

24th May Joe came they went to Auchenfoil. That was the first night the cows stayed out in the Hill park. 8 ducks set & 26 chicks.

26th May Sorry to hear that Robert is worse. ...John has come to drill.

Date (?) Robert getting better.

3rd June I was at Greenock. Robert getting better. Bought drawers.

4th June Janet went to Glasgow. Met Maria. Bought a rainproof and umbrella. Father out in the morning drilling.

10th June I at Greenock. Robert had got his last injection and was not feeling well. Old Baxter in.

13th June Janet Miller called on Robert. He was much better. I called on Mrs Currie when in Greenock on the 10th.

14th June The sports day[1]. Janet at them. Mrs Miller came and went back to them.

15th June Janet and Maria at church. Jenny Miller & girl McNab came ... (?)

18th June The sports. Maria at them. Heard last week that uncle John's Mrs Crawford (?) was ill.

22nd June Father got a black cow at Paisley. Willie walked it home. Rather wet. £17.15/-

24th June Robert came home from the Infirmary not too well. Father and Ria stripping turnips. John Thomson, L Liggie (?) hoed potatoes two days.

28th June I took the loan of £10 from Willie. Ria at Glasgow this week. Got a pair of slippery shoes.

5th July Joe came Sat night. Not having holiday. (?) job is finished. Doing one at Stranchins (?)

8th July Maggie Orr and Wee Willie came.

9th July Janet away to Tignabruich.

8th July Commenced to cut hay. Willie did …(?) Turner came 10/- a week.

12th July Mary Holmes came from Dunoon. Looking well. Mrs Olding in big room end of July. Mrs Olding and I went to Dunoon.

1st & 2nd August Blairs … (?) Helped us with hay in field below school.

11th August Janet & Janet Orr at Rothesay.

7th August Mary came at 4 Mrs Thomson at 3 Dr Plumer (?) … (?) water in milkhouse, uncle John.

12th August Uncle John out. Put up 4 stacks. 4 before that, two Baxter & Blairs men. I had the bile.

14th August Uncle John helped to put up 4 stacks, one Baxter & Blairs men, our Willie & Jennie & J. Bell.

15th August I paid for Roberts insurance (?) £6.8.11, that is £1.8.11 he owes me as I owed him £5.

29th August Tinnie Holmes came an afternoon. I got £1.8.11 from Robert. I owe Willie £4. Got other £14 7 £15 before that makes £33 in all.

18th August Father and Robert went and got a black and white cow at Paisley. It belonged to Mrs Orr Newton.

26th August Commenced to give our 11 cows a little bean meal.

30th August Alex Crawford came with a bunch of heather.

31st August Robert was at church for the first time in ten months. I was with him getting bit of his fever (?)

25th August Joe came.

29th August Wee quey calved a bull. 10 months at the bottled milk and the pay is one week behind.

6th October The Oldings came a visit. 3 weeks since we got a white cow besides Mrs Orrs. Give 4 gallons a day. Ria went her holiday. 2 nights in Glasgow. Got black hat with white round it. Janet was at Mrs Oldings last week. In Greenock she bought blouses.

8th October Robert paid the doctor £5.10/-. I gave him the 10/-. Mary Paton and the Sands were in.

10th October Mrs Holburn came and spent a nice afternoon.

11th October Janet went to Glasgow and Tinnie came back with her and stayed the night on going to Faulds and Auchenfoil. She met and spoke to telegraph wire man.

15th October Robert took in a cart of hay to Roger.

16th October ½ a ton of potatoes to Roger & ½ a ton before that.

17th October A big party at Mathernock & one at Mrs Hankinsons.

12th December Janet at Greenock. Got Ria cloth for skirt. A surprise party at Blairs tonight.

Robert and Willie at it.

11th December Mary with little Mary and Jack.

14th December Ly Holmes came a weekend.

10th December Old Mrs Harper died. Mrs Bell made Ria's jacket

17th December Got a cheese from Murray 51 lb at 8d

Christmas James and Polly came and stayed two nights.

In 1912 & 13

To Ria Millar one shirt 4/-, one silk blouse 7/-, for hat 2/-, for cup 1/-, J & C 31/2d,

Murray boots 7/6, stamp(?) 2/6, plate 2d, pot 1d, flower 1/6, Apron 6d, James boots (...?) & socks 8/3 (Total) £1.14.91/2 Long boots soled 3/6, piper(?) dress 4/6, hat 1/6 i.e. 6/-, Apron & flower 10d11th June(?) Got 2/3 ...for father and Willie for (?), for white hat 5/-, for slippers or shoes 2/-,

For minagery (?) 9d, 15th July pair of new c... boots 8/9 and for ones mended 1/6,

(Total) £1.8.4 + £1.14.91/2 = £3.3.11/2

---

1. **Sports Day:** This was an annual event, held in the evenings at the same time as the Kilmacolm Agricultural Show. A note in the programme booklet

produced for the 1935 Centenary of the Show, states: "The Great War put an end to the Annual Sports Day in Kilmacolm."

1914

January New Year's day No one in but Robert Orr & Joe at night. Marion Holmes came & went up to Faulds & came down next day & Mary Paton went home with her. Robert and Willie went with Robert Orr & were at Dippany. Duffs, Buntains, Orrs, Telfers & Langs.

6th January Mrs Colville came to stay a fortnight.

9th January Ball at Syde school. Ria at it.

10th January Surprise party at Carsons (Robert going to it) made up by …John Crawford and James Ross.

14th January I had a bad day of bile. Big mill at Blairs.

15th January Wiggin Wingham came in and asked … (?) Mary Holmes sent a … of bacon.

5th February Tinnie Holmes died of jaundice. Buried on the 7th.

11th February Janet and I were at Glasgow. Spent £5.16/-

17th March Robert took to his bed with rheumatic pains. Soon got better with Humphry's treatment.

1st May …Holmes & Mrs Mitchell came.

9th May Mary Holmes the weekend.

19th May Lizzie Holmes came one night.

23rd May Miss Mary MacDonald and her mother and Joe. He has got a gaffer's job in Govan.

19th May James' firstborn son, William Leslie.

17th June Aunt Aggie and Bob from Auchenleck.

18th June Janet at Paisley seeing… her teeth.

19th June Mrs Orr Newton in wee room seeing to … (?)

L-R: Granny Orr, Mrs Mary Black, (nee Orr), Grandfr. Wm. Orr, Robert Orr, Mr Steel (best man), Joe and Janet Johnson, Jenny and Mirn Black, Lizzie Holmes (bridesmaid), Wm Orr, Jean & Barbara Johnson.

16th July Janet got married to Joe Johnson in the Tontine Greenock, 51 at it, 45 adults.

24th July They came back weekend. Were at church

31st July Came for Sat. James and Polly met them staying here a fortnight then they went to Lamlash. James and Polly went to see Janet. She has got a piano. We are giving the cows green corn sheafs this fortnight back. Good white cow had twins & is giving 5 gallons a day. 1 gallon more than last year

20th August The boys with James McGill are taking home the last raik (or saik?) of slabs from the Port to put up the hayshed. The corn is ready for cutting.

21st August Commencing today by (?) man speaks through his nose are (?) 6 (?) can just do it (?)

26th August Uncle Willie came and helped us at the corn

28th August Janet came the weekend. Joe came the next night.

4th September Remston (?) calved – a bull. Took (?) and died.

Hugh Laird and Jean Telfer were married, staying in Duke Street

6th September Father and I at church

7th September Robert went to Paisley and bought a cow from John (?) £12:17:6.

10th September We finished putting in our corn and Uncle Willie went away next day. He worked better this time.

12th September Letter from Janet. Getting on fine.

21st September Robert bought a cow in Paisley, white one £17:10/- Gave 4 gallons a day.

9th October Peggie Crawford got married to John Menzies in Tontine Hotel Greenock.

15th October Our Willie went off to his job in Glasgow. Staying with Janet.

17th October Robert went up and had tea in Janet's. All went to the pictures & Holmes.

18th October I wrote to Congalton.

20th October Mrs Colville came with Mary (?) and Anni Marshall. We are giving our cows soft meal (*or meat?*) this week back and turnips cut.

24th October Mary and Marion went to see Janet first time. Willie and Janet and Joe came too.

20th October Janet, Joe and Willie came Saturday night.

24th October There is disturbing news of the enemy invading Britain. Hope it comes to nought.

27th October Taking in the last of our turnips – a large crop. Giving the kye cut turnips three times a day and the beanmeal mixture three times a day to continue all winter.

1915

January Ne'erday Had James Wife and son. Willie Joe and Janet. Robert and Willie went to Glasgow and came by Lang Dennistoun.

James, wife and W.L. boy came day after Ne'erday. Janet, Joe and Willie came Ne'erday Friday. Robert, Willie and Frank Blair went to Glasgow, Denniston at night.

James and wife went away on Monday. Janet and Joe Sunday night. Willie and Robert went to Auchenleck on Monday night. I sent an apron… (?) W went away next morning.

25th January I owe Willie £15 and another £10 that he paid to Austin Laird. £25 in all.

27th February Willie, Joe and Janet came. I gave her two feather pillows. Snow on the ground. She stayed and is going today to Paisley to see Jessie Donald.

5th February (Tuesday) We thrashed half a stack.

27th February Mrs Colville came … (?)

28th February Had David Carson & wife & Liz Blair. I took very ill with cold and had bile next day and was not better for near a fortnight. Willie staying at home for a fortnight. Robert and him at Auchenfoil for a stop (?) yesterday. 25 eggs a day.

1st March I owe Robert for book (?) dept £30 and besides he has paid £20 for the hayshed which is to his credit.

6th March Wee white cow had a bull calf. Keeping it. 10 cows milking. 33 6d sold and three gallons and the calf to 20th March and after.

16th March Janet and Joe came and went to Rothesay the next day for good.

28th March Mrs Colville

April Sent Willie £2, two from 25 leaves £23 which I still owe Willie and on 17th April I

gave him £100. On 1st May I gave him £2 which leaves £21 I owe him.

7th April Mary had a son born, James. *[Dad's cousin Jimmy Black — PJJ]*

10th April Mary Holmes came & she and I went up to Auchenfoil this day (Sunday).

15th April I went to Johnstone. Colville here. She gave me £1 (Thursday). I also went to Greenock same day.

17th April James and wife came for a week. 22nd John Miller was buried.

24th April Mrs Colville went home for a fortnight after being 8 weeks.

1st May I was at Rothesay. Mrs Colville away a week and we have been busy setting potatoes. Uncle Willie came to John

Miller's funeral on the 22nd April. John Miller left £3039 and heard (?) from Willie Miller the day before ... (?)

5th May I walked to Orrs Newton. Ria came for me at night.

8th May Mrs Colville........ came here. Stayed other 7 weeks, 26th June. Gave me £3 in all

13th May Mrs Currie and wee Peter came. Mrs Colville and them went to Auchenfoil on the 14th

25th June I went to Rothesay. Janet had a son that night to be called William Orr. *[Dad's older brother, who died in the Spanish Flu epidemic — PJJ]*

28th June Father a sore throat these 3 days. Ria went to Greenock. Got a knitted coat 10/- Marion came on 10th June She and I went to church. Next day she went to Rothesay, stayed 2 nights. Father has to cut the hay at Dyke... and Uncle Willie helping.

15th July Marion went away. Got some flowers.

30th October 9 cows milking. 302 penny's worth (?) James McGill shawing in afternoon and carting in in morning (?) 2 old cocks died.

18th December Mrs Orr came over first time since Janet went away in July.

22nd December Maclean paid £1 for fishing. Milk pennys 327

Photo of horn gramophone by alerkiv on unsplash

17th December Robert bought a gramaphone £1:15/-. Sold three cows this month – 2 black ones and young Peggie, £15:10/-, £16:10/-, £17:10/- £49:10/- and 15/- for a calf.

22nd December Snow and frost. Jennie (?) went away at the term.

1916

January 2nd Liz Blair left Frank for two nights. James Robertson who had been with us for 3 months left a week after Ne'erday. He got 6/- a week.

17th January We sold Kinloch's cow. Got for it £24:15/-

22nd January Whiteford sent out 2 carts coal.

Mary's baby James aged 9 months had a bad cold........... Getting better.

End of Jan James is confined to bed with a cold.

1st February Mrs Bell Carseknowe died. I am taking her hens 3/6 each 16 (of them) and 3 ducks £3:2/-(total).

5th February Willie came home. Gave him the loan of £20. James ill yet. Robert & Willie went to Auchenfoil. Had a good crack with Johnie.

April We got 2 cows from Andrew Smith, one £19 the other £20. One gives a good 4 1/2 gallons a day the other 3 ½ and we got one from Mrs Orr about £18, a good cow. Tom, the horse, cannot rise when it falls Looking after another. Uncle John awat to the island of Giggech (?)

12th May Mrs Colville went away. I went with her. Got bedroom paper – 6 pieces @ 6 pence a piece. She had been 4 weeks. About the first of May we sold the bonnie white cow for fat. Got £16 for it. Sold a big fat one before that and got £19 for it.

13th May Ria went to Glasgow weekend. Saw Mrs … (?) Janet came with wee Willie. He's now a year old. She went over to … (?) And Mary had been down that day alone. Janet goes away today Friday the 19th May.

18th May Ria went to Auchentiber with … (?)

19th May Ria went with Janet and stayed all night. Marion Holmes (Mrs Forbes) came a week later, half of May.

5th June Willie gave up business in Rothesay and came home. Got a job in Houston – the second time.

Uncle John came out and was harrowing down the potatoes and grubbing. Selling 25 gallons of milk at 1/7 ½

6th June Mrs Orr and Jessie Buntain were over – a cold day. Willie went to his job this morning.

16th June Uncle John came out. Had been the weekend with Jenny Miller and Mary Holmes. Mrs James Black called in on her way to Blackwater. I am cleaning the wee room above scullery by degrees. Father commenced to hoe potatoes himself.

17th June Robert and Willie are going to Rothesay today.

July Our Mary went to Rothesay. Jenny Holmes had taken a room from our Janet for a month.

16 Marion Forbes had a daughter. Her father had been here a fortnight. He went away on the 10th of August.

10th August Got a wee white quay £18:15/-. Been out this year for cows £144 & 1 horse £39=£183

15th August Our Janet and baby came stayed 3 nights. Ria went to Rothesay with her. Came back that night.

14th August Sold Peter Douglas white cow. Got £21.

19th August Baxters Bob and John came and put in the hay. Bobby over day before.

20th August Sunday The Glasgow holiday. Robert away to Greenock to see John Currie.

None of them were in. Called at Lynedoch Street.

19th & 21st August The foals (?) made £21. Sold to Blackwood 3 hens and 1 cockerel.

26th August June a cow in Paisley £23. 31st July a cow in Paisley £24 10/-

Mary Paton & Peggy Duff went the weekend to Mary Holmes.

28th August Robert bought the wee black cow £21.

15th September Jessie Donald & James' wife & two boys have been here a fortnight. Going away next Monday. Going to Auchenfoil today. Mrs Miller came on the 13th. I gave Mary a writing pad for her birthday.

25th September Robert got big brown cow. Doing well. Uncle John's one calved this week and the big brown cow – both quays. Calves to Smith, one £1, the other £3. A man woman and child lodging in carthouse. Man at potatoes. Have written for Mole Willie. Have commenced to give R. a pound a month. Got 1 first of October 2 before that. One first of November. Gave him a pair of stockings.

26th September James and I went to Rothesay... (?)

28th September I was at Greenock about my silk coat. Saw Mrs John Currie. Mrs Currie had a daughter the next day, 29th Sept.

30th September James went to meet wife in Paisley. Robert and Willie went to a fete at Bridge of Weir.

Ria at Glasgow. Got velvet for a blouse for Mary.

8th October Uncle Willie returned to help with the potato digging – stayed 6 weeks till the turnips were in. Getting 5 a stone for turnips and 1/8 for potatoes.

10th October Paid of my own £5. 2 for Willie.

14th October Janet came to stay a while. Joe working in Greenock and staying with his sister. Wee Willie 17 months old, very tall & is just walking about a chair. Polly and Rachel Laird one night a week again

1st November The sacrament. Father and I at it. Uncle John a fortnight at Harrowgate in November. An action by James Barr. Deduct for receiving of money got for furniture he lost.

21st November Mrs Orr paid us a visit.

24th November Going to ask Mac up tonight.

24th November 26 gallons

4th December I got from Willie to put in Bank for him £7:15/-. He was at Paisley lodging last week first week 4/- for room and 13/6 for food. Got the first instalment of interest for £50 in cheque bond 18/5

1917

1st January A quiet New Year. Wee Willie took ill the day before. He soon got better.

4 times (?) and one after for Robert, he was rejected for the army.

7th January Robert got a cow £24:5/-, an old cow good milker 34 gallons milk 2/- the gallon. James came 3 days at Xmas. Polly and weans stayed in Glasgow.

20th January Mary & Marion & Jenny were a day in Glasgow. Saw Jenny Holmes.

27th January Ria broke a tippany (?) bottle core… (?) Let it fall through.

1st March Mathernock roup. Drew about £2000. They have gone to Neitherwood (?).

2nd March Mary Paton and Peggie and Annie Duff were down. Had John Crawford.

3rd March Janet went to Glasgow. Met Joe went to concert.

Willie came from Loch Doig (?) Went with cart on Monday morning.

4th March Our communion. Ria and I at it. My new fur coat & bonnet & fur on. Getting about 8 eggs a day 3/6 the dozen.

7th March My birthday. Got a blouse from Mary Black with white spot. Pastry from Ria, & biscuits from Robert. James had no mind of it. We have 15 cows just now. In Feb Robert got a cow £26. Kept it a week. Not well. Sold it next Monday. Lost £9 on it. Bought another for £27. Doing well.

24th March Willie came after being away 3 weeks. We are 3 days without sugar. Owing to the war it is scarce. The war has been nearly 3 years now & there is some sign of our side moving the Germans back from France but there has been a terrible slaughter & suffering. History will can tell of some of it. Sold two cows in March, £26:17/- for one and £30 for a calving one.

28th March Janet went to Auchenfoil and called in at Faulds. Polly telling her that James Baxter is to get Dykefoot.

31st March Going with a Bears head. Some snow & some frost – Joe came the weekend from Glasgow. He is in lodgings there. Took away with him on the Monday morning 1 ½ stone of potatoes. There are no potatoes to be got in Glasgow, Paisley, the Port and Greenock. The potato merchants have to give up their business.

1st April Ria at church – last week I sent her mother the loan of £1:10/-. Took it out (?) her book.

2nd April Gave Ria her wages today, £1:10/-. We are to get 1/9 a stone for pots. All the month of May potatoes were 2/- a stone. Ria talking of going to Glasgow to learn typewriting.

23rd May Janet went over to Orr Newton. I had bile three weeks running, once a week. A rat attacked a chicken in shed.

All the money I have just now is £460 & £400 in Gateside. 1918.

20th June Ria went away to Glasgow the end of May to stay with her mother and to get into a shop till she could learn typewriting. Janet saw her a week later – no shop then. James has been rejected the army again. We are getting Sissy Carson to help with work. I have let my big room for July, 2 beds in it. 15/- a week.

30th June The ladies came to big room, Mrs Ritchie and daughter. Janet and Joe went to Dunoon for a fortnight. No work for Ria yet.

4th July Wed Jessie Marion and Annie Twigg came. Walked out & in. Thought it would not be often they would do it. (Annie died next year). Gave Sissy Carson £2 for work. Got word Ria had got a job in a fruiterer's shop. Janet came home before the fortnight was up. She had a bad cold and baby too.

14th July Willie came his holidays (13th). Joe and he went to Rothesay next day the 14th. Next day Sunday he took ill and on Monday he was taken to Glasgow in Laird's motor and operated on for appendicitis, just in time. (Most providentially).

21st July James and wife & family came for a week then go to a small cottage in Peebleshire.

22nd July I took bile for 2 days and was very ill with cold also.

21st July Mrs Colville and a lady teacher had been for a week and went the day James came.

29th July Sunday Robert went on byke to Johnstone then took car to Glasgow and saw Willie. He thinks he will be home in a week.

30th and 31st July We had Sissy Carson at the hay out about ½ past 9. Gave her 2/6.

6th August Willie came home from Glasgow. I went in Laird's motor for him. £16:16/- to pay for boarding, £20 for surgeon, £4 for Laird.

21st August Willie drove me to Killochries then came for me to Orrs

27th August Robert bought a cow £32. Heard W. Brewster has stopped selling bottled milk. Sending it to a dairy in Greenock. Change for (?)

29th August Willie in Glasgow.

31st August Our maid Annie came and Miss Donald same night. Lizzie Blair was down. Wee Willie just commencing to say "Ta"

1st September Willie drove me up to Auchenfoil. Heard eggs owing to the war have risen to 4/- a dozen. This is the 4th year of the war with Germany and not looking very well yet. Costing the nation about 8 millions a day. Joe came weekend. Finished working in Glasgow. Thinks he will get a gaffer job next week.

3rd September Willie drove me to Bridge of Weir. Saw Flora then went to Monkland(?) Don't care to go back for a long time. We commenced to cart…… (?) the next day….. (?)

1st October Robert got a cow £27:10/-. One a fortnight or so before that £28

8th October Got another cow £30. Getting about £3 a day for milk. 6/8 gallon (?) Joe has got a house at Craigieknowes and Janet will be going off next Saturday 20 October. She has been here for a year. Joe has got a gaffer's job in the Port £4:15/-. We finished putting in our corn on the 9th October. Got 2 boys for two three days to gather. James Todd, Adam Carson, Robert Carson, Syde.

13ᵗʰ October Willie coming tonight from Loch Doon. Was a fortnight ago the weekend owing to Ayr races. Been a month back since illness.

15ᵗʰ October Mrs James had a daughter.

29ᵗʰ October Walter Scott came… (?) Willie £50 leaves £119 to be paid up yet. Paid less interest £5.

30ᵗʰ October Miss Lauder (?) who has been 4 (?) weeks from Rothesay……………………to Auchenfoil one day………………………………………(*indecipherable*)

21ˢᵗ November Finished our potatoes. Miss Lauder went to see Janet.

3ʳᵈ November Uncle Willie going (?)

6ᵗʰ November Miss Lauder went off (?)

4ᵗʰ November a car came for Willie………………………………… (?)

8ᵗʰ November Robert………………………….. (?)

15ᵗʰ November Mary had twin girls, one died stillborn, the other to be called Maggie Lang.

16ᵗʰ November Uncle Willie and I went up to see her.

17ᵗʰ November Father's birthday. Mary sent a pair of slippers; Janet a shirt, bonnet and hanky.

20ᵗʰ November I went to pay rent. Saw Janet's house for first time, nice enough. Our maid is waiting on, very glad.

29ᵗʰ December James and Leslie came. Got Willie coming from Ayr at Kilmacolm station. It was a Saturday. Janet and Joe did not come till Hogmanay. No strangers at the door, except Mr & Mrs Gossy (?) on New Year's day. Heard that Uncle John was at Rothesay and Jenny Miller or Mrs Tainsh and Bain were going there. Getting a lb of butter. I ... Frank Blair, sometimes 3/- the lb. Frank has measles. Robert and Willie went to Gryfe (?) on Ne'erday first time.

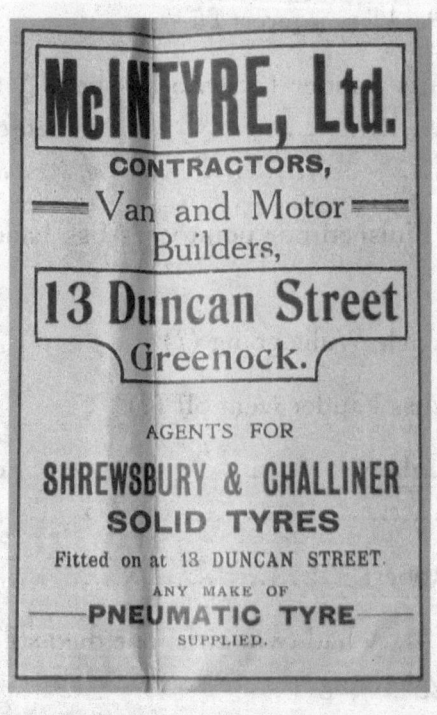

1918

5th January Robert went to Findlays.

28th January Robert has got a young cow £27.

February Joe has got a job in Glasgow, Harland and Wolfs.

2nd February The last of our own rearing cows off Blair. We had to put it away to butcher for £2:10/-. It was about two months calved, took a chill and never got better. Got a cow beginning of January £34 & by the end of 1917.

11th March Willie came home from Ayrshire & has gone to England this morning. Robert and he at Auchenfoil last night (Sunday).

14th March I wrote to Willie first time to England.

15th March Mrs Orrs cow calved – a quay. (Baxter got it £2.) It brings its cleening (?) Potter took it away.

14th March Mary was down alone. We have got word that Joe has rheumatism & has left his Glasgow job. Eggs are still 5/- a dozen. Have a hen set. The hen had just one chicken. It died.

17th March Had Pollie to take away cleening (?) Got him again the following Sunday to give it medicine. The next Sunday getting better but fallin off.

25th March Smith's big one and its neighbour calved. Smith's big one threatened to cast its calf. Vet roped it.

22nd March Janet and Joe & wee Willie came. Went home at night. Joe a good lot better.

25th March Uncle John came out to sow corn.

26th March Smith's big cow down with milk fever. Have sent for Pottie. Heard today that Mrs McLay, Ducal, was drowned on her way to Egypt as a Dr.

Uncle John out today again. Heard again that it was not true. Smith cow got better.

19th April Took 3 cows to Paisley back early sale. Got for one £37.2.0 & £25 on 17 & 18.................. *(pencil writing indecipherable-JHJ)*.

22nd April Mrs Colville came on 10 day... (?) She is not very well today and talks of going home. Uncle Willie has never come this year yet. Uncle John says we will have scunnered him. The last time he was he just went away the week before Ne'erday after being most of the summer and spring.

29th April Uncle Willie came and I was at Greenock and saw Janet. Mrs Colville went away after being a fortnight. Two girls came for her.

4th May Joe came with Robert and two beds. Gave him for them £3.

9th &10th May John was out harrowing down pots. Willie Neilson's death in paper. In his 69th year.

10th May Frost in morning but a grand day. Cows getting their dinner (?) out. Sold in April 3 back calving cows. Got word they were not in calf. Two of them £23 for one old cow & £20 for a light tented (?) one. Sowed turnips 10th May.

11th May John Baxter would be at Willie Neilson's funeral today.

6th May Set a hen. Auchenfoil eggs.

11th May Annie did half of the byre on Sat – whitewashed it. Put the ….in the new tank I got for it. Cost £2.10/- at Yonerston (?)

13th May We sold 3 back calving cows about 3 weeks ago. Got word two of them came a bulling. Robert away today to see about them. Got letter from Janet saying Mrs Miller has got the girl I wanted.

21st May Janet had her second son. called John Holmes. *[Dad's birth! – PJJ]*

27th May Marion Holmes and her 2 years old girl came for a week. She lost a 10/- note for me and I gave her another. She went away 3rd June.

1st June Joe came up suffering from rheumatics

3rd June Annie Ferguson came. Thinks she will do fine. Lovely weather. Got 7 chickens out own hen again (?) 2nd Set other two hens.

3rd June I went and saw the presents at Pomillan. They were numerous. Called at Killochries and Newton. Robert at Greenock with the two cows fat that had been sold before for backcalvers. Got about £38 for them.

5th June Buntains wedding to Smith of Auchen… (?) Her presents were numerous and £56 in money.

6th June Madge Ward's wedding to Mr Lang. 31st May Robert Lang Barnshake went to Stirling.

Father commenced to hoe potatoes.

7th & 8th June Annie went out in the afternoon to help Robert to hoe. Father and I did the bottles.

9th June Robert went to Janet's Sunday. She is coming for Willie next Saturday.

8th June Word from Willie. He has left McAlpine and has gone somewhere else. Mrs Agen (?) 4 Church St Marsh by Sea.

13th June Onning (?) calved a bull, keeping it.

15th June Janet and Joe came and took away Willie. Robert drove them home by Auchenfoil. A letter from Willie. He is working now at Marshe by the Sea. *[Probably Marske by the Sea, North Yorkshire—PJJ]*

17th June Uncle John came out first time for 6 weeks. Had had a touch of sciatica. The woman we had hoeing and thinning turnips is finished. Got £1.13/-

18th June Uncle Willie came. I just had written for him not to come as the hoeing and thinning were done.

19th June Black cow with white spot calved. A quay calf.

22nd June Father and I at church – the sacrament. A minister from Greenock. Paterson not home from Italy yet. We went in our own machine. Mac with us. A cold blowy day. A girl hired a fortnight from the Port. Mary Cambridge. Afterwards she and other 3 had trap room for a fortnight.

July In July Mrs Lonlit and family came for a month. For trap room £1, for ……. (?) £5

About middle of July James came for a while. After a week or so Polly came with weans. Gave them big room and bedroom.

11th July Duncan McGregor came for 10 days. Helped with hay.

6th August Uncle John came out. Got 6lb of gooseberries – 4d the lb.

7th August Lizzie Holmes and Ann Stevenson came for two days.

8th August They went up to Auchenfoil. We hear that Maggie McDougal Auchentiber is very ill at Johnstone Hospital.

6th August Our Mary and John and 3 kids went a drive to Braes etc. M> McDougal died. Trouble in head.

September About 1st September got word that Mrs Colville died in S. Africa.

About 1st Sept Uncle W. came for corn and Janet came for 6 weeks.

End of September James and wife are intending going home. James a lot better.

13th September Mary's birthday. I sent her Granny's ring with 3 verses of poetry.

Jessie Donald went away. Had been for 2 weeks & 2 days. Gave her a 10/- note.

Gave Janet Granny's silver and purple brooch & James her ring she got from Uncle Smillie, Polly a string of red corral beads I got from Granny. I think Mary got 3 strings.

20th September Janet and her two boys drove to Auchenfoil with James in gig.

26th September James and family went away.

28th September (Saturday) Ria came Went to Blairs that night. Her and I went to church next day and on Monday she went to Auchenfoil. It had been wet weather for a fortnight. But that day they got in 24 stacks and the next day was workable too.

1st October Ria went away. Coming back with her mother on Saturday. We will nearly get all our corn in today

2nd October Sat Black cow and a calf to Greenock. Got our corn all in.

4th October James Baxter Dykefoot took ill on a Friday at Greenock and was buried the next Friday

5th October Maria came with Annie A… (?) 12th Maria went away. It had been a wet week.

11th October October – Acute pneumonia.

14th October Got the price of one calf, not the other one & the cows – the cow was condemned.

4th November Robert got big cow at Paisley. Paid £44 Calved next morning. Milking fairly well. Milk 3.8 per gallon. About 20 a day. Robert got two cows about 6 weeks before that – not good milkers.

15th November Maggie Lang (?) Black died aged 1 year to a day. Meningitis. I went up next day Sat when it was buried

23rd November Ria and her lad came. Went up to Auchenfoil. Marion Holmes & wee girl came. Went back in two days. Had been at Blackwater & Lawparks. Coming back on Tuesday. Robert looking after a girl in the Port. Miss Braidwood. Willie still in England. Mrs Agen 4 Church St Marsh by Sea, Yorkshire, England. My servant Ann Robertson left at term - a fortnight before I got another.

M. Holmes did not come back. The other maid came and stayed about a fortnight and left one night to go to Pennytersal on Sunday then Robert got a young girl to come from the Port but she just waited 4 nights then I got Ria who is out of a job to come the weekend.

1919

January Willie came home at the New Year and is working at the Port and staying with Janet. James did not get at the New Year because he had just 2 days. Janet came a fortnight.

7th January The s….. class dance. W. & R. at it.

10th January Robert at Paisley today. Uncle John brought out the milk cart. (Uncle Willie went home the middle of December.)………….

End of March Robert myself and father all had the flu for 5 weeks. Getting better. Jean Manson came one day when I was ill. Mary came two weeks to nurse then Janet 3 weeks.

3rd April We put in the first of our pots. today in the Home. James and Leslie are going into Glas on their way home. They have been a fortnight. It has been longer cold this spring than any we remember. Willie put the drains at back byre. Uncle Willie came and stayed a fortnight.

17th April I had bile on Sunday. Mrs Brown and her sister Lizzie called. I did not see them.

.... (?) and family called.

2nd June Mary and Annie Douglas got Mary in the Burlington House (*or Home?*) Glasgow. Jenny Crawford got married to Hugh D. Kerr on the 5th in the Tontine Greenock.

12th June Willie has got the building up in the close and is painting it.

9th August Uncle Willie went away after cutting all the burn sides and helping in with all the hay. Binnie's (?) sister Bettie went away. After being 5 weeks gave her £1.10/-. Willie working at a different job yet was at nothing on the 8th and got paid up by Watty Scott (?). Robert and he walked home from Greenock. Mary and John were at the ... (?) On the 8th and Mrs Gray Monklands was at Auchenfoil next day.

Joe came up this Sun morning.

George Mason and his son & John Todd came on bykes.

2nd September Jessie Donald came. Uncle John came out next day. Uncle Willie came & we commenced to cut. Uncle John driving a man and wife came to bunch (?) slept in stable loft. Got ¼ an hour. Cut the Home in 2 afternoons. I heard from Emily Fleming. Coming to see me next week. Have not seen her for 55 years. Willie has got all the floors laid (?) and the (?) John went away on the 8th of Sept after being 4 months. Have sent for more wood to do the windows. Emily came & her cousin, a Miss Wilson from the Home (?)

27th September Jessie Donald went away. Railway strike on so Ria who had come the day before, first time since March drove her to near Johnstone. James came a week & Polly next day & 3 weans. Stayed from Tuesday till Saturday. I bought a pair of English blankets from Renfrw shop. About the 20th Joe got us a nice sideboard for £15, £1.10/- to himself.

26th September Bunin (?) sister came back. Nice help now. Was down at Mac one night & met Mrs Murray.

29th September Ria went away. Robert drove her and the Edwards to B of W. Got 5/-

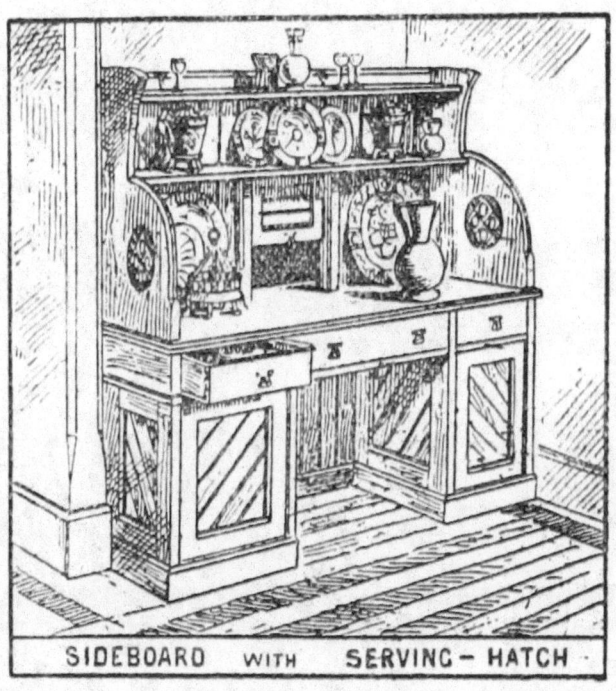

SIDEBOARD WITH SERVING-HATCH

1920

1st March Got for interest £5 from ………….. (?) After being without a maid I …now have two, Liz Spiers (?) & Kate Peacock

About 20 March Willie got a business in Greenock. Coming home this weekend to finish off work here.

26th April Uncle Willie came to help put in seed……. I know my two maids are leaving at term

15th May Uncle Willie went back to Glasgow. Potatoes all in

14th May Lythgow's dance at Kidston Hall. Robert with MacLaren at it.

16th May Father and I go to Johnstone tomorrow to pay off bonds £413. About the beginning of May James got a daughter called Marion King Holmes.

17th May We went to Johnstone in motor then it came back for us. I was very bad with the bile all day.

4th July John McGregor called in on Sunday wanting a room.

5th July Chattie (?) Thomson came in motor. Archie Currie & Willie came in… (?) Commenced the hay but thundery weather.

8th July Agnes Buntain's wedding day. Sent her a pound. Miss Gannon (?) was a week. Boarding £2.10/-. Archie Currie stayed 10 days but wet weather.

16th July I went to Greenock in milk motor.

21st July Grand day. Ricking park below the hedges.

12th July Mrs Scott son and daughter for a fortnight in bedroom upstairs. Chattie….. and went home on the Saturday

2nd August Robert gave Willie £20 first instalment of £100. … £80 to get. Uncle Willie came middle of July.

18th August Gave Robert £12 for……..

22nd August I gave Willie £25 out of 45 he has to get for milk cart

25th 26th and 27th August Bobbie Baxter, Will Blair and Young Scott came and put in hay with their bogey. I gave them each two 5/- pieces. Willie Young has been held up (?) for about 5 weeks in ……….. Stepends barn.

31st August We stacked our hay 6 stacks…. the shed full. Bobbie Baxter, Wull Blair and Scott (?) …. with horse and hayrick-lifter 4 … days in great help splendid weather there's a wee bit to cut below the School.

12th October Mrs Colville died in Johnstone Hospital, result of a shock.

5th October James took ill. 11th Mary and Janet went to see him.

19th He is getting a little better.

November Uncle Willie went home end of October. Been 3 1/2 months. Gave him £6. James allowed up a little about the 2nd November.

29th November Lizzie went away for a fortnight. Was not going to come back but did come. Janet came the 29th, stayed a fortnight with John and baby Joe. I gave her £2:10/-

19th & 20th December James came home and stayed.

1921

February I took the Flu. Was ill about a month in 1921

24th March Robert has been in Greenock Infirmary for 4 weeks – appendicitis. About a month before that he was off the milk cart with rheumatics. Willie had to go with it then and now Archie Currie has brought home the cart for 3 weeks. Mary was down today. 3 weeks in March Smith's cow had a quay calf. We are keeping it.

Blair has 2 calves, one from Dippany (?) he is giving us 26 gallons of milk just now. Getting £25 a week.

29th March Polly and two girls came through for a fortnight.

24th March Robert came home from the Infirmary and took it easy for a week. Liz went for a weekend….. James McCullagh went on the ran dam (?)

3rd May Archie Currie went in milk cart after being a fortnight. He helped to set the tatties and painted the house outside. I got Smillie money £3. 15/- end of April.

End of July Polly and 3 weans came. Hay all in the week before then the weather broke and Baxter has not got all in yet.

5th August Paying for two cows today £77

30th August Mrs Maggie Black went to a home in Glasgow, Claremont Home, to be treated for exema. We hear John Kinloch is in a Home in Glasgow – some inward trouble.

September Jessie Donald came. I have had a swollen sore finger for 2 months. Thought it might be the bone but I am glad it is getting better. Had a letter from Mary Holmes asking me to Rothesay one day last week but could not go. I intend going to Greenock on Wednesday to see Janet. James' wife went with Madge (?) last week to Bridge of Weir

7th September James Kinloch is ill with. I went with Janet to Inverkip.

24th September My finger not quite better yet.

15th December James has been confined to bed for 6 weeks. Don't expect he will ever rise. Polly been here for more than a month. Mary down yet. Janet a fine stay at the time (?)

1922

Middle of March Got £5 interest from War Loan. End of March got Uncle Smillie's £2.0.9

End of March Got Uncle Smillie's £2.0.9

30th March I was at Greenock and saw Mrs Currie. Jessie Donald has been here for 6 weeks sewing some for Mary and myself

On January 24th James died. It is now the end of March and Polly and two boys are here still. She attends the hens.

22nd April Bessie Millar got married after her son was born (Mrs Meason). Willie owes me a balance of £3.16/- May 1922.

12th July We commenced our hay. Very wet. Before that. Uncle Willie came.

13th July Polly went with Janet to Largs.

28th July Polly went the weekend to Glasgow. Brought back the boys. The girls (?) at school all July. I had Mrs Simpson from the Port all July. James bedroom £1 a week then a daughter of hers, Mrs Paton came for a fortnight.

10th August I went in milk motor to Greenock. Janet came back with me. James Kinloch died at Branchal in July 1922. Lizzie Crawford got married to Mr Kerr in July.

14th August Uncle Willie went away after being a month helping with the hay.

1st September Got interest £5

2nd September Jessie Donald came. Bought cloth for two shirts. Some nice days now but not many without rain, the wettest summer I evr mind of and cold always broken by thunder.

15th September I met Janet & John at Prince's Pier and went to Tighnabruich to see Kate MacLachlan & Mr Henderson.

22nd September Uncle John was out and drove the .... (?) as the corn in mid park. Mary Millar and her man came and spent the afternoon. Quite nice.

4th October I paid Willie insurance money £25.2/-. He also owes me 8/- for shirt and £3.15/-. I have an IOU for this. Jessie Donald went off today. Mr Murray out looking for leak in pump pipe. We have just got a few huts up. Eggs 3/- a doz, 3/6 in Kilmacolm.

10th October One cart of coals from Whiteford. Not so smooth sailing with Polly having her two facedness.

29th or 30th October Jenny Lang died at Branchall aged 71.

9th November Got a girl, Lizzie Gorrie. Doing fine. Meg and Mary Campbell went away. Ina Millar got married in December 1922. Came here now and again for a week putting in her time till she joins her husband who has gone to Australia.

28th November James Baxter died at Burnbank aged 68

14th December George Scott Hillside hurt his left arm in the Mill and got it taken off above the elbow.

15th December Uncle John out. Polly at a party at Hankinsons at night.

16th December Tom came back. Had left his place to ... Polly going away at Xmas. Mrs Carruth Birton (?) died in October.

Clyde Steamers at Greenock, c1880s

1923

4th April I met Janet at station. I had little John Johnson with me.

'Little' John Holmes Johnson, aged 5 or 6 - the editor's father

We went and saw Uncle Willie (?) Ria drove me in and out. Have got my first dozen of pure bred eggs set. Heard about Mrs

Orr servant. We have David Laidlaw as servant, a lazy conceited thrawn ill-natured fellow. We have got all the corn sown on the 3rd of April. Mrs MacLaren at Liverpool her Easter holidays sent me a lovely cake in the shape of eggs. Robert saw Jessie Donald a fortnight ago. Gave him £1

March I was down at Miss Mac's one night and met Miss Clayston and Mrs Smith, Slates

12th April A letter from Polly saying she was getting a boarder and that Jean was lame since getting out of hospital after the scarlet fever. Willie Black Auchenfoil has not been well for a month and not at school. Our Willie not looking well.

End of May Janet came for a fortnight. Great Fete at Kilmacolm On June 16th. Drew £800 to pay debts of Institute.

1st June Liz Gorrie painting the house outside and windows. Wee Gally (?) went away today not feeling well. Jacky Smith came yesterday.

First week in August George Mason came went by Mary's.

28th August Ria came with Mallick (?) Going to satel (?) in a week. Our Janet came to take John home to school on the 21st.

18th August ... (?) And Mrs Roger came while she was here.

31st August Very wet weather. Has rained every day for 6 weeks or more. Baxter (?) was to have been today to take in. Robert ill this morning with rheumatics away with the milk. Had to get the doctor. Kept bed for a fortnight.

21st October The pains are not all away from him yet, tender feet. I had to go with a stick, some days two sticks but getting better. Taking a little kruchen salts every morning. Robert on hands getting a motor car.

I gave Robert in exchange for charge £7, for motor £6.10/-, in loan £20 (I don't remember if I got it back.)

1st December Marion Holmes and Chrissie came.

3rd December Our motor came and a wee man (impident) to teach Robert the way.

5th December I had a bad day of the bile.

6th December Our Parliamentary election day. I got a drive in young Burnets (?) motor.

9th December I had a letter from Mrs Holborn.

10th December A letter from Jean Duncan (?) and… (?) I wrote to Polly. Commenced this week to sell potatoes 1/3 &1/5

1924

25th January Potatoes selling now at 1/6 a stone. I went in Robert's motor to Port Glasgow first time. Nice and handy. Willie and Joe have bought 9 Terrace Road. Robert got home today (25th) 3 new suits. A railway strike on. Mr Ramsay MacDonald on for Prime Minister social government. Eggs selling 3/6. My brother Willie died aged 73 years and near a month. Born on 28th December. I fell about a month ago on the floor and cut above the eye.

16th February Father took a weak turn. Liz went home to come back that night but did not come. Came on Monday glad to see her back.

23rd February A roup at Steels Blacks Home. Robert got two cows, one calved.

26th February I wrote to Mary Holmes. Liz Holmes at West Kilbride. Jessie Donald to come on Thursday for a fortnight. Willie at ..... on Saturday night 23rd. We sowed our corn a week later than Frank and a week later getting in our seed potatoes.

The cows getting their dinner (?) on the hill park from the 5th May. We have a man called Andy helping Robert to sow manure and lift the midden. We sold some hay to Dougliehill, Kerr Netherwood, Scott Hillside and John Kinloch.

July Janet went a fortnight after here a weekend (?)

August Mrs Douglas and 3 children came and stayed till 11th August - £4:10/- + £2

5th August Leslie and Jack Orr came.

14th August I made 3 lb blackcurrant jam for Mary. Robert has gone to the Port...a visit of John Laird and then Robert Laird. This month had John Currie & wife & 2 on the 9th

16th August I had the bile bad and a very sore leg.

Sandy Graham and his wife and daughter came in............. (?)

29th August Leslie and Jack Orr went away after being 3 weeks.

5th September Robert took me to Mrs Orr in motor. Met Mary Buntain and Agnes. Our Liz painting outside. A letter from Marion Holmes saying Liz is going to be married on the 14th of October. I was at the wedding, our Janet and Joe and Willie.

November Liz staying here 3rd half year. Have got a man Harry Coats 12th May. Harry and Rob are white-washing. Mary Healy came. We got her for Black's Newton. Janet came a fortnight at the term and left wee Joe. He got on fine. Some old turnip seed has not come through.

2nd November I was at the doctor (?) with Miss Maclaren.

8th November Our Janet came up the weekend. Willie and Joe have got up their showroom and storing (?) fairly well. Our potatoes all dug end of October. Turnips nearly ....11th of Nov and a good crop. Pots......

11th November I sent Polly £3. I sent Jessie 10/- her birthday. I am going to cut a night… (?) Skirt for myself.

22nd December Neill brought 2 bottles

1925

16th April Neill brought other 2 bottles. Lamont was killed by sawmill at Auchenfoil.[1] We are scaling lime park above Hankinson. Cold weather, hailstone showers. John McGill ... man in May this year. John Laird had to leave Ladymuir. Got a small place near Crosslee and James Holmes had to leave Priestside for Jackie Telfers and James Holmes and wife bought a house in the Port. John Breslin left Hatrick and went to Ladymuir and James Black had to leave Gibblaston. He bought the Home Farm of Tillichwraes (?) Mary Holmes came the end of May and we went in and saw Uncle John and Janet Barr. Miss MacLaren is away ill at the Infirmary. Jessis Donald came 9th of June had been a week at Janet's. Liz is staying on but getting ill to put up with. Father able to walk to the Height.

19th June I went to Greenock. Took bile in Janet's.

23rd July Janet and I went to Mount Clair well ... (?) good day.

27th July Our first haylifter came and we are putting in with it. A grand sunny summer in 1925. My own blackcurrants made 23lb

29th July Liz went to Glasgow half a day. J Barr and Miss Lindsay came out

1st August All our hay in now. Never remember it in so soon. A letter from Polly. Her boys did well at school. Jack got a first class house (?) ... (?) Certificate for his work in the class and a prize for being Dux in the Preparity school. The Rector prize a beautiful book. The Earl of Elgin gave the speech and the Countess presented the prizes and Jack had the honour of presenting the Countess with a bouquet of white carnations.

5th August Janet and I in Glasgow – getting my black coat and her a navy blue costume. John and Joe Johnson here this month.

10th August July Jessie Kinloch and David Brewster were married.

17th August Janet and I went to Greenock and the Bank.

19th August Liz went to Port Glasgow the afternoon. Jean Black & Mrs Orr came.

12th September John Currie and wife and wean came. Our Janet and two boys came same day. All got a drive in in car.

13th September Liz went with Mary Hank to Bailieston a weekend. Father got a posy from Neil

Mary Orr's birthday. Sent her a dish ...(?)

14th September Robert went to Paisley and bought two cows, one of them was Smiths.

15th September Liz Holmes and Marion Forbes came. I had bile but managed to talk to them.

18th September One of the cows calved, a quay. Car left to get sorted. Liz went for bottles in ... (?) Cart.

6th October Marion and Jean Orr were to go to school today. Jack went to Leslie's school last month – the John Watsons, clever boys.

5th October .... (?) our potatoes... (?) first time doing fine. Liz Gorrie... John Wilson... (?)

6th October I wrote to Mary Holmes.

18th October First night's frost killed the dahlias. Miss MacL very queer. Our Mary down.

25th October Liz went off this morning in her high horse motor going home (?) Getting too cheeky not to get away again till she............when she ....Liz left at the term. Went to Dumfries. Stayed two days. Came back to Chapel. Left Chapel 13th Jan 1926 then she went to Haddowkiston (?) We have got Liz Smellie for a maid, a young cheeky randy, but when in a good mood works not so bad.

---

1. **Lamont killed:** The Belfast Telegraph printed the following news item: WHIRLED TO HIS DEATH - SCOTS LABOURER'S TERRIBLE FATE - While working a threshing mill at Auchenfoil Farm, Kilmacolm, Renfrewshire, William Lamont, farm labourer, was caught in the main shaft and whirled round it. Death was instantaneous and his body was badly mutilated. Deceased had been employed on the farm for about sixteen months, and it is understood he belonged to Perthshire." (Belfast Telegraph, 18th April 1925)

1926

January Janet and Willie came on Hogmonay. Joe on Ne'erday. Liz Gorrie went to Chapel in December. Liz Smillie came here. Willie Holmes came on 6th January. I had bile next day. Janet went away on the 6th. Rob got a cow in Paisley on the 6th. – 24 pounds. Calved next night

GRANNY ORR'S DIARY
(1925~1944)

Mrs Marion Orr, née Holmes

Editor's Note: This is the second diary kept by Mrs Marion Orr of Gateside Farm. It covers the years 1925 to 1944. In his transcription, my father noted that half of this diary is written in pencil and indecipherable. The first page was unreadable and the next two pages had been torn out.

Granny Marion Orr at Gateside farm, with Grandfather William Orr, son Robert Orr, daughter Janet Johnson (née Orr), and grandsons John and Joe Johnson

1926

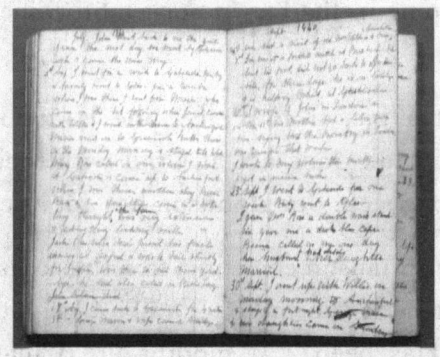

- J. Campbell Fyfe's Home number – house in Kilmacolm 298 Kilmacolm.
- Glasgow telephone Douglas 395
- Galbreath & Fyfe Writers, 95 Bath Street, Glasgow
- Peter Gatherer & Sons Grain Seed & Wool (?) Merchants, 21 Crawford Street, Greenock
- Black's phone Number 440
- Willie's phone number 357

<u>February</u> Old John Laird, Dykefoot, has been very ill but getting better. George Love died and was buried on the 5th Feb.

Mrs Orr Newton is recovering from a bad attack of influenza & pleurisy.

22nd February I wrote to old Ria a letter. Smellie went away at May term and we got Lizzie Burns. Father took ill a little before the term with a bad cold & bad spit - could not come out of bed for about 2 months and very weak.

5th August Finished putting in our hay – 7 stacks. Grand help with the men at the hut at the Mill & splendid weather. Janet came up for a fortnight. Had Liz Hol (?) and her man. While she was here had Mrs Currie, Archie, Mary Jess & John's wife in July.

8th August Sunday Janet and Joe came. Janet stayed all night & took the boys home in the big motor. John came back next day with Robert.

9th August Got a p.c. from Polly. She is at Girvan with the Forrests & Leslie and Jack are at Crail with their uncle James. Coming here next week. Joe Johnson has got a second motor.

14th August Jean Manson came in a taxi to Mauls Mill & walked up. Robert took her in in motor. Father Orr getting better and able to be up. Has been 2 ½ months ill. A man came to sort piano.

27th August We finished cutting corn at Millan wood. Greir & Wackly W...(?)

28th August Dunoon sports. Mary at Mary Paton's and Jenny Holmes 10th ... (?) John Johnson went away the day the Orrs came. 18th August. *[He would have been 8 years old-Ed.]*

John Laird Faulds died at Branchton on the 23rd August and was buried in Kilmacolm on the 25th.

19th August Janet Barr & Bessie & Miss Lindsay with Willocks ... (?) Came & spent the afternoon.

28th August Janet Orr Newton, Sandy Ainford's wife died – a stoppage of the bowels, weeks illness.

September Maggie Orr and Lizzie Orr came. Walked it from station and had to walk back for Robert had the motor away at Johnstone. Joe Johnson got a motor this month. Willie getting more work to do. Looks as if they are going to succeed at last.

Evelin (?) Orr got married in the month of May of this year. Married in a church and a reception in a hotel – about 100 at it but they dirtily left the Gateside ones out of it. (but that is a common occurrence) James Orr and wife & Eric (?) came in their motor one Sunday just for a show off. Good cheek. She is a perfect snob. Evelin's name now is Roe & she stays in a hotel in London. He is an agent for something.

Money in Bank £417 + £80 + £60 + £100 + £3 = £660 plus DV £590 = £1250. In Aug 1927 £1200

3rd September Leslie and Jack went to Mount Clare. We have 5 stacks up. Janet and Robert coming tomorrow.

I heard from Bessie Barr that Janet was real ill for a week.

4th September They came took our photos at cirnbeam

[Note: The mysterious 'cirnbeam' may have been misread in translation, and was perhaps meant to be 'the hornbeam' as in the tree behind them. See the photo referred to by Granny Orr, overleaf-Ed.]

Granny Orr (seated) with daughter Janet Johnson, nee Orr, and son Robert Orr at the 'cirnbeam' Gateside

5th September I had the bile.

6th September Chain (?) road came for our cow that Pottie took the cleaning from. It went through it and fissiled out

4th September Janet Barr died after 10 days severe suffering. She was buried beside her husband in Kilbarchan new cemetery on Bridge of Weir road. Her niece, Mrs Graham Taylor (Bessie's daughter) gets the house and its contents. Her brother Tom gets the rest of her fortune (very much one-sided). Willie Holmes and wife came one Sunday 29 August and took our photo at front door. Mary Holmes at Gourock this month.

13th September Our John paid us a visit. Staying with Jenny Miller. Had been taking a drive in a motor to see Bessie in Glasgow by Bessie's husband two days before going back to Rothesay to stay the winter.

15th September The two boys went to Glasgow on their way home. Had been at Auchernfoil. I gave Mary her……. (?)

4th October Our maid took appendicitis and was taken to Glasgow Infirmary by Burns (?) Lizzie Gorrie got me Peggie.

27th October Sent Polly £1 from B

28th October Sent Jessie £1 from B. I am busy putting grey fur on Janet's blue coat.

25th October A snow storm and severe frost for a fortnight.

September & October we had as many as 10 men some days helping to take in corn, dig potatoes & cut trees (?) Got dinner, tea and supper and 2/- the half day. The coal strike has been going on for 6 months, bad time.

September Lizzie Gorrie got married to John Jack.

November Potatoes rising from 6d to 9d a stone for blues and Kerrs pinks, golden wonders. Rob is ½ Frank sold his at the beginning for less than £3 the ton.

1st November Robert went to Paisley and got 2 cows. Came to £42. Father has paid his share and Robert owes me his £14 (Now) Paid. 1926 Agnes Ross and Wull Crawford got married middle of November and went to Branchal – a daughter born to them not many months after.

December Old Davidson the shoemaker got married in December.

16th December Janet Black's 20th anniversary of her birthday. *[Dad's cousin Jenny – PJJ]* I gave her my engagement ring.

Coal strike ended after 7 months. Getting coal at 1/9 per cwt. It was 5/- a while.

21ˢᵗ December Mary Crawford Dippany and James Ross got married (a son born to them on Oct 21) and came home to Maul's Mill the night before Xmas 1926. Mr & Mrs Ross went up to Syde.

29ᵗʰ December Old Mr Bell called. Robert went over at night and heard … was told John Black had a lump on his knee.

30ᵗʰ December I had a letter from Bessie Barr saying she had nothing of Janet's to give me.

1927

1st January I had Janet and family-it was a Saturday. Willie at night. Joe on Sunday. Polly the Friday before. Willie Holmes on Monday. Went away on Wednesday.

9th January My flowering shrub is out. There came a very heavy storm beginning of February. Blew in our byre window and did much damage elsewhere.

8th February Robert sorted the netting round the garden and kept the hens out.

9th February I wrote to John.

At the b… of January Mrs Crawford, Dippany, took ill and had to be taken to a Home in Kilmacolm first and then to Paisley. Lost heart after Mary left her and got married. At Auchenfoil they have got a ….. motor and Mary &Donald and John and Jimmy came down one night in it. Willie Black is not so well, rheumatism through him. Father Orr taking weaker turns.

26th February Mary came down and Janet came up. Both went home at night. Mary went down to Mauls Mull and then up to Syde to see Mrs Ross who was quite cheery.

28th February Robert took a cow to Paisley but took it back again, too cheap. I had a letter from Jessie Donald saying John Craig had died and Mrs Hutchinson. Robert called on Jessie and gave her 10/-

3rd March Roger is to get ½ a ton of golden wonders. Father's going about today not so bad. I am putting a row of Boxwood to the foot of the garden path and no hens are coming in. Want to finish my pedigree books and have peace.

1st April Sowed corn in lea (?) above Hankinsons. Sent Jack his birthday.

5th April Set potatoes below Hankinsons. Finished the field on the 7th. On the 8th Polly came on her way from Greenock. Marion has the measles. Gave her 10/-

9th April We have 4 calves, 2 bulls & 2 quays.

13th April I took the Flu off Robert. Was very ill a fortnight. Willie was ill too and Janet not very well. Joe bought a private motor off Leperstone.

June About June 1st Father got so silly on his legs that he had to stay in bed. After a fortnight he rallied a little and was able to walk round the bed

15th June 11 chickens out that is 30 altogether. Some dozen did not come out and some eaten by rats. Will set some yet.

20th June Other 11 birds

28th June Set poison for rats.

25th June Joe Janet and boys and Norman came in motor coming on Wednesday, Greenock holiday. Father confined to bed these 5 or 6 weeks. Can just walk round the bed but fairly well. John Black and Mary and some weans were at Auchenleck on Saturday. Same day as Joe was here.

29th June Jessie Donald came on the 29th. Father not up these two days. Janet and the boys walked up from Village. Going to Sutherland next day in the motor.

1st July A letter from Polly saying Jean had passed to get into the Watson school and that she herself was coming next week to see us. She came and went back to Glasgow that night.

11th July R has paid interest till end of June.

3rd July Willie came his holidays. Made the chicken half of henhouse. Sent payment (?) to Glas on the 6th. Stayed in Caly Road, went to Isle of Man next day. Came back on Friday the

7th July Ann Stevenson & Crissie Forbes came, stayed a little & went to Auchenfoil and stayed a night. Ann expects to get a permanent school after the holidays.

9th July Robert went to see Miss Dickson first time.

11th July We have for servants, Jimmy McGinnes (?) and Jenny Robertson. His sister and chum came to see him today (Sunday). Father not able to stand on his feet. He hits (?) himself.

14th July Mary with Donald, Willie and Hugh came down to see Father.

15th July Janet came and stayed a week & I went to Greenock and saw Willie's place and went to Mary Holmes in Greenock. Miss Leaf (?) facing the sea.

1st August The MacPhails came & stayed a fortnight in room upstairs.

4th August The 3 girls Black came with Donald.

5th August Leslie and Jackie came.

6th August (Saturday) John Currie and wife and daughter came. I was very tired and had bile next day.

7th August Leslie and Jack went to Auchenfoil.

13th August Janet and Kate Carmichael came. J not speaking.

16th August Jenny Black went to Edinburgh to stay 2 days with Aunt Polly.

18th August Jenny came back well pleased with her jaunt.

19th August Wee Joe had a near escape from the hay lifter.

Granny Orr's grandson, Joe Johnson beside hay rick, Gateside farm.
(The editor's Uncle)

15th August Jimmie McGin had a narrow escape from the hay lifter falling on him.

20th August We are in the midst of stacking

September The boys Orr stayed all the month at Auchenfoil. Came back here on Friday and went to Janet's next Wednesday, stayed a night and went home on Friday about the 8th September – going to school on the 22nd September, Jean to go with them.

22nd September Mary came down spoke about Mac & her stones (?) at the gate. Maggie Orr came on the 15th.

Sandy Graham called on the 30th. Dis not let him see Father. Our corn is all cut but it has rained for 3 days & 2 nights and we have none in. Much of Scotland is flooded, disease in the potatoes, a very wet summer. Robert in Glasgow today (22nd) looking after his potato digger. I have taken 3 bonnets to pieces.

23rd October Polly & Marion were in Glasgow for 3 days. She came here today. I gave her a Wraes flower for Nan. She got 10 and a rabbit. The same day Mary and her daughter Jenny went to Glasgow with Joe and got Jenny a fur and other things. Marion got one the year before. They went to Jenny Holmes. I have got a new velvet bonnet. Father keeps on pretty well. Polly thought him looking better. Uncle John came a fortnight ago. He thought the same. Robert drove him to the Buntains and then to the Village. I have not finished my book (?) yet.

26th October Got half a cheese from MacFarlane Shearer 1/1 1/2 the lb

1928

1st January Robert took a cold and I took it off him, the Flu and Father took it too. It was too much for him and he went off his food. Up till then he ate fairly well and on the 9th January he passed quietly away. Mary was down and helped and Mrs Kate Carson was over at the end. I was in bed and lay for 4 weeks. Funeral private. Maria came and attended to me.

Grandfather William Orr, Marion's husband

25th February Ria went to stay with Janet. She was flitting that week to Lyle Street.

Uncle John was a week at Netherwood. They took him a drive here and to see Willie Buntain. Went home the 9th

11th February Mr Mitchell and John Currie came.

5th March I am sorting in the garden.

28th March Mary Holmes came to see me. Gave her Granny's vase and T. ladles (?)

7th March My birthday. Got a Jug (?) from Janet, a Shetland shawl from Mary – her Mary had knitted it, her first one.

9th March Marion, Jenny and Mary came down at night. Mrs Orr and Robert came in motor at night. Got on all right.

10th March Ria not back from Greenock yet. Will be 3 weeks in 2 days. Robert and Tommie Casey at the drum (?)

14th March Sold our gig to Frank Blair for £2.10/- He is taking his milk to the station to the Co-op Society. I am started to finish my P. Book.

15th March Robert and Jim Morten at Johnstone. Called on Mrs Bright. She was in bed with a sore leg.

20th April Kate Bell (Mrs David Carson) died suddenly of heart trouble. Burial on 23rd at Kilmacolm – 9 motors at it.

28th April Good weather for setting potatoes – biggest part of 5 acres set. Janet Blair came today. Had been last night at Gourock House with Mrs Currie. My first setting of eggs out, 10 chicks, 2 died. Got a dozen from Mrs Carson. Lizzie came with them& put them all together, doing fine. This is my third week culling.

1st May Heard about May Scott.

6th May I went to Greenock to get frock sorted. Went and called on Mrs Currie in Gourock House. She is 81 and no grey hairs. J and J not getting on well.

11th June I went to Rothesay as the guest of the Misses Clarke at Mount Clare. I stayed till the

21st June enjoyed myself very much. I wrote my name on their writing book also the following lines:

Although to leave ye a' the noo my hert's a wee bit sair
I'll hope to come anither day and see you at Mount Clare.
And may the Power above look down and keep you in His care
And a' the blessings that ye need attend you at Mount Clare.

I came up to Greenock and stopped a night with Janet and on the 28th she and her family went to the Highlands in their motor. The next day was our Sacrament. John was at it. He went back to Rothesay the next day. I sent some roots to the Clarkes. I had got some Roots from them and a Royal fern and a Hydrangea

23rd June I went down and saw young Mrs Ross.

28th June I had old Mrs Harald to tea. Nice old lady. Mrs Ross and baby came up. Her first visit.

5th July I went to Pomillan and Newton. Willie Buntain getting more feeble and very blind. Mrs Orr had been ill with bile, getting better. A letter from Jessie Donald. She had fallen down the stair and broken her arm. Was getting better. Maria left me on the 2nd July. Kept house when I was at Rothesay. Did fine. This has been the most cold and wet summer ever I mind of. Frost in the mornings in July and cold blowy winds. We commenced to cut hay about the 15th of July and in 10 days had two fields rucked and all the rest cut – the weather was very favourable after all.

20th July Jessie Donald came. Arm much better. Able to sew with her right hand.

22nd July Have made 30 lbs of jam. On the 17th our wee maid, Mary Lamont went away for a day ... 3

28th July Mary's father came to see Mary. She had been complaining to get ... (?) She is waiting on. Not a bad worker. Joe came in a temper to take John back. Mary's father got a £1.

30th July Beggar man got waistcoat & shirt 1/-

10th August Jessie has been 3 weeks. May Scott had a daughter last week.

8th August Lizzie Holmes and her man came. Robert went off for (?) tonight. He and Tom are about finishing the drains. 3 stacks up last week. Waiting till the rest is drier. A letter from John last week. Mr MacPhail not so well. One from Ria. Not any rooms let yet.

28th August Jessie Donald went home. Our maid Mary Lamont went with her – been 5 weeks. Uncle John came a fortnight before that. Stayed in Netherwood from Wed to Tues. Jennie Miller came with her two children in July.

31st August Janet Willie and Joe were at Joe Ross' wedding at Burlington House.

1st September Jim Manson & Jenny Orr (Mrs Black) came in taxi then John Currie, wife and daughter came. The Curries had been at a family gathering the night before. A farewell to the daughter of my cousin John Holmes and her husband & second cousin Mr Paterson, grandson of Mary Kerr Hatrick.

2nd September (Sunday) Jean Loutit & Jessie …Alan came. Boys walked home with them.

4th September Tomorrow is Marion Black's birthday. I have given her the … that her great grandmother had bound (?) and some sweets. She is going to Edinburgh tomorrow to stay 2 nights. Old Mrs Harald came down today to ask me up tomorrow.

5th September I walked up to Carseknowe. Robert was away with the motor to Greenock. At 5 o'clock he came for me, all quite nice.

6th September (Saturday) Two days very wet but today good. Some corn cut & needing drought

7th September Wet again. Yesterday old Mrs Bain came down to speak to Miss MacLaren about paying for torn books. Came in to me and had a long talk and tea then Rob took her up in motor.

8th September Janet and Joe came a drive in motor. Mary Lamont went away & did not come back. On the 11th her father came and said she was not well.

12th September Janet and Kate Carmichael were at Auchenfoil. Joe came for them in motor.

13th September Mary's birthday. Gave her Coliles plate white with pale blue rarol (?) flowers. Jenny Holmes came that day to

Auchenfoil. Mary came down with her. Annie Cairny came Good worker.

15th September Polly came for the day.

18th September Her sister Nan and the girls came.

19th September Got a letter from Mary Holmes.

22nd September Corn all cut one afternoon. The boys Orr went away.

30th September John Currie and Mr Mitchell came to wind up the Estate affairs. The father of Mary Lamont came for her clothes and money and the MacPhails walked up from Greenock, the 3 and a companion.

2nd October Maggie Orr and Lizzie came. Rob gave them a drive to Mill. Bought one semit from Dalzel 9/6

6th October Janet came up the weekend- I gave Willie a reduction of 3

10th October Had in a big squad at potato digger. The byre about half done.

17th October Finished our potatoes. I had the bile next day.

27th October Willie Holmes and wife came. Brought gramophone with them. Mollie not better yet.

28th October Our communion, sent for Mary Holmes but she could not come. She was flitting. One room May (?) Andrew Laird spoke to me in the seat. Got another semit for Willie. This girl, Annie Cairny, is a good worker. Just getting one egg a day.

27th Put £15 in bank.

31st October Halloeen. I am alone. Rob at Haralds. Maid at Mill. Tommie out.

1st November Dalziel came. Got semit for self. Willie Orr called, barn finished. Johnnie Davidson went off the High road but wanted back on it. Maid shawing turnip Swedes very small. Got Burmah Oil money 1st Nov

9th November Janet came with Joe's sister from England.

11th November Mary came down for the day. Went to Maul's Mill. Macs getting the byre floor lifted and keeping the cows in. Wrote to Mary H. and John.

28th November Term day. The man Tommie left. Going to Campbell Crawford Branchal. The maid Annie Cairny left to go to Straven. Rob went to Glasgow and got a lass. Came home on Friday. Mary Smith a clever wee lass. Man did not come home.

29th November Mary Holmes came a surprise visit. Had been at Dykefoot. Jenny Black came down and stayed a night & two days. Jammie (?) stayed 3 nights.

December At end of December a letter came for Mary Smith to go home and nurse her mother. I did not want her to go but she went off in the morning and walked to Glasgow. She might be three weeks. Got no money.

1929

January 1st week in January got Netta Healy, a stupid girl but very willing to work. Before Xmas Rob and I took cold. I got better, he got worse. Very sore throat, a month and two weeks before he was getting better. Dr Ferguson attending. No one at the New Year. Mollie Holmes not well. Janet and the boys came for a week. Joe went to England. Got £100 from Mason (?)

8th January I wrote to Maggie S ... (?) in answer to her own boys names is Archie Allan. He knows Mrs Watson, Polly Speirs. Netta Healy came for 3 weeks. Took mentally ill. Mother came for her after being a week without a mind. We got Lizzie Plagin (?) She came on the 5th February. A severe winter, hard frost & snow & very cold for many weeks. Robert smashed his motor this month. Something broke and it ran down the Clune Brae.

End of April Willie became sole proprietor of the property at 9 Terrace Road, Greenock.

5th January A roup at Cauldside. The man Buntain died suddenly with the flu' - it was in nearly every house. At the roup Rob got 3 calves and 1 cow, some turnips.

28th January March 1929 Mrs Marion Currie died suddenly. I had been to see her the day before. She was staying with Mary J at Gourock House. Willie was at the funeral on the 30th. She was aged 82.

3rd April A man came along and Rob engaged him, John Glabreath, a good worker. Slept in bothy. Archie in Trap room. James Ross getting better of pneumonia & pleurisy. James Scott of Green very far through.

9th April Had Mrs Harold 4 hours cutting pots.

11th April She came at 10 o'clock till ¼ to 4

15th April She came at same time.

22nd April Mrs Harold finished cutting – would not take anything for it. I gave her a cardigan, fawn colour.

25th April Lizzie Roger went to the salvation station in Glasgow. We have been putting on lime on Redland for corn yesterday and today. John Galbreath helping elderly man. Snowing today.

11th May Cattle Show. John at it. Got colder. Did not get out.

18th May Polly came from Glasgow. She had been with Marion for Nan to take to Seamills. John Currie and wife came.

20th May John Campbell & wife came. Have taken a house in Rothesay for June & asked me down.

29th May I got a letter from John saying Mrs McMillan had died suddenly and wee Gordon was with his granny in Greenock.

1st June Very nice warm weather. Great heat all over. 24 deaths from it in New York yesterday. My maid that came last week went away today. Would not stay any longer. Cathie Kilpatrick. Archie Allan left at the term – getting too great with Jessie in Dippany. Going to Donald Laird.

4th June Janet came and stayed a night. Helped to clean the big room.

5th June Mary Holmes came.

6th June Mary went to Lizzie Holmes in Rothesay for two nights. James Black came for a week and helped to milk. A new lass came on 7th June, Martha Spence.

8th June Motor at Anderson Garage. Stuff to get.

9th June Two girls up from Port. (Sunday)

31st June Polling day – school holiday. The two Johnsons came on their bikes & stayed a night. Janet Miller and her two came. Had been at the Old Mill. Archie whitewashed byre and part of close. Bought two pairs of drawers from Dalziel for Rob, 3/9 each.

11th July Aunt Aggie and Mrs Lang died at Auchenfoil.

25th July Highland Show at Alloa. Robert and I at it. 37.000 that day, a lovely day. Held on Lord Marrs Park.

Our hay was all ricked the day before. Mary Paton a week at Auchenfoil. Willie Holmes two girls at Auchenfoil the week before Glasgow Fair.

20th July Robert went and saw Rob Holmes. He was at home from the Infirmary. Very ill.

28th July I have 3 hens hatching out chickens. Not many coming out.

1st Jessie Donald came and stayed till the 30th, covered a mat for Mary and sewed for me. She is getting the pension now. Commenced in June.

In July Jack Orr passed (exams) One of eleven that got into Fettes College. The Orrs going to Tarbert in August.

8th August I wrote to John. R & L Barr (?), Mary Holmes.

9th August Sanitary man came to see about the further improvements. Today 1 dozen of chicks out of 4 dozen eggs.

10th August Wrote to Mary Jessie. Got an apron from Jessie Donald.

11th August The Youngs (?) went away in their nephew's car.

23rd August Mary at Kilmarnock Dairy jaunt (?)

24th August John Currie and wife came.

25th August Robert and I at Alloa Show.

4th September Agnes Scott collecting 4/6

5th September Marion Black's birthday. Gave her my father's Bible, bottle of scent etc. A letter from Polly saying Jack's clothes for Fettes College would cost from 30 to 40 pounds – his name on every article. Robert getting through most of the drains in the meadow, second field for this year.

10th September Robert Holmes & wife came. He is staying a few days, getting better of a severe illness, bloodlessness, taking calf's liver juice. He stayed 10 days, the last day at Auchenfoil. Leslie Orr came on the 19th. Stayed till the 25th Sept. Went up to Auchenfoil for 3 days. Going to the Royal High School in Edinburgh on 1st October for 2 years. Jack Orr went to Fettes College on the 18th October 1929.

23rd September Janet Blair came in Flin's (?) motor at night and had a long crack. Flinn went on to Auchenfoil with old Mr Kinloch.

25th September Cut our corn last week. Put in 4 stacks yesterday. Weather favourable. Mr Watson called got a bonny bunch of flowers.

30th September Glasgow holiday. Jim Stevenson called at night. Had been at Auchenfoil. Got our corn all in – 9 stacks. The following week John Galbreath thatched them, two very wet days in the week.

6th October Willie Crawford had a supperation throat. Johnnie Black Auchenfoil in bed, kidney trouble.

8th October Watson called again. Got flowers.

9th October We commenced to howk the potatoes, the neighbours nearly finished with theirs. Finished ours in about a week.

24th October Mrs Buntain Pomillan died. Buried on 26th.

28th October Mrs Baxter, Senior died at Burnbank. Buried on the 30th. I went with Robert in the morning to Janet's. Joe not well. Removing his sale room to another place and his shop to 58 Rue End street.

29th October John Galbraith commenced to plough the braeface above Carsons.

31st October Hallowe'en Our maid Martha Spence & Lizzie Rogers went out dressed and got fun (?) and tea in two houses, Harolds and Blairs. Martha went next day for a weekend to home.

2nd November Rob went upo to ask for John Black who was very far through. He met Willie there. That was Saturday night. He died on Monday morning the 4th November. Jenny Holmes & her man called in Jean Black's motor on their way to Auchenfoil. He is to be buried on Wednesday the 6th November 1929.

List of women at John Black's funeral:

Mrs John Black, Mrs James Black, Mrs Skeoch, Mrs Bain, Mrs McDougal, Miss McDougal, Mrs Scott, Hillside, Mary Duff, Mrs Cuthbertson, the three girls Black, the servant, Mrs Laird,

Faulds, Mrs Muir, Mrs Anderson, Mrs Jean Dunlop, Mrs William Orr, Gateside, Jenny Holmes or Stewart, Mrs Rachel Laird or Stevens, Marion and Lizzie Holmes at the cemetery.

8th November We thrashed 6 stacks today, big mill. Janet came up with Robert. Joe had gone up to Glasgow the night before to see a professor. Not well.

28th November Our maid went away, Martha Spence and the next day Isa Gunn came. John Galbraith went away on the 30th to Campbell Crawford.

27th November I wrote to John. I had been to see Willie Buntain on the 26th Nov. Had a letter from John on 3rd Dec James Black, Auchenfoil, died suddenly at Paisley on the 13th Dec, 5 weeks after John's death. Just as big a turnout as John's. Buried beside John in the New Cemetery.

25th December My maid went home for a night. Came back next day.

26th December Mary Holmes came all the way from Falkirk to see me – a cold showery day.

24th December Joe went to the Victoria Infirmary.

30th December Janet and two boys came up for a week.

1930

1st January Ne'erday. Our John not so well.

6th January George Laird died coming from England.

8th January Joe left the Infirmary

10th January A letter from Malcolm Currie. Mr McPhail, Mont Clare, died the day before

20th January Mary came down for a day.

21st January Willie went to see Uncle John.

24th January Kilmacolm Farmers Ball. I am finishing up my scrap book.

30th January Mrs Harold down. After being ill, a fortnight after an operation on the bladder my brother, John Holmes, died in Rothesay Hospital on the 21 February 1930. Taken by Wyllie & Lochhead to Kilmacolm Cemetery. Service in St James. Left his money in equal proportion to all his nephews and nieces.

4th March I took a bad cold off Rob. Just getting a little better the following week.

20th March Mrs Orr Newton and Rob came over for an After-daylight. Both looking well.

25th March Houston Steeplechase – Rob away to it. Very blowy but fair.

29th April Robert went up to Mary. Don Laird had been bothering her about valuation.

30th April Agnes Buntain called on her way to Miss MacLaren's.

1st May I answered Mary Holmes letter and asked her through. Wrote Maria. Wrote Polly this week. I am sorting garden walk, putting ashes on it & delving a bit every day.to get out bishop weed.

2nd May Harold nailed up the hen house (*tool?*) doors ¾ hours. I have cut potatoes myself for 3 days. Robert working late every night preparing pots and turnip ground (?) Set black hen in tin bine over own eggs 13. David Carson went down to see Mac last night.

3rd May David Carson for change.

5th May Mary Holmes came for 2 nights. Robert busy with field on the brae. Kennedy helping at night pots. I cut them all myself. Harold could not come. Bobby had a smash – hurt.

8th May Set third hen, second from door.

9th May Robert finished putting in pots & turnips.

6th May Mary Holmes and I went over to Annabella

22nd May Liz Holmes and John Campbell came. Went up to Auchenfoil – walked up and down. Got a lift in motor farther down.

24th May Joe Johnson very far through. I have to delve all the garden myself and take out all the bishop weed.

2nd June Glasgow holiday. Marion Holmes, Willie's wife, had been at the Old Castle with 3 children and called after. Chrissie Forbes & Molly Holmes were at Auchenfoil

10th June I went by Auchenfoil to Greenock. Saw Joe. Very thin. Hannah came in.

11th June Robert & Maggie Missin (?) commenced to thin the turnips. Maggie Simson (?) - the worst servant ever I had. Most illbred & nasty, a' dirt.

30th June Joe Johnson died on Sabbath day. *[my grandfather —PJJ]*

1st July He was buried in Greenock Cemetery. Funeral private. I was there & Mary & Donald Black & our Willie. He left all in order.

3rd July Jessie Donald came on 13th June in Black's motor, 2 weeks ago. Staying a month.

13th July Mr Patrick came for Jessie.

10th July Willie and I went to see Jenny Hunter (?)

14th July Willie went a jaunt to Edinburgh. We are putting up hay in ricks. A terrible illbred big Irish lass.

15th July Miss MacLaren died in Islay on her summer holidays. Buried in Greenock. Janet was flitting this week. From 49 Baxter Street to 21 Lyle Street. George Mason came for two or three days.

16th July Jim Smith came for 6 weeks.

17th July Mr & Mrs Patrick took me a drive in motor through Houston. I called on Miss Galloway. She is very thin.

15th August All our hay in.

16th August Mr & Mrs Currie came

17th August Willie at home weekend as much his business is increasing. 12 of a staff – 8 men joiners and upholsterers, 2 women polishers, a bookkeeper and Mary Witherow is a shopkeeper in Rue End shop.

18th August Robert away to Greenock in motor to take up some things that belong to Joe's two motors that he bought. I expect Janet and boys on Sat Coming every fortnight for a while.

September Wet. Bad corn weather all month except towards the end. Folk had to bring it in not too dry 3 days before the end of September. We got ours all in. It was dry weather but not too good. Keeping up since and it is now the second of October. We have commenced our potatoes. Have David Anderson helping us this fortnight – a queer man, bad speaker. Had been at the war. Addicted to drink. We had a man called Murdoch helping with the corn

Middle of September Jessie Donald took a shock. Was taken to Crow Road Hospital. Our Janet went to see her. Leslie and Jack Orr came to see us. Jack went first back to school. Leslie two nights at Auchenfoil. Was going back to school (The Royal High) on the first of October

One day in September 1930 there was a first divide of Uncle John's money. All pleased. Nothing done about Auchenfoil yet.

6th October Heard James Crawford Dippany had taken a shock. The greatest airplane R101 came down on the 7th. 47 lives lost. Cost £1,000,100. David did not come back… got another. Men and women in Bothie helping with pots. Just commenced the digging (?) yesterday the 7th Oct.

8th October Our maid Jamesina Morrison is out tonight to meet her lad who comes from Greenock. Robert was asked to go Millers in Greenock tonight but did not go.

16th October James Crawford died (Dippany)

18th October Janet came the weekend.

19th October Our Sacrament and I was at it – did not know till the day before. Willie could not go. I wrote Polly a week ago. I wrote Mrs McPhail a month ago, no answer.

Our maid Jamesina Morrison came a month ago, £2.10/- a month. A good servant. Was home a weekend on 18th October. Brought me a blue tea canister

November Sent Polly her usual donation. Got a letter from Mrs McPhail. Janet came a weekend 14th November.

24th November Mary was down at night. Much bothered with the milk. Thinking of retailing it.

25th November Ina down at Ross's.

26th November Robert away with potatoes to Port. Willie … (?)

List of deaths since 26 October 1929. This is December 1930

Mrs Buntain, Pomillan 24th Oct; Mrsd Baxter Burnbank 28th Oct; John Black Auchenfoil 4th Nov; James Black, Auchenfoil 13th Dec; George Laird, St Andrews 6th Jan 1930;

Mrs McPhail, Mount Clare end of 1929; John Holmes Mount Clare 21st Feb; Joseph Johnson 30th June; Miss MacLaren, Syde School 15th July; James Crawford Dippany 16th October; Mrs Maggie Skeoch, 21 Dec.; Hugh McColl of Rogers

Kilmacolm cemetery, Photo © wfmillar (cc-by-sa/2.0)

1931

<u>January</u> John Laird, Cairncurran died Jan 1931. Mrs Crawford, Dippany Nov 27 1930;

<u>February</u> Born at Margaret's Mill, the second son of James Ross, early in Feb 1931;

End of February heard that Mrs Love, Cairncurran (*mistake*) had taken a shock

<u>21st February</u> I was in bed two days with cold and bile.

<u>28th February</u> We had the big mill – thrashed 5 stacks, one left. John Johnson has got a job in a baker's shop, 3/6 a week[1].

<u>19th March</u> Mrs Orr and Robert called at night. Ina Morrison is our maid.

<u>June</u> I went to Pomillan & Knockbuckle & Orrs.

<u>6th July</u> I stayed 4 days with Janet in Helensburgh. Mary went two nights. Our maid is Maggie Brodie.

<u>12th July (Sunday)</u> Willie and Robert went in motor to Kil taking the bus to Helensburgh.

24th July Donald Black was murdered. Shot at the roadside near home, coming from Mathernock at half past 11 at night. I went up to Auchenfoil. Shot by a servant man at Mathernock name Colin McMillan. *[See chapter 65 for a fuller account of this tragic event, based on newspaper reports at the time—JJ.]*

Leslie Orr has won a scholarship and is going to the school another year.

24th July Mrs Orr and Robert came over at night to talk about D. Black.

27th July I have a very sore throat. Got better in 3 days.

4th August Janet came with Maria.

5th August James Adam & wife came. (Paisley)

6th August Old Mrs Harold came from Carseknowe.

8th August John Currie and wife came.

14th August Mary Holmes came. Had seen Aunt Liz away. We finished putting in our hay, a good crop. Leslie and Jack Orr helping a week & Sam Martin, Sam Laurie and Pat.

15th August Jean Manson came. Becky Twigg disappointed her. I wrote to Jessie Donald in Crow Road Hospital.

22nd August Janet came the weekend and helped to clean my big room. Mary came down at night. Rob went up and helped them with haystacks. 3 afternoons.

25th August Today he is thatching our own. The black and white big cow calved a week ago. Not very well getting better. Sold the bull last week. Got £13 for it. Jack Orr went to Girvan a week ago & Leslie was to go hiking.

29th August Robert and Frank Blair at Dunoon sports. Maggie Brodie getting cheeky, refusing to do as she is told.

7th September Sent the black and white cow to Greenock. Sold the black & white cow at Greenock. Got £7 for it. Supposed to have a wire in it. Also sold a young quay £13. Getting most of our corn cut this week. Old Sandy Walker called with … (?) Orr.

9th September Jenny Hunter called with two ladies, daughter of Maggie Laird Branchal then Liz Holmes and John Campbell came. Willie came with man to sort the shed for cows and … for corn. Polly sent a letter, Jack and Leslie away to Manchester.

14th September Greenock holiday. John and Joe Johnson away on their bikes to Kilbirnie. Our Rob and Willie away to Glasgow.

19th September John Currie and wife& the Misses Scott came and Mary Jessie – John McNab also came. A good day. Commenced to stack.

22nd September Have got up 8 stacks – weather keeping up. The trial of Colin MacMillan for murder lasted 4 days. He got off, not guilty although it could have been proved he was guilty. Witnesses were never asked. Mitchel and Smith who spoke for him were unscrupulous rascals, all to win their case. *[see chapter 65 – J.J.]*

At night Mrs and Robert Orr came.

23rd September We put up our last stack 10

28th September Glasgow holiday. Mr and Mrs Forbes came. They had been at Auchenfoil.

29th September Letter from Mary Holmes. She had had the flu and was at Glasgow last Friday. Robert started to take down the hedge at the top of mid park. The motor at Glasgow getting lights sorted. Got 3 rabbits from White who was shooting at Planting.

17th October Finished our potatoes, park at school. Digger and many gathering. Polling election on. Ramsay Mac, Prime Minister.

Colin MacMillan is trying to get a job near Mathernock.

20th October The motor getting sorted again. Two days with milk cart.

November About 20th November they got a private car at Auchenfoil, a Riley.

18th November Wed night Robert and I were at Auchenfoil

25th November We hear they have got an offer of £55 for the Green house. Got a letter from Mary Holmes. Mrs Morrison, Milton, was severely burned about a week ago. Getting better. We hear Sandy Lang is ill, sore tongue.

27th November Mrs Crawford, Dippany died.

4th December Grace McCrimmon (?) came, always crying. Went off on a Sunday 4 days.

1st December Mr & Mrs Black, Devol, came to stay at Belleview. Frank Blair without a house-keeper. He got one afterwards on Xmas day. Chrissie Forbes & Molly Holmes came.

29th December Robert and I went to Newton.

31st December I went to Port bank. Visited Mrs Harold. Janet came home with me. Stayed till 5th Jan.

1. **Editor's note re Granny Orr's 28th Feb. entry:** My father told me that the talk of the bakers shop while they were filling the paper bags with rolls, was all about Einstein's theory of relativity and the speed of light! He used to run round the hilly streets of Greenock delivering rolls before going to school. He was 12 and ¾ years old when he started in the bakery.

1932

5th January Very wet stormy days. Robert ploughng the Home. Commenced today.

6th January Jessie Blair (or *Black?*) Mrs James Kinloch was buried same day was old Mr Davidson, shoemaker and Mr Conway.

2nd January Polly and Marion came this week the divide of Auchenfoil money was (uncle James). We have still Sam & Bob Laurie sorting ditch at foot of Hill park. Sam ploughing in the forenoons.

20th February We have had summer weather this month. Rob has lifted the dyke between Midpark and stackyard and is making the stackyard before the house in the field beyond the garden. Maggie Black is my maid's name. A good worker. Her lad is Donald Espie. We have still old Sam.

12th February Rob and I went to Pomillan. Mrs Orr & Rob was here a week before that. I have been working in the garden for two weeks. A little every day. Maggie helping to delve one side of walk and Rob is doing the other. This month Robert sold two cows. About £15 for one and £5 for the other. The Auchenfoil ones have the measles the last fortnight. This is the 20th Feb. 6 of them down with it but getting better. The school teacher, Mrs Browning, sent me 5 tulips. I sent her a pot of bulbs. I had the 3 Orrs & Maggie Buntain & Frank Blair this month.

26th February Jessie Donald died in Crow Road Hospital. Buried 1st March in Hawkshead Cemetery. Rob and Willie at the funeral.

March Rob Dunlop died in Peacemuir. 21st Robert Holmes died. 24th Mary, Robert & I at the funeral in Kilbirnie. Drove in Black's motor.

8th April Mary Holmes came and our Mary came down to meet her & we had a nice crack. We were near finishing the cutting of potatoes. Maggie Scott called collecting for church.

11th April I took cold off Robert in my head & it turned like flu. Could not eat much for 5 days. Greenock holiday. Willie Janet and the two boys went to Edinburgh to see Polly and the Zoo. Very cold weather. The two boys Orr came here. Went up to Auchenfoil next day when Leslie got a telegram asking him to go home that night to see about a job.

15th April Our potatoes are in & corn sowed. Getting a young cow from Frank Blair tonight, the thinnest cow ever I saw but milking considerably well.

25th April Willie Buntain died aged 85. Leslie Orr got the job in the staff of the Educational Office Edinburgh. He will be 18 years old next month when his salary will be 75 pounds.

6th May I went up at night with Rob to Auchenfoil. All well there. Garden much improved. Jenny fond of flowers. My maid, Maggie Black, is going to be married at the term. I am helping her to make a hearthrug out of my patches. I am stopping helping Polly after this term.

9th May Getting all our turnips in tonight.

End of May Mrs Orr Newton & Robert, our Robert and I went up to Auchenfoil one day before the May term. Mary Holmes went to Burngill, Houston & Dykefoot before the Bains went to Knockbuckle. Old Sam Martin is still with us. He and the maid are hoeing potatoes in the Home field.

2nd June Janet came and papered the kitchen.

8th June Janet and Mary and our Robert went a sail to Tignabruich and had a nice time with Kate MacLachlan.

9th June Lizzie Baxter died in Larkfield Hospital, aged 35.

10th June Robert Orr Newton has got the farm of Langside and he is taking our Robert to see it tonight.

14th June Robert, Frank and John Black went in Black's motor to Monkland.

11th June Paisley Show. Rob got a 3-piece cake dish.

15th June Ginny (?) calved – a big bull calf. Calf died up on the field above Hankinsons.

17th June John Currie & wife came. They went to Auchenfoil. Our Janet has taken a house at Arrochar for first fortnight in July

23rd June Janet came up and varnished the old dresser. Kitchen not all varnished yet.

17th June Robert Holmes Kilbirnie came. Stayed a week at Auchenfoil. Molly Holmes went there the same week.

22nd June Mary went in motor with Maggie Black and Mrs MacDougal to Rothesay(?) Mary came in a little.

23rd June It has been dry for 6 weeks. Some rain today. Corn and potatoes growing well. Baxter has a hay field cut. Our Rob getting a little more milk sold.

25th June Robert Holmes called in on his way home from Auchenfoil. Molly Holmes went last night. Robert away to Johnstone Tug of War.

1st July Willie and I went to Arrochar and stayed till the 6th. Wet weather all the time and not good yet. Have got no hay up.

6th July Robert Orr was married to Bella Lyle of Scart in the Cargill Hall, Bridge of Weir. Robert and Frank Blair at it. Teacher has her house let. We have 6 boy campers at Planting.

12th July Got our first ricks up.

13th July Ann Stevenson came to Auchenfoil.

14th July Mary and John Black drove Becky Holmes home.

9th July Maid, Lizzie Agnew went to Glasgow and stayed till late next night.

13th July I wrote to Mary Holmes and Polly.

15th July Got a letter from Mary Holmes.

21st July Old Mrs Harold came down to see me. Young Mrs Harold still in bed. Something wrong with her stomack.

23rd July At our last hay field ricking below Hankinsons. The two Johnsons up this week. Sam and another man & Mrs Ferguson.

Lines I made about Arrochar:

O Arrochar! O Arrochar
Ye'll see nae mair o' me
For I hae got enough o' ye
Until the day I dee.

Your high hills & bare face
Make no appeal tae me
I wadna gie the bonnie glens
O' Kilmacolm for thee.

But every yin is no alike
Tis well that that should be
So Arrochar will still be grand
For many a yin to see.

24th July The anniversary of Donald Black's death. A memorial in the paper with the words "His sun went down while it was yet day."

2nd August A letter from Polly.

3rd August John, Marion, Jenny & Mary Black came down at night to pull gooseberries. Got 18 lbs. We have got 4 stacks up, one to put up and rest in the barn. Have old Sam Martin & Scabby Maggie and the two Johnsons helping also the maid Lizzie Agnew – her father came to see her yesterday.

6th August John & Joe went home the weekend. We would have finished our hay stacking today, only it came on very wet.

John & Joe came back second week in August. Got 5 haystacks all thatched about the 13th – first year before the house. 5 calves this summer, 2 others died in decline (?) in August. We have got other two young quay calves, 7 in all. I think there would be about 100 lbs of Gooseberries this season.

15th August The Johnsons went home last night, coming with their mother next weekend.

11th August Young Willie Crawford of Gibbleston died aged 3 years.

15th August A very violent thunderstorm. Some foxes & horses & cattle killed.

16th August Our Robert off on bicycle to Kilmacolm to go to Curries. 6 lb of gooseberries with him. She was not in. M. Orr got them.

19th August Opening roads in corn. Sam talking of going away soon.

31st August We finished cutting corn.

9th September We have just got one stack in. Weather broken.

1st September Jack Orr came. Helped up with the first stack. Because of it being showery he went up to Auchenfoil on the 8th September. A lot of neighbouring boys and men come to perform athletes twice a week. Robert can pull up 20 stones. Maid goes out almost every night in the week.

10th September Jack came back from Auchenfoil. Still wet weather.

13th September Jack went to Auchenfoil to go by milk car to Greenock to stay a night with Janet.

14th September Aunt Madge came in car with Jim Wright & Jean W. & Marion Orr. They are staying the month at Seamills.

15th September Rob with 3 men hutting the corn.

16th September Put in two stacks. Not good. 12/- to pay men.

17th September Getting tea in the afternoon.

19th September Finished stacking. 15 stacks. Two three days good this week.

23rd September Friday Janet came by bus. Went off next morning with Robert.

28th September Robert and I went up to Auchenfoil. Commenced to dig potatoes. in the Home park. Some damp.

5th October Janet came by bus. Stayed all night. This has been a wet week.

8th October Robert finishing the thatching. Sat heard that Jenny Holmes was away with appendicitis and that Jenny Miller is also in an Infirmary in Glasgow Victoria Hospital. I cannot walk with ease without a stick this year.

9th October Gave Willie £50.

12th October Janet, Miss Kennedy and Kate MacLachlan came in Kennedy's motor. Went by Auchenfoil.

19th October Rob and Willie went to P in Glasgow.

23rd October Commenced ploughing this week in the old stackyard. Showery weather. Lizzie Agnew cut the corn stacks.

28th October Janet came by bus stayed all night. Jenny Holmes has been through an operation – her bladder.

31st October Jenny Holmes (Mrs Stewart) died in the Glasgow Infirmary after a successful operation (suddenly)

Janet Miller is over hers & is home. Mrs Bobby Carson had twins, a boy and a girl, a week ago.

October & November Mrs Carson (Bobby) has been ill for the last two months.

3rd November Mary had gone to see Jenny Holmes on Monday but she was dead on Sunday. She stayed in Glasgow 3 nights. Called in here on her way home. We had the big mill today. 5 stacks.

9th November Rob up helping at Chapel – big mill.

17th November About 4 stacks corned (?) at 2 o'clock boild (?) ham (?)

December Early in December I had the flu, not very bad but not so well for 4 weeks.

17th December James Blair was knocked down by a bicycle on the road between Pomillan and Stepends.

24th December Christmas Eve Saturday night. Willie brought me a nice big bun. His business is increasing very nicely. The two Johnson boys are here this week, staying till the year comes in, school takes up 4th January 1933. John brought me a big box of sweets and Joe a good writing pad. From Auchenfoil we got a parcel – R. socks, W. a knitted waistcoat, myself a cardigan and from James Black I got a box of sweets and a nice note. I sent him a crown piece. We are well served with this little lass, Maggie MacKinnon. She is going to Glasgow tomorrow 29th to a party of the Salvation Army. She did not come back that night, forfeited 5/-

1933

1st January Janet, John & Joe came yesterday. Stayed 3 days. On the 2nd Polly came with Mr & Mrs Alex Crawford. Next day Leslie and Jack came, stayed a little then went up to Auchenfoil. Got a drive in.

2nd January A Conference in Glasgow. Mrs B. & Marion, Willie and John Black at it.

4th January James' birthday in 1880. Robert went to Barfillan with Andrew Smith.

6th January A party of young ones at Dippany

9th January A letter from Mary Holmes

13th January Writing M. Holmes.

10th January Marion, Willie and John Black down.

22nd January Janet & boys were the weekend.

27th January I was not so well – sore … (?) And diareia. Rob and Frank at Campbells. Got a letter from Liz Gorrie (Mrs Cuthbertson).

30th January Robert at a Council meeting.

31st January Rover had 10 pups, 4 died, 5 drowned. Kept one, called Oscar, black and white

8th February Had big mill, wet half day.

9th February We have no man. Robert busy with potatoes. Selling to MacCallum & Horsely, grocers, £25 a ton. Lifted a pot of snowdrops.

10th February Frank and Rob over at Orrs.

1st February, the hybrid Roda Howard …was nipped in the bud. End of Feb more buds came out.

18th February Janet and the boys came the weekend.

20th February A man came, George, a ploughman. 15/- a week. Walks to Greenock at night. Wee pup 3 weeks old getting playful and bigger every day. Robert off to Port with potatoes to Horsely's. Going to Greenock.

24th February Mrs Mary Black in bed, result of a rack.

27th February She's getting better. I gave W. £26. Very cold weather with snow showers for a week past. Too hard to plough.

7th March My 80th birthday. Willie has given me an ebony stick.

6th March Maggie Black was out (?) of a place & came to see me.

24th March Beena (?) came and stayed the weekend. Her man not working but she was & was quite bright.

22nd March Our Mary came down and spent the day.

15th March Janet came the weekend.

1st April Sent Jack his 2/6. Robert busy ploughing the home & Andy Reid lifting potatoes. A good crop but cheap, got 32.5/- at first then down to £1.15/- and some just get £1 & lifted up at the house.

3rd April Molly & Chrissie & boy Holmes called in Easter Glasgow holiday.

6th April Mrs Orr came over to see me.

12th April Greenock Spring holiday. Willie here but no callers. Very glad to get peace.

11th April Maggie Scott collecting. Gets 4/6 for church. Mrs Harald talking about leaving Carseknowe. We are having Andy Reid for another week. We are driving lime.

12th April Jack Orr came & went to Auchenfoil. Stayed one night. Went to Greenock in the morning. Went to Mount Clare and stayed two nights then went to Glasgow on Sat night.

17th April Cutting potatoes. Got Sarah and her man. She helping me to cut.

19th April My right leg got very sore sitting cutting. Will not manage it long. The Johnsons are here, their Easter holidays.

30th April Maggie Black (Mrs Espie) came and helped for a week. A man and Gibbie at setting potatoes. Mrs Ferguson and another setting. A nice letter from Jack Orr.

May Our 13 quays went to Gibblaston on 2nd May. Cold weather. In May the first Rodes flowers & at 21st Mount Clare ones came out dark red.

21st May Molly Holmes & Marie came to stay at Auchenfoil a night.

14th May I got a clecken of chicks from Auchenfoil.

20th May Old Sam came back.

1st June Mrs Mary Black & John & Rob & I drove in Black's motor all the way to see Mary Holmes at Falkirk (Lauriston). Got a grand day. Enjoyed ourselves. Called in at the Threeply coming home. The daughter Jean was to be married in a week's time, the 9th of June. Saw a lot of presents and got tea. She is going to a farm beyond Lochwinnoch. I was very tired next day.

5th June We have Sam whitewashing also we have Gibbie doing odd jobs. He was sorting at the burnside today. Robert is away at Johnstone sports. Got 1st prize at tug o' war. Got a nice alarm clock.

7th June Whitewashed the byre. Very warm weather. Thunder going about. The McGlinns away in Jamie Ross's motor to Wemyss Bay.

12th June Sam & Rob hoeing pots. First two buds on rose bush at foot of tree.

10th June Maggie McKenna went off to Glasgow. Did not come back that night, forfeited 5/-. Janet came up. Not be back till we go to Largs.

17th June Mr & Mrs & Miss Currie came. Gibbie came & Sam & him will be at the thinning turnips & weeding thistles. Rob went up to Auchenfoil at night, Sat.

19th June Mrs Ross & Annabella with kids went off in a caravan to Prestwick for a fortnight.

About the 20th our Mary went down to see old Mrs Ross at Margaret's Mill. The place looking well, a new bothy and henhouse and a garden. Came in when coming home.

22nd June Jean Manson and Becky Twigg called on us, went up to Auchenfoil from 1 till half past 3 then here till ½ past 6. Enjoyed themselves well.

21st June Our maid went the trip to Port Bannatyne. She is working away all right. Lovely weather but thundery. Laird contractors phone number 195.

1st July Janet William and I went to Largs for one week. £3.8/- each. Mrs Robertson, Planetrees, met a Mrs Donaldson there.

12th July I went to see Mrs Orr Newton, ill on Sat. Maria is here. Came 7th July. She came for a week.

13th July Jim Stevenson came. Went up to Auchenfoil with Janet and Ria.

14th July Mrs Orr died, Newton. Aged 76.

17th July Willie Hepburn died aged 26 or 27

28th July R and I went up to Auchenfoil. Janet Blair & Conny Craig & Jim Craig came after…(?) Molly Holmes called on her way to Auchenfoil. Stayed two nights.

29th July Charlie Stevenson called Sat. He stayed a night at Auchenfoil, went home on Sunday night. On 31st Ann Stevenson went to Auchenfoil. Reeni came stayed two nights.

1st August Robert's birthday. Janet came. Went home at night.

3rd August Robert and I went in car & saw the Grays at Carruth. Called on Janet Orr.

4th August John Orr came over for R to help with hay.

10th August John Johnson has been most of a fortnight helping with hay and corn. Lizzie Holmes and John Campbell came one afternoon. We are painting windows with green and white. Have commenced to cut corn in Home park. Joe and John & M.

McKenna (?) bunching. I sent a letter to Mrs Holborn on the 9th in answer to hers.

7th August Sam left us. We are doing without him

13th August Sun Good day. 14th wet.

15th August Thundery showers. Cut the sod for the …(?) + garden at the foot of it. Robert went to Glasgow for bottles.

7th August Sold our first two quays, £35.13/-

15th August Paid Kilbirnie (?) man 3/6 for apron.

22nd August Jack Orr came and helped with corn & stayed a week. Did not wait at Auchenfoil.

26th August Got up 2 stacks – Robert and J. Orr and J. Johnson. Dunoon Sports. Robert did not get. Lovely day.

27th August Rained all day.

16th September Robert went to Edinburgh. Stayed from Friday night till Sunday night.

17th September Went to Paisley. Bought two calves.

18th September Commenced our potato digging with digger. In 5 days had them finished digging but (?) one day.

20th September Willie got top teeth out in Port Glasgow.

23rd September Sat J & J Johnson came got brambles. Good crop. The Johnsons were all up the weekend on the 16th. Mary taking our eggs (?) Janet sent photos of J and J to the Highlands. Not pleased with her own.

30th September Janet came up and Rob and I went in motor to cemetery

October Has not got an answer from them

5th October Maggie McKenna was very wild over contradicting her about old Ned skaling lime. Will need to put her away. She went off for half a day.

7th October Mary came down on Sunday as John was going to the Green. This is our Harvest Thanksgiving. Beenie came last Sunday 1st October. Stayed a night. Mr Marr, the minister, called on the 4th of October.

Mary came down in the motor at night with John.

14th October Janet came up her monthly weekend.

15th October Our sacrament. Willie and I at it. We stopped retailing milk a month ago.

2nd November Mary Holmes came the afternoon. Cow not well sent to Cham (?) next day.

13th November John Duncan died after (?) weeks illness. Peter Morison (?) at Knockbuckle.

23rd November Jenny Black went to a home in Glasgow to get her tonsils out. Came back in a week's time.

28th November Maggie McKenna did not get a fee. She is waiting on – a terrible liar and fraud (?) but not a bad worker.

30th November We have Greer sorting Barrows. Been 4 half days at one, comes to 10/-. We have 17 young quay calves. Maggie McKenna is staying on for £9. 22nd November, Jenny Black went to Glasgow for one week and got her tonsils cut at a home.

5th December I wrote to Polly.

7th December I wrote to Mary Holmes.

8th December I got a letter from Mrs Holborn & I got a letter from Polly saying her aunt Mary died on 20th of November at Rothesay.

9th December Janet and family came the weekend. Beena came. They papered the lobby – Greer did not manage to sort the clock. He is sorting barrows and putting felt on roofs. R lifted £30 out of R.B. today. W getting on.

22nd December All the Johnsons and W at Witherow wedding. Robert has got 20 calves

28th December Maggie McKenna is going to Glasgow for a day.

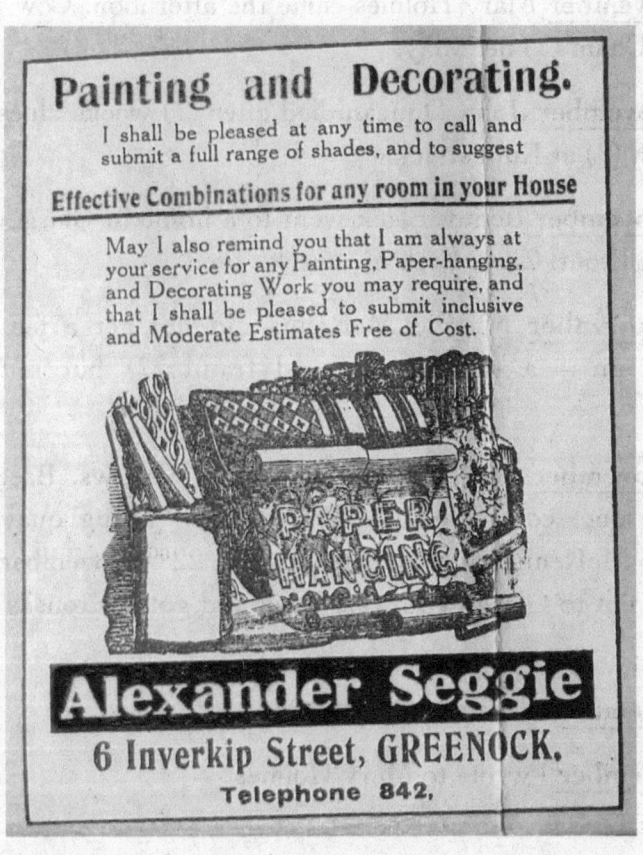

1934

1st January All the Johnsons and W up. Polly came two days before. We had the thrashing machine in December. I had a letter from Polly and wrote to her in Jan. Wrote to Mary Holmes on 31st Jan. The thin white cow died this month & a cow worth £20 died 6 weeks ago. Another young cow bad with scours. Robert at silver wedding party at Hankinsons then at a party at Blackwater on the 26th.

1st February Rob away to Port Glasgow.

3rd February Frank Blair R and Willie at Glasgow. Janet and boys weekend. Maggie raging and flyting nearly every day.

10th February Mary Paton or Black died at………. Our Mary was with her. Buried at Kilmacolm. Our Robert at it. Greer here still. Shed nearly finished.

27th February Sent to Greenock a little brown cow that would not stop scouring, that is three milk cows this year we have lost and a calf with sore eye. Another calf we got at Paisley died.

1st March Party of married ones at Blackwater. Broadfoot got 68 bags of potatoes & some before.

7th March Rob & I up at Auchenfoil.

13th March Rob went to Greenock and heard he has to get over £3 for cow that scoured. Janet Miller unexpectedly paid us a visit this same day.

14th March I sent with John Black 6 ½ dozen eggs and got a letter from Mary Holmes.

15th March Got a letter from Polly. Leslie had passed with honours his exam for Mercantile Law.

27th March Mary and John Black came down. Gave them 11 ½ dozen eggs. Our maid Maggie McKenna, a terrible ill-natured jade went off in the huff today after a blow out about nothing. Came back in afternoon.

12th May Show day. Maggie went off again. Did not come back till midnight

28th May Maggie. We put her away. She would have worked for £7 but on no consideration would we have kept her. A young girl from Miss Irwin came but did not wait long. A woman, Mrs Mitchell, came for 6 weeks last half of June.

1st July Janet and family and Willie and I went to Ayr. Mrs Tennant 13 Newmarket Street. We stayed two weeks. Beena and Mrs Mitchell (deaf Maggie) kept house. Greer got cheeky with Robert and was left when I got home. A dozen chickens died.

24th July Mary and Willie Black and our Rob drover to Denny and got chickens for Mary. They called and had tea at Mary Blair's Bonnybridge.

25th July The Farmers trip to Edinburgh. Rob went up to Auchenfoil with a letter from Willie. Joe and Angus here this week. 24th July was anniversary of Donald Black's death. A place is vacant in our hearts that never can be filled.

13th August The two girls came, Jean and Marie. Going away from Auchenfoil tomorrow.

15th August Commenced our corn cutting, big park up the road, finished it in 3 afternoons. Jack Orr came today and Leslie came on the 17th. The two girls came the week before then to Auchenfoil.

17th August I wrote to Mrs Tennant, 13 Newmarket Street Ayr and sent her a little book with one I had from her.

18th August John, Joe Johnson & Jack, Leslie Orr all went up to Auchenfoil, got the Blacks and walked to Corlic at night. All 4 staying at Gateside and helping with corn.

19th August Sunday Robert has gone to Glasgow.

24th August We finished our corn. 5 boys besides Jack and Leslie helping.

27th August Monday Got up a stack but came on rain. Polly and Mattie came and Jim Stevenson went to Auchenfoil and got a drive in for 9 train. Leslie sprained his foot.

28th August Thunder, rain. Gave P 5/-

September About 6th Maggie Buntain died in a Home in Glasgow.

13th September Mary's birthday. Sent some sweets and the Porterfield cup. Are getting in all our corn today. 15 stacks. Showery weather but we were fortunate in help.

15th September Janet and family came weekend.

20th September Robert, Frank Blair went to Tighnabruaich. Joe came up at night to feed 7 calves. I wrote to Mrs Duncan, answer to hers.

24th September Wrote to Jean Manson. Glasgow holiday Chrissie Forbes & chum (Miss Buchanan) came. Molly and Marie Holmes day before. Robert went on bike to Greenock. Was at Janet's and Lootits.

2nd October Agnes and Maggie Buntain came an afternoon and had tea. We are at our pots digging – broken weather. Two lads from Greenock helping. Tommy and John.

About the end of August Jock Laird (the Masher) died. About 30 years after my brother Robert, they were great chums.

3rd October Just 7 in Syde School. Mrs Browning teacher.

10th October Janet came with Mrs Gillies.

13th October Janet & family & Ria the weekend. The bulb of woreless broke but Willie sent another and it is all right.

17th October Rob at Blair's digging. Ours finished yesterday. Got wireless insurance. Got a lot of brambles this year. Got our photos from Chrissie Forbes – Rob and her and I & her chum. Eggs down to two a day.

26th October First two carts of potatoes to Macalum in Port. It has rained wet weather since middle of July. We have two boys and the maid, Nessie Devine.

28th October I wrote Mary Holmes.

29th October R. has gone to Greenock to see Banker

November Early in the month I went to see the Buntains in Knockbuckle. They were removing into a house in the village, Fernie Bank – the next week.

26th November Had the big mill. Had Janet and Beena. Had Beena a week and a half. Got a wee girl at the market but she left after 3 days. Nessie Devine went away the 24th Nov – the wee girl's name was Cathie Casiday, paddy and catholic. This one's name is Mary Milne, sister to the boy we have, Tom. She came on 6 Dec. I am nearly finished with Janet's rug. She comes on Sat.

7th December A letter from Polly.

19th December Mary Holmes came. Gave her a brown silk tea cosie. Mary Milne went away after two weeks.

25th December I got a lot of cards and photos from Bessie Millar, taken when we were in Ayr. Mrs Browning sent a lot of grapes & Mrs Gillies a cardigan. Willie is getting a showroom up all right after the fire in his yard. Also getting windows put in the wall of Terrace Road & quite busy.

1935

January John Orr and Jenny Bain were married in the Kidston Hall on 4th Jan. 70 at it. Going to live in Killochwraes old staeding. Jenny Orr not letting her into the Newton.

11th January I am getting better after a week's cold. No maid. A maid came at night with her mother & a friend but the maid …….and went away the next day.

Bessie Miller's address in Troon – 5 Golf Place, Troon (Mrs Menson)

28th January Mary called in on her way home from seeing Annie Black …loch whose daughter had a motor accident.

29th January Robert took a young cow to Greenock Market. Got £15.10/-

4th February A letter from Mary Holmes asking about Annie Lang's accident. Annie Lang got 11 stitches on her brow.

8th February I wrote to Polly. Spoke about David's wife.

12th February Peggy Granges sister came and Peggy says she is to go home. Robert ploughing above Hankinsons

28th February Peggy came back. Marion, Jenny, Willie and Hugh came at night. Our Janet was up and we had good fun with games, Consequences

7th March My 82nd birthday. Jenny Miller came out and spent a pleasant afternoon. I was feeling very fit and cleared the ... at roadside in forenoon. Rob and Alex Milne at Port with potatoes. Got a table cover from Janet & something nice from Mary. Got a new flash light and a lot of other nice things from Willie.

9th March Rob was at P. in Port Glasgow. Was at Glasgow the Sat before with Willie. Heard that Hills 6 storey Mill was burnt. A surprise party at Dippany.

18th March Thrashed the last 6 stacks. Janet came up.

21st March I got a PC from Polly saying Leslie had won his degree of Bachelor of Law. To be capped in June. Bobbie Carson home after being operated on for a perforated stomach

About the middle of March a little Robin Red Breast disappeared after lingering outside my bedroom window all the winter months. The same thing happened last year. It never came back all summer.

April Janet is not keeping so well.

13th April John and Joe went to Edinburgh for a week. Robert Orr, Langside's son died this month and a young son of J. Black, Devol also Murray the minister's wife and Scott the joiner also at Barscube. Had Beena from the 8th 4 days then Nellie Simpson 3 days.

18th April We have commenced to set potatoes two Milnes and Joe Cassels.

5th May (Sunday) Willie and Rob away a walk. Tomorrow will be jubilee day of the king and queen. Special sports on the village and all over the country including bonfires. Sarah (?) from Greenock has been here a fortnight come Tuesday.

2nd May Set a hen, Auchenfoil eggs.

6th May Jubilee day of the king and queen. Mr and Mrs MacNab & Janet Blair came. Also Chrissie Forbes and another girl, Ruby Dale.

16th May Set two hens. Wrote Mary Holmes.

22nd May Archie Currie & wife & Janet came.

29th May W. sent to R. 100 – I have 5 chickens out.

10th June John Johnson took up duty in the Royal Bank, Kilmacolm, as clerk. 17 years of age. *[The editor's father!]*

13th June Janet and I went to Glasgow & got new coats. Rob and I doing without a maid this fortnight.

16th June Rob went to Rothesay and met C. Holmes & Ruby.

17th June Old Gibby has come to help at thinning turnips.

November I have not written anything since 17th June, 5 months ago.

18th November Rob and Ruby took a fancy to each other and after 5 months got married in her mother's house Glasgow on 29th October – just brothers and sisters invited. Rob got over 40 presents.

We have had a fellow named Frank from Greenock for some months at 4/- a day. He made the cart shed in the Green and sorted many a thing about the place.

18th November Got a letter from Mary Holmes and one from Maggie Skinner. The young wife is shaping all right. We are selling our potatoes to Mitchell, a dealer. He takes them away. It has rained so much since harvest was cut that Gibblaston, Branchal and Chapel did not get all their corn in – too slow. Jenny Hankinson got married to Mr Carswell. A farmer near Paisley on the 6th November. 170 asked to the wedding. Rob and Ruby at it in the Lorne Greenock.

23rd December Jack Orr came & went to Blacks, Johnsons and Glasgow at night. Had a fine week near London. He is getting a donation of £40 a year for the three (years) he is at St Andrews from the John Watson Institution.

Royal family members on balcony, Buckingham Palace, Silver Jubilee of George V and Queen Mary, 6th May 1935

1936

7th March My 83rd birthday. Got a nice grey fur cap from Willie & other things.

14th March Janet & family came up the weekend & I went down with them to Janet's new house, Richmond Villa, 33a Newton Street, Greenock – a good and beautiful place.

25th March Mrs Perpoli came for a week or more. Not feeling well and depressed.

13th April Janet and family and Ria came with me to Gateside. Robert busy ploughing for seed. One park of corn sown. Ruby at Glasgow the weekend. Jack Orr broadcasting from St Andrews.

December I have not written for some months. Robert's baby girl Ruby was born on the 24th of July 1936.

I have been staying month about with Robert in Gateside and Janet in Richmond Villa.

15th December Janet and I had a visit of Mrs Witherow and Maggie to tea. This week they are getting the electric light in at Gateside.

16th December We had a visit from Jack Orr. He is still doing well at St Andrews. He goes to London next week to play rugby. James Ross has started a butcher's shop in Greenock this month in Ann Street. John Johnson going to a party at Orrs in Edinburgh at Hogmonay. William Thomson goes about once a weekend to see Jean Orr. Alex Crawford died in Larkfield. This month King Edward VIII abdicated the throne for the sake of marrying Mrs Simpson who had divorced two men in America. Peggie Fleming left Gateside this month and went to Frank Blair.

17th December I sent £1 to church funds. Thomas Dunn died suddenly – missionary.

33a Newton Street, Greenock.

1937

<u>February</u> After being at Auchenfoil for a fortnight and at Gateside a fortnight I came down here the first of February

<u>2nd February</u> Malcolm Currie came from M. Jessie's to spend the evening with us. Looking well.

<u>3rd February</u> Mrs Gillies came over here.

<u>7th February</u> Robert called on us. Came from Paisley. I am feeling quite fit and able to sew. Sent a letter to Crissie Forbes for my photos to send one to Mary Miller.

<u>14th February</u> Mrs Tainsh, Marjory and John (came) to spend the afternoon.

<u>16th February</u> Chrissie Forbes came and brought ½ dozen photos. Robert called

<u>18th February</u> Mr & Mrs McNab spent the evening with us.

<u>19th February</u> I wrote my first letter to Mary Miller in S. Africa. Her address is Mrs Neil McKay, 140 Main Road, Seapoint, S. Africa. I am staying my month at Richmond Villa. John is getting

visits from Willie Thomson. They go to pictures. Thomson goes often to see Jean Orr in Edinburgh. Willie Orr goes every weekend to Gateside and has done it for years. He is getting on well in business at 9 Terrace Road.

After being four weeks at Richmond Villa I came up to Auchenfoil on the 29th Feb – In Greenock Janet and I had visited Mrs Gillies, Maggie Orr and Mrs Witherow. Maggie Orr's lodger died this year after being 10 years. She has got another.

2nd March Mr & Mrs Laird Faulds came over to Auchenfoil at night

3rd March I took a sore pain in my left side of my head, very sore all night but got better in a day or two before I went to the communion. I got a white shawl from Marion and a nice posey from our Willie

7th March I went with Willie and Rob to the communion at St James. Weather clear and cold.

12th March Two Lairds, Cairncurran and two Dunlops from Knocknair and 3 MacDougals were at Auchenfoil that night I took sore pain in my right shoulder, same as I had in my left. I had to stay 3 weeks at Auchenfoil then one week at Gateside. I did not feel well for two,three days. Robert got the 7 last stacks thrashed – Marion Black, Mrs Dale and Greta helped.

29th March I came down here to Greenock. Lost my black stick.

31st March Jean Manson called. She is staying with a lady in Gourock by name, Mrs Forbes.

1st April I have written to Mary Holmes and Ria Perpoli.

Early in April Robert came for me to go to Gateside as Ruby was ill and had to get a complete rest. I came back here on the 17th

May. Ruby was a lot better and was to be at Gateside that day.

16th April Mrs Duncan and Maggie Buntain came to see me at Gateside – a fortnight before that Jean Loutit and her lad came and had tea. About the end of April our maid Agnes Gillies came to Gateside. She was a good worker. Had curiously turned feet and herv teeth out.

May King George the sixth and Queen Elizabeth were crowned (12th May) in Westminster Abbey. Janet and I were listening to the great ceremony at Gateside on the wireless. Janet was papering the kitchen there a yellow ground.

15th May John Johnson went to London with (Robin) Park. He had passed his examination (the Associate Members examination of the Institute of Bankers in Scotland) before and was awarded by the Bank £5.

19th May Janet and I went shopping. I tristed (?) my dress in Prentices. Met Mrs Black and her sister Miss Jessie Orr.

21st May Joe Johnson was at a dance in High School.

21st May Robert came down. Ruby and Agnes getting on well. I have engaged two rooms at St Andrews for us – first two weeks in July.

6th June (Sunday) Marion, Mary and Jennie Black (were here). Marion, Mary and John Black had been the trip to Iona that week – a very wet week.

3rd June John Johnson went to the Highlands on a bike to Sutherland.

15th July Janet Willie and I came back from our fortnight at St Andrews. Polly stayed two nights with us. Mary Holmes a day after staying another fortnight at Janet's where we visited Mary Jessie & heard about Ally Currie's death in July & we met

Miss Morrison in the street. She will come and see us when I go back.

2nd August Marjorie Tainsh went to stay a fortnight with Janet as her father and mother were a fortnight at Carnoustie on holiday. John Black has been ill with rheumatic fever for some weeks now and is very weak & ill yet.

I came to Gateside for a fortnight. Good weather. Rob has got some hay in. Garden like a wilderness with weeds. I am doing a little to sort it every day. Wrote to Mary Holmes & Ria & Janet this morning. Wull Blair & Peter (?) & Joe Johnson are helping Robert.

30th August I came from Gateside to Greenock 1st week 7th September 2nd week 13^{th Sept} Mary's birthday. Janet and she went to Glencoe.

10th September Mary, Willie Janet and I went to see Geordie (Mason) in Uddingston. Got a good reception, a beautiful clean house. Willie hired McGarva's taxi

11th September Jack Orr came to Richmond Villa then went to Auchenfoil and stayed there 2 nights then went to Gateside to help Robert with the corn stacking.

15th September Jean Manson came.

27th September I went up to Gateside by Auchenfoil in their motor on a Sunday. The following Friday Ruby went to Glasgow. Robert went next night and they both went to Edinburgh next day, a Sunday. Returned to Glasgow that night & Robert came to Gateside. She came next day.

10th October (Sunday) The Harvest Thanksgiving. Robert went alone to it. That day there was an upheaval.

11th October I went up to Auchenfoil

17th October I and Willie went to the Sacrament.

19th October John Black who was only now getting better of his rheumatics, his mother and I drove to the Braes & called in at Monklands. Were warmly received at the Braes by the two Misses Caldwell's. That same week the same three went to see Auntie Maggie. She was in bed ill.

27th October I came down with Willie Black, a Monday night. He went to see his girl.

31st October Mary and Bob Ross were at meeting Sunday.

1st November Willie went to Glasgow on business.

2nd November Polling Day in Greenock. Got our lum swept. Cost 4/-

5th November Guy Fox day. Good day. Jean Manson called. She boards in Gourock now. Our Robert called at night. Gave me back a loan. A nice Rock tree Jimmy Black sent us today. Going to put it in the front of the house. 31 buds on it. I posted a letter to Mary Miller today. Her daughter is engaged to be married in South Africa. Their address is, Mrs Neil MacKay, Sea Point Road.

6th November Willie set the Radio there (?)

7th November 1st November, a Sunday night, I took ill with diarrhea. Very bad 2 nights and 2 days. After 7 days I feel myself getting better.

14th October Mrs Dale and Greta & Andy were at Gateside (a Sunday). Ruby and Baby went to Glasgow with them that day. Robert joined them next day to get a cooking stove.

15th October We have had more than a week of very fine summer-like weather. Sunday Mary, Jeny and Willie Black today. Mary had been off her usual for 2,3 days a week ago.

Robert going to Paisley in bus met Tom Fulton. Had a great crack with him about the Speirs. He is a connection. His mother was Ann Speirs.

Willie was at the Misses Miller.

16th October I sent £1 to St James Church. Janet got a washing macjine about 6 weeks ago. It is a great help to the washing. I washed a few things today but not quite better yet.

17th October Willie Thomson came and took John off to Alhambra. We wish he would discontinue his visits. They don't tend to any good.

19th November Robert came to 33 Newton Street.

24th November Mrs John Currie called and asked Janet and I, Willie and the two boys to go a night for tea. I am mending a broken ornament.

25th November I wrote to Mary Holmes 30th I wrote to E. Blair.

2nd December Willie came with…… firewood. Polly came to Janet's.

29th December Robert at Paisley t….. calves. Blair's old cow calved – a quey the week before he was at a roup at Neilston and got 5 calves.

4th December Polly had been at Auchenfoil. Had gone up there in milk cart after being some days at Janet's where theyt had gone to Largs and Paisley & Mary Jessie's. Mr McNab not so well. Heard today that Mrs Holmes, Bardrainey has died, aged 93. (Mary had been ill with bile.)

4th December I have been a week at Gateside. I intend going up to Auchenfoil on the 6th for a fortnight. Robert took in his beats from the grass on 4th Dec - never saw them out so long before. Rubu went to Glasgow yesterday the weekend.

1938

3rd January I came down to 33 Newton Street to stay a month. Had been 7 weeks away.

12th January Heard about John Laird's baby son being dead.

13th January Our Robert fell from hay loft and sprained his foot.

16th January John Johnson went up to Kilmacolm old kirkyard & saw the Holmes tombstone (and took following notes)

A square plot on each corner a small stone marked 1690 also the letter H marked 1690.

..........................1789...........................

The burying place of Messrs Holm in Langside, John Holm Burchhill, Robert Holm, Bogside, James Holm Castlehill and their successors – James Holmes, Nittingshill, son of Robert Holm. His son John Holm, Priestsode died 14th August 1875 aged 85 years and his son Robert Holm, Wraes died 24th August 1895 aged 80 years. His widow Mary Speirs died at Wraes 1899 aged 85 years. 1690.

21st January At 33 Newton Street. I wrote a letter to Polly. Had a visit of Jean Manson. She is liking her lodgings better. A letter from Ria –she is getting on fine with her furnished rooms, getting them all let. Willie got them furnished for her. John, Joe and Hugh Black are having ... (?) and doing fairly well. Janet sewing flowers on a table cover that she got from Marion Black. I am making a cushion. I go up to Auchenfoil next wek.

24th January Rob sent to Janet one bag of potatoes. Joe made good marks at his exam. We all got an invite to Alice Renfrew to tea. Heard Miss Morrison is ill. Got a nice bundle of ... (?) From Willie. Willie got a posey from P. Scott.

27th January Janet, John and Joe and myself went to Alice Renfrew's party (?) I took her a cushion cover.

30th January I came up to Auchenfoil.

31st January Mary went to see Aunt Maggie and stayed two nights. Went to Watterstrong (?) on Wednesday and John brought her home. I am to mend her old fur coat. Very stormy weather.

5th February I wrote to Mary Holmes. Mary went up to ask for Mrs McKendrick.

6th February It has been very stormy wet weather all last week – great damage done on sea and land but not in Kilmacolm.

12th February Mary and I with John went to Knockbuckle and saw the Bains. Then I waited at Gateside for a fortnight.

20th February Chrissie Forbes came to see Ruby.

27th February Mary Holmes came to Gateside. Ruby was at Glasgow with wee Ruby.

28th February Willie Forbes came on a Sunday.

1st March Willie Janet and I drove down in McGarva's taxi to Greenock.

3rd March Robert has been nursing his broken leg for 7 weeks now & is to go on another week yet. Our Mary and Jenny Black were at a party at Alice Renfrew's last night. I am sorting blankets to line a mat for Janet, also making a small rug for our Mary.

7th March My birthday. Got a nice posy from Willie.

10th March Had John Currie and wife and Mrs & Miss Tainsh. Had a nice night. Games & chat. Rob at Greenock – was told to go back in a month.

16th March Jack Orr made a bet – wrote on the pavement at St Andrews, "Kind friends I am broke." And sat down behind it with his arm out of his sleeve, one leg seen and an upturned hat beside him in the attitude of a beggar. The picture was in the Daily Record 16th March.

19th March Heard Robert was to go to Glasgow Infirmary to get his leg x-rayed. Yesterday we heard that Jenny Orr, Newton was very ill. Today we have tonight a Laburnum tree at Richmond Villa.

21st March Jenny Orr died. Our Robert got the bandage off his leg and it is getting better.

23rd March Janet went to see Marion Holmes and Lizzie was at Gateside that day.

24th March Mrs Erskine and her mother were here (Richmond Villa visit). Willie has bought a motor car £100.

26th March I came up to Auchenfoil in their motor.

25th March Jessie Blair died at Pennytersal aged 17 years. Janet and I were at John Currie's. Met the McNabs and son John.

28th March Mary has gone to see them at Pennytersal.

7th April Mr & Mrs Orr came a visit to Auchenfoil. I had a long crack with them. They used to be in Croots (?) farm, Lochwinnoch. It was very wet weather every day almost in March but in April grand weather for the seed putting in.

11th April Robert swept my room lum, very dirty. Don't mind of it being done in 60 years. I came down here from Auchenfoil on the 9th. Mr Ross took me down. On Monday morning Willie went off to Greenock in Jim Ross's motor.

12th April Robert is going to sew corn. His leg is not quite better. We got the wee room lum swept. A bit of a row. Robert selling straw to Blair and John Crawford.

20th April We have had a good week. Robert has sown two fields. He has 4 stirks at Paisley today. He got an average of £13 odds.

27th April Robert had other 4 stirks at Paisley. Got an average of £14.4/-

25th April I left Gateside and went up to Auchenfoil with Willie Kerr. Came down to Newton Street at night with Willie Black.

1st **May** I went to bed with very sore shoulder and flu. Got up the 4th of May but very weak.

3rd **May** King and Queen opened the Exhibition at Bellahouston.

6th **May** Janet went out and bought the spirit lamp for me and two rush mats for Bath.

10th **May** Janet and I went to call on Willie Orr's wife along with M. & Lizzie Orr.

11th **May** We went to see the Dramatics at the High School. Hugh Black was acting in one act, John Johnson in another. We had a motor going and coming. After having about 6 weeks of dry weather many burns dried up (but now) getting rain.

18th **May** Janet and I went to Paisley. I bought 2 cardigans & Janet got a two-piece dress – blue with white spots. Same day Willie passed (driving) test and he has got a nice car.

21st **May** Willie will go up to Gateside in his motor tonight. He did not go last Saturday – first time he missed a week for many years.

22nd **May** I went up to Auchenfoil Sunday.

29th **May (Sunday)** I went to Mary's meeting. Norman Miller spoke.

3rd **June** John took his mother and me up to see the Tomato House at Auchenfoil. I named it Gryffe Neuk - a party at Auchenfoil that night. Mr & Mrs Hansen (?) & Mrs McNeil and Maimie.

4th **June** I went down to Gateside. Wee Ruby was not so well.

5th **June** Our Communion. Willie, Robert and I went in Willie's new car. Spoke to Elsie Blair. I am to go to Pomillan next week with Mary. Spoke to Janet Miller. She had been busy cleaning for a month.

6th June John Black drove his mother and Jenny and me to Waterston. Jean made us welcome. A lovely Home and flowers. We think we are getting too much rain now for the crops and cold wind.

I am sitting in my room at Gateside and making a cushion out of the velvet that was on the top of sideboard that Mary had embroidered over 30 years ago. (It is) for Mary.

14th June Ruby is better and running about. Robert got two bull calves at Paisley yesterday.

1st July After being in Kilmacolm for a month and had paid a visit to Pomillan and saw Willie Kerr's Tomato House and myself naming it Gryffneuk I returned to Greenock. Janet, Willie and I went to Aberdeen in Willie's motor & Mary came down the night before & came with us to Aberdeen. Left at 9.30 and arrived about 4 o'clock. Next day being Saturday we drove around the city. On Sunday Mary and Janet went to her meeting. Willie and I went to St Andrews church

5th July Monday We all went in motor to Balmoral and Braemar.

Granny Orr on holiday. Having tea at Braemar.

6th July (Tuesday) We all went to see Mr and Mrs Thomson.

7th July We passed the gate of Glamis Castle & through the village. Another day we entered the gate of Gordon House, the residence of Lady Aberdeen. We saw salmon in the river Feugh (?) also a bridge called the Sheuchan (?) Briggie. *[Shakkin' Briggie, Cults-PJJ]* After being one week with us Janet, Willie and I went with Mary to Perth to get train to Greenock, (i.e., where Mary got train to Greenock). We got out at Glamis Castle gate & got our photos taken. Next day, Saturday, Janet and I went to Woolworths, a huge place & teeming with visitors. On Sunday Janet went with the Thomsons to their meeting. Willie and I went to St Andrews church.

Monday Janet Willie and I went through Magens Cathedral and Dutthie Park, 40 acres. Then Willie went to meet Polly at the Pier. She came by boat from Leith.

Tuesday we took Janet to the station to entrain for Inverness. Then we three went in car to Peterhead, about 31 miles.

Wednesday. In the forenoon Willie drove us round the beach then to Hazelwood Park, over 100 acres — a puzzle there of an intricate hedge where after being in a while it was most difficult to get out — at night.

One day Mary, Janet Willie and I went to Inverness & then to Culloden field & got our photos taken beside the Memorial Stone. Coming home we saw Rob Roy statue on a rock at Petercoultie. We returned to Greenock the middle of July. After a week there Mary, Janet and Willie and myself drove in Willie's motor to the Exhibition in Glasgow-great affair! We got a nice day.

18th July Coming back from Exhibition I stayed at Auchenfoil. Aunt Maggie was there too.

19th July Lizzie Holmes came to Auch & waited a night. Gave me her address — 223 Kingsheath Avenue. She brought me a table centre.

3rd August I wrote Mary Holmes. She answered next day. Beena wrote to Mary to know if I was at Auchenfoil. I wrote her I was going to Gateside tomorrow. Jimmy Black and his girl friend went a sail to Ayr.

5th August Jimmy Black is away with Ross in his boat. Jenny and Mary went a sail. Robert called today and paid Mary for potatoes £3.10/-. Marion went with Ina MacDougall on 1st August.

6th August Pop took me here to Gateside.

7th August Sunday Willie came in motor. Ruby not pleased, not his second day.

26th August I went up with milk lorry to Auch & went down to Greenock at night with William Black.

1st September We had Maggie Orr and Lizzie and her man and Willie Orr and his wife. Had a nice night.

2nd September Janet and I were taken in Willie's motor to Mrs Erskine. We had a nice night there.

3rd September Willie drove Janet and I up to Gateside. Came back on Monday morning.

7th September Greenock holiday. Willie is away to Ayr with Mary and Elsie Witheroe & Miss McMeechan. Showery weather for the corn. I got a letter with seeds from Mrs Glass. Had a letter from Ria.

13th September Willie took Janet and I up to Glasgow. Got Mrs Forbes to come with us to Lizzie's. We were made welcome. They have a……. house and garden. Mr Kerr in 25 Newton Street called and spoke about a book, then sent me it, "In Search of Scotland"

19th September I came up to Auchenfoil with Mary in motor from meeting.

22nd September Alice Renfrew and her sister from Canada came to Auchenfoil.

24th September Mrs James Renfrew, her three children and old Mrs Smith her mother & Sarah Smith came and in the evening Mr & Mrs Archibald & two children came with Black's motor that Mr A had been sorting. The same night came Molly and Marie Holmes & a chum Jean. Great disturbance in Britain this week over Hitler's movements in connection with Czechoslovakia

30th September This week Mr Chamberlain flew to a meeting in connection with the war & met the four powers in Munich, Mussolini, Hitler, Deladin *[Daladier, representing France - PJJ]* & Chamberlain and they came to an agreement for peace – the world was extremely glad.

1st October I came down to Gateside. Ruby and Nan in Glasgow. No corn has been taken in for 3 weeks

week until today, Saturday.

16th October Willie came in his motor and took Rob and me to the communion then I came down to Greenock with him. Ruby not too well. Just one good day in 5 weeks. Raining yet.

17th October Janet got sent from England a …. (?) And jacket 10/6

19th October Willie went to Glasgow in car – don't know who with. Home after tea.

20th October First good day for in taking corn. A good bit spoiled. A man cut bare the rose hedge. The sun (?) today reaches 4 inches above the clock.

21st October Half day good then rain. Mary Black and got her feet sorted second time. I am reading "History of Kilmacolm"

13th November I came up to Auchenfoil with Mary on the Sunday.

15th November Letter from Rhoda thanking me for present. I expected a longer letter from her mother.

20th November (Sunday) A week since I came here.

28th **November** Mary Holmes came to Auchenfoil. It was a very wet day. Was driven out and in. Called at Gateside going home.

29th **November** Robert came up. Was quite hearty. Had secured most of his corn and not a bad crop of potatoes. Ruby keeping well.

28th **November** The night of Mary Holmes visit the 5 children of James Laird, Faulds, were over, had tea and games

21st **November** James Black got a nail (rusty) in his middle finger. It was poisoned and had to be cut and got terrible sore.

24th **November** Mrs Lang, Agnes and Bessie came a visit to Auchenfoil. We had a nice crack.

25th **November** Jamie Black was taken to Larkfield Hospital. It got cut 4 times.

28th **November** I came down from Auchenfoil to Gateside. Robert was at Paisley that day. Mrs Dale came here that day. I had her in the room. Had a nice talk.

30th **November** Robert went to Paisley. Sold 6 uncalved quays …. (?) £13

1st **December** Doretha Congalton called in Mr Fennick car. Her uncle, Willie Bell, was killed on the railway near Kilbarchan 3 weeks ago. She thinks the nephew of the uncle will get all themoney. He left £3055

2nd **December** Robert at Glasgow today, getting Ruby's glasses sorted.

3rd **December** Got word today that Maggie Skinner (Mrs Holborn) died on the 25th October 1938. Her daughter wrote me from England. Got word that Jimmy Black's hand is keeping better.

10th December Jenny and John Black are in bed with colds. I cleaned out the trap room. I made ready the maid's room that's to come on Monday. Robert fee'd her on Wed.

12th December Willie called for me at Gateside. We called at Auchenfoil. Murren and Jenny were ill with flu. Mr Ross and Willie Kerr all ill. Jamie getting better.

15th December Willie took Janet and I to see Jamie Black at Larkfield.

16th December Willie took us to see Jean Manson. I heard that the maid Martha Lang came to Gateside this week and is doing well.

20th December Some snow. Willie putting himself on diet. Marie Orr going to Glasgow today.... Willie motored J & I to see Miss Morrison. She had been robbed by two men. Last week in December we had John Currie and wife, Malcolm, Mary J and Mr McNab.

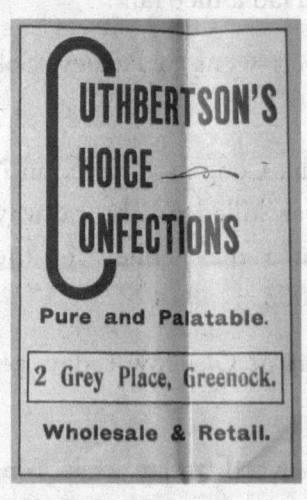

1939

1st January A quiet Ne'erday in Newton Street.

8th January I went in Blacks motor to Auchenfoil. One night there we had Elsie Blair & her father, Mary Duff, Nan and Jean Ross.

20th January Jamie Black came home from Larkfield. He had got his finger cut off at middle joint.

23rd January I came down to Gateside.

24th January Mrs Dale and Gretta came. The Law has been passed that every servant man is to get £1 a week and work eight hours a day. An elderly maid, a Mrs Carrol is at Gateside just now. Martha Lang, a young girl, just stayed a week – I am keeping very well and content.

More wars and rumours of war. Neville Chamberlain wanting all young men to enlist. A letter from Mary Holmes last week.

3rd February I came here today from Gateside after being there a fortnight & a fortnight at Auchenfoil. At Auchenfoil there was a party – Mr Blair and Elsie, Pomillan, Mary Duff and two Misses

Ross. Willie and Janet came up for me to Gateside & took me down here to Newton Street in motor.

5th February John Miller is speaking at the meetings every night for a week, good speaker. A letter from Polly today saying she is coming tomorrow. I finished decorating the …… big…. In the green room last time I was here. A month ago.

6th February Polly came. Went to pictures with Willie. Next day Janet and her went to Largs & Willie and her went to pictures at night.

7th February Polly came. Janet took her to Largs next day, then to Johnstone & Kilbarchan 10th to Gourock.

11th February Jamie Black came and took her to Auchenfoil. Staying the weekend at Glasgow. Willie took her every night to pictures. Willie goes up to Gateside, his usual 2nd Saturday weekend.

17th February (Friday) Robert called on us. Mrs Graham had her pillars cleaned. Granny's silver wedding (?)

22nd February I have had the cold since last week – in bed two days, up today. Salt nitrate sucked up the nostrils was good formit.

24th February I wrote to Maria and asked her down.

25th February Willie went up to Gateside. Willie and I were one night at Miller's preaching.

26th February Snowing.

1st March Mr John Miller is preaching in Port Glasgow for two weeks.

6th March On Monday Willie took me up to Auchenfoil. Gave me my birthday present which was next day. A good present. I stayed at Auchenfoil for two weeks. The Blacks attended the meetings well. Rachel Laird (Mrs Stevenson) called one day fat (?) & fair. I was at the meeting one night at the Port. Well attended. A good earnest speaker!

17th March A son was born to Robert at Gateside (Weight 9 ½ pounds). At 11 o'clock pm 17th March, 1939. *[Dad's cousin Robin—PJJ]*

24th March I got Smillies £1:2:1 Got the Close whitewashed. Ruby and baby son doing well. Mary Miller (Mrs Cammonay?) is … a second cousin to Margery Tainsh.

1st April I came down to Greenock

3rd April (Monday) Willie, Janet and I went in Dunlop's motor to Crianlarich – a fine jaunt. Met Mr Aidenhead (?) Have read one of his books. Willie took Janet and me to Gilchrist's shop one day. Jean Manson called another day. Maria has to leave the house she lets in Glasgow. Theresa is going to Liverpool and she (Maria) is to get her house.

16th April The whole nation is disturbed at the thought that there might be war. Mussolini and Hitler's word cannot be depended on – a pair of tyrants. All are preparing for war in case it comes. Robert Barr of Somerlee (?) died a fortnight ago. He left about 1 1/2 million – made off whisky. A most miserly mean man.

27th April We had Mrs Duncan and Maggie Buntain last night at Richmond Villa. I have been here 4 weeks. I go to Blacks on Sunday for a week and then we go to Kilbrid for a week. I bought a shawl this month – 11/6

28th April Hitler's speech.

1st May I went up to Auchenfoil for a week. Willie being at Gateside took me down to Greenock on the Monday morning and that afternoon we went to West Kilbride to Mrs Kegan, Law Farm, a clever and kindly woman who gave us very good food and a clean house. We drove through a good bit of the locality – a bonnie countryside. Went to Mr Campbell's church, the minister Mr R. Barr left £500. The following Monday we drove back to Greenock.

This month John Johnson passed his exams for the Association of Bankers. About the middle of May R. Blair of Pomillan died. Ligia (?) Blair died about 3 weeks ago (Mrs Sandy Millar).

30th May Willie Janet and I went to Gateside. Ruby was at Glasgow.

4th June Willie and I went to the Communion at St James. Mrs Dale came to Gateside & had a confab with Willie and Robert in the big room. Wull Blair has left Gateside and is staying at Cairncurran sheep still at Gateside. After staying two weeks on the Monday morning I came down to Greenock. I went to the meeting. Mr Ross speaker.

19th June Jim Stevenson got married in Belfast.

20th June Janet and I went & called on Miss Morison. Got Norman's address.

22nd June Janet and I called on Jean Manson & planned to take her to Auchenfoil.

24th June Willie took in motor Janet and I to Wemyss Castle to a garden fete. It realised £1336.

25th June Sunday. Mary and Jenny and John Black were here. Willie Black has been in Ireland for 10 days with his girl, Netta Johnston.

26th June Willie drove Janet, Jean Manson & myself to Auchenfoil. At night we three went to the school prize-giving in the Town Hall. Joe has left school. He got a certificate, made a little speech and led the whole Hall in 3 cheers for Miss Black who had got a presentation and was retiring.

27th June Willie took us in motor to the Wraes – Mary Holmes, Jenny Miller, Janet and me. Saw the Glen and Falls and had a picnic at front door.

Editor's note: Granny Orr wrote the following poem a day or two after her visit to the Wraes farm steading, her childhood home.

"Lines on our visit to the Wraes.

Mrs Stevenson, Mrs Tainsh, Mrs Johnson and Mrs Orr
We made a tryst between us four
That we would go and see the Wraes.
The time came round that we got there
And got to climb the weel kent braes,

The Ganter Glen was blooming fair
The Ganter Falls were sadly gone -
Its waters had been turned aside
Around the Hill for Quarriers Home.

The house itself was not the same
Its glory had departed
Like hers that used to welcome us
And make us feel warm hearted

Outside the door we spread our feast
While old tales we recounted
At last we all enjoyed our tea
All obstacles surmounted

And after pulling roses fair
And honeysuckle scented
We bade farewell to memories dear,
And came away contented

So many thanks to Willie Orr
Who took us there and back
Who helped us gently owre the dyke
And kept us ali in crack.

And we will hope some other time

Before the wintry days
That he and his good motor yet
Will take us to the Wraes.

Marion K. Orr 1939

29th June Joe went for a week with the Boys Brigade to Whitley Bay near Newcastle.

1st July John goes off for a 10 days holiday to trek the Western Isles.

2nd July I go up to Auchenfoil.

13th July John Johnson got a very wet week for his tour of the Highlands. Got back safely and went to Gateside to help his uncle Robert with the hay.

Last Saturday 8th July Lizzie Sheach came to Auchenfoil and one night we had Mrs Smith from Dunbarton and the folk from Kippuich. I go to Greenock this week & Dumfries next week.

15th July Aunt Polly came to Greenock. Willie went up to Gateside.

16th July John Johnson came down and went back to Gateside.

Friday Willie came up for me to go down to Greenock.

17th July Janet Polly and I were taken by Willie in motor to Dumfries from Greenock – a long journey. Came through Ayr. It was a Steeple Chase day and there was a great crowd of folk and motors. Monday afternoon we went up the Observatory. Tuesday we were at Gretna Green. Wednesday we were in Burns House where he died. Our lodgings were in Mrs McNealy, 80 Queen Street. Willie and Polly went every night to the Pictures.

Thursday we went through the country. Saw a car smash near Moffat. Gentleman driver got his rib broken, 3 ladies their foreheads cut. In the afternoon we called on Norman Morrison, near Thornhill. He was looking well. I sent a p.c. to his sister.

21st July We went and saw where Burns was buried. We did not know but it was the anniversary of his death. A fine monument over it. It is in St Michael's churchyard, Dumfries.

22nd July We took Polly in motor to Moffat to get a bus to Edinburgh after going to see the famous Beef Tub, a very mountainous country where we saw the place where Dr Ruxton flung over the bridge the pieces of the bodies of his two victims, his wife and servant maid.

24th July (Monday) Our Mary arrived at Dumfries. Next day we went and saw Abbotsford where Walter Scott lived and wrote many of his books. Getting there we went up a very steep narrow road, up a mountain side. It was a bit frightsome. Mary, Janet, Willie and me.

We all went to Gretna to see the place where couples were married. There had been 111 that month and many visitors. We saw Burns house where he died and where Jean died in the same house many years after and was buried beside him. We visited Ellisland farm and ……. heart Abbey and had many beautiful drives through beautiful country – many trees.

31st July We came back to Greenock and Willie took Mary up to Auchenfoil.

1st August Willie took me up to Gateside. Frank Connelly was helping Robert to sort the henhouse along with Joe Johnson who came up with us. Joe has been elected to study for a Gym teacher. Also he is much sought after for the football. This month Joe R Johnson was successful in passing for a Gym teacher and on the 6th October he is to go to Jordanhill College to perfect for his job for 3 years. He was some years in the High School in Greenock and was master of the house, master of the school and master of the football club and is now getting over £1 a week for playing football.

26th August The young man, James Dick of Kippuach farm Dumbarton who was here at Auchenfoil on the 7th July. I was here and met him and his sister and mother. He was cutting corn with a tractor and binder. Had a gun about him, on turning the tractor the gun went off. The shot went through him. He died that night. And this is his funeral day, the 26th August. Mrs Mary Black and John were away to his funeral.

22nd September I have been at Greenock for 3 weeks. James Black is to be married to May Moodie on the 27th September, the marriage to be in the Lorne. Janet and I were in town today. I got pair shoes in Marks and Spencer. I intend being at the wedding. I got a letter from Mary Holmes on the 18th September.

27th September James Black and May Moodie were married in the Lorne Greenock – just the near families of each at it. I, Mrs Wm Orr, granny to James was at it. *[Jimmy Black, cousin of the editor's father.]*

28th September Willie took Janet and me up to Gateside. Ruby at Glasgow for a fortnight. I wrote to Mary Holmes. Mrs Jean Brown called on me at 33a Newton Street. Mrs Maggie Ferguson is acting as servant at Gateside.

30th September Willie and Janet came the weekend to Gateside. Warsaw has fallen to the Germans and still the war goes on.

9th October I had been one week at Gateside when Ruby and her mother and Greta came. Ruby was very angry. Thought I would have been away. She went back to Glasgow. We brought up a wee pig on the milk. Did fine.

15th October I came down with Willie and Janet to Greenock. Jim Black and wife at Auchenfoil. I am making a cushion for Mrs Forbes and Mrs Stevenson of flowered velvet.

19th October Joe Johnson went to Jordanhill College. He is going to play football at Barrhead. *[Arthurlie Football Club — Ed]*

Early in October Jack Orr went to Oxford University at the Government's expense for one year.

25th October There came a letter from Jack Orr.

28th October I wrote to Jack Orr.

9th November Willie and I went to the Linn (?) Bridge of Weir but Bessie Barr was not in. Called on the Buntains in Fern Villa in the time of the Black Lookout.

10th November I am renovating Queen Victoria's picture. Robert came down tonight.

11th November Armistice Day Queen Elisabeth broadcasted to the Empire at night on the duty of women.

13th November Rob wrote for Willie not to come up on Sat night. He went. I am covering a mat for Janet.

18th November Willie went to Gateside – things looking better.

20th November A letter from John. Had been boxing.

25th November I came up to Gateside for a fortnight. Ruby went to Glasgow.

28th November Jim McDougal took his young wife, a Scott of Shieldhill to Burnbank Farm. John Baxter removed to Gryfeside Farm

11th December Willie and Janet came to Gateside the weekend and took me here on Monday morning.

6th December Bessie Barr and her daughter, Mrs Taylor, came to see me at Gateside. Robert's pigs doing fine – 6 big ones and 3 wee ones

13th December Mrs Mary Black has been not so well for about a month. Getting better. Rheumatic pains.

22nd December Jean Manson called at 33a Newton Street

28th December Robert came down to see Willie about him not coming up so often to Gateside.

30th December Janet and I have been getting presents. From Mary I got a fountain pen and from the girls a gold brooch and one with Bee on it from Mary and a Holm (?)

Willie has gone up to Gateside. I got a water bottle from Jenny Tainsh. Janet is knitting two pairs of slippers for Maggie and Lizzie.

1940

1940 Presents I got at the New Year 1940: a fountain pen from Mary. A brooch from the girls Black. A brooch from Mary Holmes. A foot muff from John Johnson. A small calendar from Annie McPhee. A water bottle from Janet Miller.

6th January Willie Janet and myself along with Jack Orr (who came to Greenock that day) all went to John Currie's and had a nice after daylight (?) W. Kerr was there and M. Currie. Jack left to go to Glasgow that night. Edinburgh next day and London on Monday to finish his term this year for his service in India. John Johnson went off that day too (8th January) to London, after a holiday of nine days.

11th January I have finished painting flowers on the big cruck (?) Willie goes tomorrow to Dunlop.

9th January Robert's pig that he got from Houston had a litter but they all died.

12th January Rob came down to Greenock.

13th January Willie went up the weekend. Ruby was friendly. They had been getting the well cleaned out. There were more than a hundred pails full in it about 5 feet deep.

17th January Willie took a run up to Gateside. He met the Misses Miller and Malcolm Currie there but they did not go in.

18th January We expected Miss Morison and A. Holmes but we had a heavy fall of snow and they did not come. – first snow this winter.

20th January Willie took me up to Gateside after one week. Ruby went to Glasgow for a week and came back the next week. The 5th of February. I went up to Auchenfoil on the same sledge that broght Ruby to Gateside over the snow which was 4 feet deep on the road, tramped hard. It lay on the ground for 5 weeks.

19th February I came down to Greenock with John and Mary Black. Mary was trying for her test in driving. She got it and so did Hugh the week before. He is now the milk driver. We came by road through Port Glasgow. The road is not cleared yet from Auchenfoil to Greenock but today (20th) it has come on rain.

20th February Willie heard from the Misses Miller that May Scott (Mrs Wm Holmes) fell on the slippy ground and broke her ankle.

21st February Heard today that Jack Smith is dead. Got operated on for a sore eye and never regained consciousness – the operation was not successful. Old Mr Telfer is in Larkfield Hospital. Mrs Telfer not well.

23rd February The top rose off the tall tree at corner of the garden. It was felled in December. Kept in bloom till end of February 24th

7th March We had a vist of Miss Morison and Miss Holmes – a good cheery chat. My birthday – I got a nice posy from W. and a cardigan from Janet – 25s. Mrs John Currie brought a cake.

9th March John Tainsh flew part of the way to Orkney. I wrote to Mary Holmes.

10th March Jimmy Black and wife, John and Marion Black came (Sunday).

12th March Had a letter from Robert. He sold the first 4 pigs at Paisley. Had a second letter from Jack Orr from Oxford – getting through his studies there.

13th March Had a letter from Mary Holmes.

22nd April After being at Gateside a fortnight & Auchenfoil a fortnight I came here a week ago.

19th April Jack Orr went back to Oxford after being at home a few weeks on holiday. John Blair died in a home in Glasgow – some trouble about his mouth. He left about £9000. Jack Smith, Auchencloich left a few hundreds over £1000. In February Willie Caldwell of the Ward died. Marion Caldwell had gone to nurse him & herself took a stroke. Jimmy Black went to the Ward to help. In March Austhen (?) Holmes, Bardrainey died. His nephew, William Holmes, has got into Bardrainey.

Janet and I went to Glasgow and bought each a coat - £4:14/-

22nd April Robert was to sell 10 pigs at Paisley.

24th April Archie Currie came alone. Jean Manson called. She stays in Greenock now.

26th April Marie Orr called on her way home by Glasgow. From Auchenfoil she got acquainted with a soldier there. The war is now at grim fighting in Norway. About the time old Telfer, Branchal, died. He left about £9000.

5th May I wrote to L. Caldwell a note of sympathy. I got a letter from Polly – Jack is to be at Oxford to study. All his time is upon the province in India that he goes to called Bihar, the language Hindu.

27th May Lysa Sheach came to Auchenfoil when I was there. Another day Mrs Land and Bessie came.

10th June I came to Greenock.

14th June Paris has fallen to Hitler.

29th June Janet and I went to Gilchrists and each got a hat.

21st June John Johnson arrived at midnight from London a weekend.

27th June Janet and I went to see Miss Whyte in Rockcliff – kindly received.

30th June John went off on foot to London. Got on time, lifts on the road. Ruby needing another cot for Robin.

6th July Robert commenced cutting hay today.

9th July Willie, Janet and I went to see the play, Queen Victoria. Very good.

15th July I came down from Auchenfoil to Gateside about the middle of May. Was at 33 Newton Street for 5 weeks. Willie, Janet and Joe and I went for a fortnight to Ayr, Plane Trees Boarding House. Ria came also. Our Mary (Mrs Black) she stayed one week. Then we had Polly for another. John came home from London & stayed one week. We all went to see Bessie Miller (Mrs Meason). Her children are getting big. John went back to see the girl Jean. The next day we went by Lochwinnoch and came the same way.

3rd August I went for a week to Gateside. Ruby and family went to Glasgow for a week. When I was there I sent for Maria who came on the Saturday following when Janet came with Willie and I went with them to Auchenfoil. Maria went on to Greenock with them on the Monday morning and stayed till Wednesday. Mary Ross called on me when I was at Gateside and came up to Auchenfoil when I was there. Another day Bessie Barr and her daughter came in a motor. They thought the farm was very extensive and everything looking well. Jack Orr who had passed his final exams at Oxford and was to sail shortly for India was there to bid them goodbye. He had also called on Bessie Lang

17th August I came back to Greenock for 4 weeks.

18th August George Mason and wife came on Sunday.

5th September We had a visit of old Mrs Walker and her daughter.

7th September Joe was at a football match at Barrhead. He hurt his foot, did not go back to Gateside for three days. He is on holiday and is helping Robert at Gateside.

10th September I wrote to John in London and on the 11th his mother had a letter from him saying that the bombing in London was terrific that week. I wrote to Mary Holmes this month and got an answer back.

23rd September I went to Gateside for one week. Ruby went to Glasgow. I gave Mrs Ross a double wash-stand. She gave me a dark blue cape. Beena called on me one day. Her husband had died and her daughter married.

30th September I went up with Willie on Monday morning to Auchenfoil and stayed a fortnight. George Mason and two daughters came on Sunday

10th October When at Auchenfoil they commenced their potato digging. Had 31 to dinner and two teas and once 35 altogether.

14th October Bob Ross drove me down to Greenock on a Tuesday.

20th October (Sunday) Willie and I went to Gateside to go to the Communion but the motor had something wrong with it so we did not get. Came back to Greenock next morning.

23rd October I wrote to Mary Holmes.

25th October I got a letter from Mary Holmes. She had been at Roseneath Castle. Same day I got a letter from Jack Orr. He was to sail next day for India. Also a letter from Robert. Janet bought two cardigans, one for each 2:8 1/2 Mine – black and white cotton. Very nice.

25th October We at Newton Street were frightened for the bombs that seemed so near us. Some tenements down and 6 killed.

25th October Jean Manson called. Not getting any better pleased with her landlady. Janet bought two cardigans at 2.8 ½ She is making a soft green dress.

31st October Halloween. Janet and I and Willie alone. Joe at a meeting in a church.

1st November Janet got a paper to see if she could take evacuees.

3rd November A son born to Mr & Mrs Black, Green.

16th November Willie took me up to Gateside. I stayed one week and went up to Auchenfoil with him on Monday morning & stayed two weeks. May Black brought up her baby son. It is called John.

9th December Bob Ross took me down to Greenock in the motor at night. He is on the night shift. He is an engine driver. Mrs Johnson got a profit of £50 on the sale of the Burma Oil paper. Also £50 from the Provident Bank from money lodged there. It is continuing the same for 10 years.

14th December We had Mr & Mrs Erskine and the mother. Mr Erskine is a fluent talker. *[Editor's note: Jack Erskine, who was an elder in the Church of God in Greenock.]*

15th December (Sunday) Marion and Mary Black. Betty MacDonald has been driving the milk motor for 3 weeks now. Hugh Black has got a Dairy in Greenock. Joe Johnson has to join the army.

19th December Janet and I were seeing Mary Witherow's …. (?) We gave her a silk quilt…. (?) £3.

22nd December Mary (Miss) and Jenny Black (Sun). Jenny wearing her engagement ring.

24th December Janet papering the kitchen green and gold colour.

I got a letter from Mary Miller with a photo of herself & daughter & baby grandson.

25th December Christmas. I got Annie Swan's life from Jenny Miller… a hanky from our Mary, card from Ria, Jean and Marie Orr. A card to Willie from Willie Martin and one to us as a family.

Annie Shepherd Swan, (1859-1943) was a Scottish journalist and fiction writer. Politically active in the First World War, she was a suffragist, a Liberal activist and a founder-member of the Scottish National Party.

26th December I sent two books to Miss Whyte – The Cross in modern life[1] & Enfelice (?) I sent a small silk neckerchief to Miss McPhee, Trafalgar Street 5 I thanked Jenny Miller by letter. Joe Johnson has been working in Hastie's Engineering Works this fortnight. He has left Jordanhill School for the duration of the war. He went back to it again.

26th December I wrote Mary Miller, told her about J. Orr & sent a photo taken at Bellise Ayr.

27th December Mr & Mrs Ross, M. Mill, came. Willie took them home as he was going to Gateside.

29th December Joe working at Hastie's this fortnight. Hugh Black called. He had got a motor car for milk driving.

---

1. **The Cross in modern life:** Available online here: https://archive.org/details/crossinmodernlif00gree/page/n3/mode/2up

1941

January Ne'erday. I was in Greenock – a quiet day. Willie went to Glasgow. I got a present, Annie Swan from Jenny Miller. Mary Holmes did not write.

4th January John Currie and wife and Malcolm were up for tea.

7th January Willie was in Glasgow and visited Jean Loutit.

11th January I went to Gateside. Ruby came home with Robert on a Wednesday.

13th January Willie came back for me. Stayed the weekend and took me to Auchenfoil on Monday. I was two weeks at Auchenfoil. Mary and I were in at Mrs Lang's one afternoon. Old Mrs Barr was ill. Heard John Orr, Newton was not very well.

28th January Janet and Willie were at McNabs.

1st February I came down with the Blacks on Sunday. On January 31st I wrote to Polly. I got a letter from Mary Holmes in January. Marion Holmes (Mrs Forbes) in bed for a month – sore leg.

7th February Janet and Willie and myself were at Mrs Langs, Renane Fernia.

8th February Malcolm called and talked a while. Willie at Gateside.

15th February A letter from Polly telling us about Jack. He had lande in India. Got a great reception. Dined with the Governor whose daughter had been at St Andrews with him. The chief secretary showed him round the place. The prison was one in which there were 2000 prisoners. They all stood at attention and saluted. He was taken to a court in Blagalpur as his position there as an assistant magistrate. He says he doesn't even need to tie his own laces. His servant stands by handing him each garment as he dresses. He has another who looks after all his laundry and another who goes all his messages. He is to have a tutor for the Hindu language. A letter from Robert. He has got a horse from Service in Greenock to replace the one that had to be shot.

16th February Sunday. Mary and Willie down.

18th February Tuesday. Malcolm Currie came for a week. I wrote to B. Lang. Told her about Jack being in India. I told her what I knew of her pedigree.

26th February Malcolm Currie went to Auchenfoil.

28th February I wrote to Jack Orr – first letter to India

3rd March Polly came from Edinburgh.

5th March Janet and Polly went to Paisley. R saw to me.

6th March …. (?) Spoke to Janet at the door.

7th March My 88th birthday. I got a nice sum from W. and a few other things from others. From Mrs Tainsh Annie Swan.

8th March Polly went home by Glasgow. Stayed 6 days at 33 Newton Street. She said they had to pay £200 to replace what had been lost at sea.

15th March I went up to Gateside with Willie. Stayed till the following Saturday. Bob Ross took me up to Auchenfoil but Willie went to Gateside that Saturday too but made it up with Ruby.

18th March There was a party at Auchenfoil- a Dunlop Knocknair, 3 MacDougalls, 2 Misses Laird, Cairncurran. That was the third party.

20th March I wrote M. Holmes. Sent back Francis Gay's letter. The bombing was back at Clydebank and Glasgow.

24th March Malcolm Currie after being 5 weeks here at Auchenfoil left to go home to the Highlands.

1st April Got a letter from Mrs Brown. Her last surviving sister Abigail had died. A big bombing expected in Greenock on the 11th of this month. I am staying here till after.

3rd April This is my third week at Auchenfoil. Lizzie Skeoch came yesterday. She has 5 people from Clydebank. Isobel Wright is also here. Robert came up. Very cold backward weather for seed time. Mary attending a doctor in Greenock about her legs. Getting sore and stiff.

7th April A big bombing here at Auchenfoil. Windows blown and at Garshannon ... (?) Lost a horse and ... (?) Craig some sheep. Janet and I first night in our wee dugout. A deadly raid on Greenock with German bombs. The people next day fled from the town in hundreds. Took shelter any place. In farm house in Kilmacolm. 200 in Auchenfoil. Many of them staying night and day. Great destruction in houses and broken windows. Ria stayed a fortnight here in April. She was bombed out of her home in Glasgow. We are short of sugar more than anything else but butcher meat is scarce.

8th April Mrs James Renfrew and 3 children came up for refuge but there was a quiet night.

9th April During this month Robert's old horse he got from Greenock died. Old John Laird and his son Robert came out for eggs and to see me at Auchenfoil. I expect to go to Greenock tomorrow. The 14th.

15th April I came down here. Bob Ross took me. John Johnson went away today to Haddington to his regiment, the Royal Artillery.

12th May Have been here at Richmond Villa 4 weeks.

13th May Robert came down on bike to see the ruin in Greenock. On the 7th May we in Richmond Villa the night of the big raid had 11 windows bombed out and doors jammed. By the 16th we got them patched up till better sorted.

14th May We got two men to give shelter to – William Rankin and his illegitimate son.

17th May Joe went to Galston for the weekend.

19th May Janet and I were disappointed in not getting to Gateside for a week because of our lodgers. I will be 5 weeks down here on 20th.

22nd May Ria came and stayed one night.

29th May W. Kerr came to speak about Ria. He could not take her in the meantime as his house was filled up.

30th May I was out for an hour cleaning the walks in the garden. Willie was at Gateside yesterday with Davie Rowan putting in seed.

1st June Willie and I went to the Sacrament. Met J. Miller, Miss Blair, the two Buntains and the three Langs. Same day we came by Gateside. Heard Frank Blair was to be married on 6th June. Robert and Willie gave each a £1

3rd June Posted a letter to Mary Miller. I worked in the garden fully an hour while building a wee dyke…… (?) D. Rowans.

5th June Still sweeping up the garden walks. John Black was at Fife seeing John Laird. He stayed a night in Edinburgh. Our two men lodgers are getting along not so badly.

17th June I wrote to Jack Orr. Told him about the raids on Greenock.

20th June Had a visit from Jean Scott and her two grandchildren.

21st June Ria came for the weekend. Getting on all right in Glasgow – getting odd jobs. John Johnson has been a week on holiday from Haddington. Joe finished with Jordanhill College.

1st July Lizzie Holmes came to Janet's. Went home at night. Janet and I went to see Jenny Miller that day.

3rd July Janet and I came to Dunoon for a week and Joe leaves for England tonight.

5th July I wrote to Bessie Lang today. Mary came to Dunoon for 6 days. Our Willie just got one night. J. and M. went a bus drive to Glendaruel.

9th August Willie Janet and I came up to Gateside. They went away on the Monday morning.

15th August I wrote to Jack Orr and to Mary Holmes. I stay this week here then go to Auchenfoil. Rob busy at his vegetables. Hay not all cut. I wrote to Jack Orr on 17th June. Got no answer. That's 3 letters to him.

16th August I went up to Auchenfoil and stayed a fortnight. Met Mrs Walker there. Jenny to be wed on 1st of Oct.

12th September I have been here at Greenock a fortnight. Willie, Janet and I have been invited to Jenny's wedding at the Douglas Hotel Glasgow. I wrote to Mary Holmes today. I had a parcel from her – 4 towels to be sowed and a writing pad.

10th September Robert came down.

13th September I gave J 10/-

14th September John has gone to Glasgow to meet Joe.

15th September I wrote to Jack Orr.

18th September Janet and I at Glasgow. She got a furry coat and I got a dress for JB's wedding.

24th September I got a letter from Polly to read. She had sent it to Willie. She is waiting on Jean's event in London. John Johnson is helping Robert with the harvest. Got leave from the army. A letter from Mary Holmes saying she would give my curna (?) to Jane. It was the one with beads on it. Made of curtain of Gateside sideboard. Sunny today after a fortnight's good weather.

1st October Jenny Black's wedding to Wm Kerr of Gryffe Neuk. Janet, R. & Wm & myself were at it in the Douglas Hotel. Janet had on a lovely velvet dress, navy blue. The couple went a tour in their motor.

7th October We had the Misses Scott to tea. Ardgowan Street.

11th October I go up to Gateside today. It is 9 weeks since I stayed a week there.

8th October We had the Misses Scott (Ardgowan Street) to tea.

10th October We had Maggie and Lizzie Orr & Mrs James Lang her daughter and boy & girl to tea.

11th October Mary Holmes at Gourock sent me a note to visit her. I had no time as I go to Kilmacolm tonight Saturday. Mary Holmes called on Janet the following Tuesday. Ria was in Greenock for a few days.

18th October I go from Gateside to Auchenfoil tomorrow for a fortnight. Joe Johnson called – his first visit since going to England. Got about 7 days.

25th October I have written Malcolm Currie from Auchenfoil. Jimmie Black got exemption from the army. 51 people getting dinner at Auchenfoil – tattie gathering and corn stacking. 3 of the boys got killed going home by walking along the railway line.

29th October John Black went to Ayrshire and bought a tractor and a plinso (?) Combined price £450.

William James Barclay Craig of Monklands on active service in Sept last.

30th October I wrote to Mrs Craig Monklands, also to Jack Orr – my 5th letter. I wrote to Jean Manson in Glasgow.

1st November I wrote to Bessie Lang to come to Greenock. I got a letter from Malcolm Currie. I go to Greenock on 3rd November

4th November I wrote to Polly in England.

7th November Janet and I went to 60 Ardgowan Street to tea with the Misses Scott. Jessie Houston (?) there. John Johnson came that night. Went off next night Sunday.

9th November I wrote to Mary Miller (MacKay).

11th November Armistice Day. Robert was down.

12th November Got a letter from Jean Manson. She had not been so well in Glasgow.

17th November I wrote to Joe Johnson.

18th November I wrote to Jenny Miller (Mrs Tainsh).

In October Mrs McNeil sent to Janet and I two table covers. In November I got a blue silk cushion from Netta Johnston.

This month I went up to Gateside for one week. Robert was busy with his vegetables, disposing of them. They repaid him not so bad.

December I went from there to Auchenfoil for another week. – busy there exchanging furniture with the Green farm.

Willie is to be married to Netta Johnston on the 17th December, 1941. I came back to Greenock on the 14th to be ready for the weding.

17th December Willie Black was married to Janet Johnston (Netta) 40 at the wedding. They go to Green farm.

25th December Xmas Day John and Joe were both at home. Ria (Mrs Perpoli) came to stay with us in 33 Newton Street. She gave us two half sets of beautiful china and other ornaments. Joe went to see his pal at Galston today. We all got a card from Mrs Martin (?) Joe stayed one night at Galston and one at Auchenfoil.

30th December I wrote to Mary Holmes and to Miss Whyte. Joe went back to England to his new job.

31st December Janet got a letter from Marion Holmes. We have still the two men upstairs.

1942

January Ne'erday. I spent it in Greenock with Janet and Willie and Maria in 33 Newton Street. No visitors but all quite happy. With peace and plenty & favourable news of the war. Over 20 other anti-axis nations have signed to help us.

4th January James's birthday – died in 1922. I did not get many presents this Xmas – a writing pad from Mary, pair of bedsocks from Miss Whyte. Gave her a good calendar. Got a nice letter from her.

18th January I came up on this Sunday with Willie to Gateside. Heard in the afternoon the sd news of Mrs Dale's death the night before.

19th January Robert and family went to Glasgow.

20th January They went back to the funeral. I was in bed two days with cold.

24th January I have been at Gateside for my week. A heavy fall of snow. Roads bad.

5th February I have been at Auchenfoil a week. I had a letter from Mary Holmes last week Also one from Mary Millar and John Johnson. I have answered a letter to George Mason, telling me about his daughter's husband's death.

2nd February I posted a letter to Bessie Bain (?), the Line (?) Bridge of Weir. I got an answer saying her eyesight was bad – that is more than a year it has been bad.

6th February I wrote to her daughter, Mrs Graham Taylor, Lyle Burn (?) Bridge of Weir instead of her mother.

Robert came up today and had quite a long chat. Wee Ruby is extra clever at her lessons.

Willie Kerr is building a bathroom here in the close for James' end.

7th February I have been a fortnight here on Monday morning when I expect to go to Greenock with W.

I gave old Hugh his usual tobacco. I was two days in bed here (cold) but I am better.

13th February I wrote to John Johnson

15th February I got an answer from Jenny S. Taylor – quite nice.

18th February I wrote to Mary Holmes from 33a Newton Street.

19th February I got a letter from Mary Holmes. She wrote the same day as I did.

22nd February Marion Black and Betty came (Sunday)

26th February I wrote to Mary Millar.

25th February I wrote to Jack Orr, to Patna.

7th March My birthday. A good posey from W. A calendar from William Martin.

8th March Sunday Mr and Mrs Mason and John Johnson came. Snow on the ground.

9th March Willie managed through the snow to Gateside for vegetables. John Johnson came and gave me a gold brooch. The war still going fast and furious.

11th March Robert down today. Gave him two pairs socks.

13th March I got a birthday present from Mary a cardigan B & T. Janet whitewashed the kitchen white and green

20th March I got a letter from Wm (?) Martin. I wrote to Polly.

22nd March I gave a cushion to Marion Black – one side my old black velvet cape, the other side yellow (?) I wrote to Mary and sent Wm Martin's letter to read.

25th March I wrote to Mary Holmes

26th March Janet went to Glasgow to see Marion Holmes. I went to Gateside a week before the 24th of January. The next time I go is tomorrow the 18th April, that is 12 weeks.

22nd April (Wednesday) I came here on Sunday – 3 days ago. I am writing a letter to Polly. Robert is getting his seed put in. About the 1st May I was at Auchenfoil for 2 weeks. James and wife, son and Mrs Moodie were there. A mare had her first foal but died.

10th May I have been here 2 days at 33 Newton Street. Very cold weather.

16th May Had a vist of Mary Jessie and at night John Currie and wife.

20th May Had Hugh Black and Isobel Wright.

24th May (Sunday) Had Mrs Mary Black, young Mary & Jenny (Mrs Kerr) & Jimmy & wife. We have vegetables growing in the garden at No 33.

28th May We had Mrs Walker and Mrs Barbour. A postcard from John from Oldmeldrum

31st May Willie, Jenny and me were at John Currie's Sat night.

29th May Robert was down – looking well.

2nd June John came at night for a fortnight.

5th June Mrs Tainsh came. Brought syrup.

6th June Janet and I thinned the cabbage and turnips. Willie and I go to the Kilmacolm sacrament tomorrow. Willie and John at school sports today. After all the sports did not come off.

7th June Willie and I went to the sacrament. Saw Mrs Tainsh, the Buntains, Mrs Brown and Gally Wallace.

Gateside garden — as it once was.

10th June Was out in Gateside garden today. Everything is going to wreck and ruin, except some roddys, lilac, laburnum & broom all in flourish. Robert has too much to do. What was called

Willie's garden is complately ruined & every small tree uprooted. The name for it now is "Ichabod" – the glory had departed.

1st July We went to Largs for a fortnight-4 Boyd Street. Had a visit of Mrs McKellar. Our Mary was with us the first week, Polly the second. Mary and I went to Rothesay and saw the Misses Clark. Willie was with us.

18th July I got a letter from Jack Orr today.

22nd July I wrote to Mary Holmes. Next day she sent me a p.c. of Queen Elisabeth.

24th July Ria went to Glasgow. - saw Mary Holmes and Marion. Ria is not very cheery these days, has not heard from her daughter in Australia. We are getting our broken windows put in by the Corporation of Greenock.

26th July Marion and Betty came on Sunday.

27th July I sorted the flowers in the front .... critics and in the afternoon Janet Millar and Bessie came. Janet Miller then saw the Curies in the Bowling Green.

28th July The second good day for a while. The Russians are hard pressed. A letter fro John and Joe yesterday. John will be going away shortly.

16th August Willie took me to Auchenfoil.

18th August I wrote to Joe Johnson at Portsmouth.

19th August John Black went to Keppuch on John Ross's motor bike at 1 o'clock. When coming back it had to be sorted. Got home about 4. It is raining every day – bad for the hay getting in and outside work.

22nd August It has rained for a fortnight. Mary Crawford came up in her wee bogie from Margarert's Mill to see me.

28th August Betty took me over to see the bridge that Willie Kerr is putting up at Gryfeneuk. It is very nice and imposing looking.

30th August I came down to 33 in Mary's car this day Sunday. Joe has been here a week on holiday. He's up at Gateside today.

September I wrote to Miss Whyte early this month and sent her "A Run through Kilmacolm" She thanked me kindly for it

13th September Mary's birthday and Joe's – made a dumpling for it. Joe got two nights and went back on Monday morning. He is getting very tired of Portsmouth.

14th September Ria is here still but is getting very unsatisfied and taking not…….. (?) We are wishing her well away. We will offer to pay her rent in Glasgow. Robert has three land girls helping with his weding. Is keeping just one tinker & family on and getting a tent for them to put below the bridge at Carsons some good day.

18th September Robert came with his tinker.

19th September A good day. Have got down from Gateside the bonny peony rose. Ria doing better but cried out in her sleep last night. - dreamed the Negros had got hold of her.

October Maria left us 21st September to get a place in Glasgow. After a week came back and stayed a weekend, quite pleased to know that she is going to get a job End of September we had John Currie & wife.

2nd October Robert and Tinker came. We had a visit of Mary Holmes. She had been at Greenock a fortnight.

5th October I set a gooseberry bush in 33 Newton Street

17th October Gave Janet £1:5 – clear - Frank Blair left Craiglinchach for good. Robert Orr, Langbank, took him away in his motor to stay with him. Young Frank and his wife did not treat him well. Have had a wet week cannot get the corn secured – The battle still raging but have hopes of final victory. I have caught a cold. I was ill for a fortnight.

31st October A show of sheep dogs in Greenock. Janet and Lizzie Orr were at it.

1st November The first ten days we have had it good all summer. It let all the corn and hay get in dry. Robert got a subsidy for growing potatoes, £100.

5th November This day Britain received good news of the war. General Montgomery with the eighth army defeated the Nazis under Rommel near Egypt and charted (?) them.

11th November I wrote to Mary Holmes and Miss Whyte. Joe came his holiday from Portsmouth before going overseas. (Changed a £1 with Janet on the 12th Nov.)

13th November I got a letter from Mary Holmes. There is good news of the war yet.

16th November The Duke and Duchess of Gloucester were in Greenock today and Gourock.

24th November A letter from John in the far east.

19th November First son born to Jenny Black. Kerr to be called William. James Black's wife had a son a fortnight ago to be called Alan.

11th December I came down here from Auchenfoil.

30th December Robert was here yesterday.

31st December 2 days ago I sent Miss Whyte a calendar and book – Kilmacolm History. I sent Jenny Tainsh a bed jacket (pink and green). I got from her a book, Frances Gay. Gave Mrs Black black silk stockings. Got from her a Bn and White cardigan. I wrote to Polly asking for Leslie, a fortnight's time. No answer yet. Leslie was in hospital in Edinburgh with a sore throat. A letter from John Johnson a week since, saying he was in hospital with an attack of pleurisy. I wrote to M. Holmes a month ago, have got no answer.

Deaths in 1940 and 1941
1940 19th April John Blair, Pennytersal
Robert Blair, Pomillan
Smith of Auchencloch, husband of Mary Buntain died in
Feb 1940
In February Willie Caldwell and his wife died at the Ward Farm
also Marion Caldwell of the Braes
Arthur Holmes of Bardrainie
Mr Telfer of Branchal in March and Jimmy Black died in
January of 1941
1941
Near the end of the year Jenny Black of Auchenfoil (Mrs
Bain) and
Lizzie Black of Auchenfoil (Mrs Paton)
William Crawford Chapel
Mr Ross, Carseknowe, Kilmacolm
1942
David Taylor, Branchal 8th January
Mr McKenna, Garshannon April 1942
Jean Manson died 9th May, 1942
John Douglas died this year
Dr Gregory died and Andrew Smith
Sandy Graham, late of Blackwater

John 11:25 Jesus said to her, "I am the Resurrection and the Life. He that believeth in Me, though he were dead yet shall he live."

Eccles 2:16 "Be not righteous overmuch, neither make thyself over wise. Why shouldst thou destroy thyself."

Proverbs 25:17 "Withdraw thy foot from thy neighbour's house lest he be weary of thee and so hate thee."

> Jack Orr's address in India
> J.W. Orr, ICS,
> ARP Officer
> Patna, Bihar.

Watercolour painting of Gateside Farm by Jo Johnson, editor of this book.

1943

4th January I wrote to Jack orr to Patna. Also I wrote to Jenny Taylor (Mrs G. Taylor)

6th January I wrote to Wm Martin. Malcolm Currie called. Stayed a day after.

11th January I wrote to Mary Holmes. I wrote to Bessie Millar thanking her for her photo of the family and her daughter going to be an actress.

10th January Sunday Our Mary down and Betty. I got a reply from Miss Whyte 6th January.

2nd February I wrote to Polly. She is in England.

3rd February Malcolm Currie called one afternoon.

4th February A letter from Ria. She's not so well. Willie at Glasgow today.

July I have been ill now for about 5 months, since my 90th birthday am getting a little better.

8th July Hugh Black, Auchenfoil, got married to Isobel Wright Greenock. Took up house in Bentinck Street. He was only 21 years old. I am staying with Janet at 33a Newton Street, Greenock.

24th July I am still in bed yet but no worse.

22nd August I am still in bed. Mary is down this weekend. I am still getting a little better but not good at walking without a stick.

30th December I am still in bed but get up a little at night – play draughts with Janet. Robert was down today and I had a letter from Agnes Barr (Mrs MacKellar or Mackellvie).

Granny Orr with her daughter Janet in the garden at 33a Newton Street, Greenock

1944

Mrs Orr is to give Ria £1 next time she comes. Today is 23rd July 1944. I Mrs William Orr am still confined to bed but have no pain & can take my food & can enjoy reading & can still get up every night for a few hours. Now in my 91st year

Queen Elizabeth born in August 1900

13th August Mrs Orr paid Ria £1 me next time (paid).

4th September Janet to pay next time. I (Mrs Orr) am still here.

The diary ends here.

Granny Orr died at 33a Newton Street, Greenock, at 6.30am, on Wednesday 15th August 1945, aged 92. The death was registered on 16th August 1945, by her son William Orr.

The Shooting of Donald Black

BACKGROUND AND TIMELINE

Granny Orr's grandson, Donald Black, was shot dead in the early hours of 24th July 1931. He was just short of his 23rd birthday. His mother, Mrs Mary Black (Granny Orr's daughter), had been bereaved of her husband John Black (Donald's father) just less than two years before.

On the evening of Friday 24th July 1931 Donald walked over to visit his girlfriend Mary Duff, at Mathernock Farm, about a mile across the fields from his home at Auchenfoil Farm.

Early on Saturday morning, between five and half-past five, Donald's mother called to wake him as usual, but he did not answer. She discovered his bed had not been slept in and sent Donald's 13-year-old brother John over to Mathernock to find out where he was. The folks at Mathernock said Donald had gone back to Auchenfoil about 11.30 p.m. the previous night. John then followed Donald's homeward route along the farm tracks which exit onto the main Kilmalcolm to Greenock Road, past Horsecraigs cottage, just up the hill from Auchenfoil Farm.

The following extracts from the contemporary newspaper reports, trace the timeline events.

THE DISCOVERY OF DONALD BLACK'S BODY

Port Glasgow Express, 29th July 1931

"The night before" [i.e., on Friday 24th July 1931] "he had gone out after stating he intended calling on his sweetheart, Miss Mary Duff. daughter of a neighbouring farmer, Mr Duff of Mathernock, as he had been in the habit of for some time. He spent a pleasant evening at the farm-house, and left for home about half-past eleven. Like other farming people, the Black family are in the habit of retiring early, and no surprise was occasioned at Donald's absence when they went off to bed at the usual hour. On finding that Donald had not been home Mrs Black, fearing that something was wrong, called a younger son, John, and after explaining the matter to him, she told him to hurry over to Mathernock in order to learn if his brother had left, and when. Taking the shortest way across the field, John did not take long in reaching his destination. Mr and Mrs Duff were startled to hear of Donald's inexplicable absence, and could throw no light on the matter except to inform John when he had taken leave of them."

Dundee Telegraph, 27th July 1931

"Donald had been wearing a new pair of shoes with specially patterned soles, and his brother managed to pick up his footprints, but lost them on the hard surface of the main road. The footprints came to view again on the softer soil at the side of the highway. Then came the discovery of the body."

Larne Times - Saturday 01 August 1931

"When he reached the top of the brae which looks down on Auchenfoil Farm, was horrified to discover his brother lying dead."

Port Glasgow Express, 29th July 1931

"The body lay face downwards on the grassy verge beside a telegraph pole. The clothing was saturated with blood, and there were also stains on the grass. There was a waterproof coat over the left arm, and nearby was the victim's walking stick. John Black ran quickly to his home and informed his mother, brother, and sisters of Donald's fate. Police Sergeant Gray, of Kilmacolm, was summoned by a brother, [John] who cycled into the village, and a doctor was also sent for. After examining the body the sergeant got into communication with Mr W. G. Young, County Procurator Fiscal at Greenock, and the police at Port-Glasgow and Paisley. The first examination suggested that deceased had been struck by a passing motor car and thrown against a nearby telegraph pole. The fact that there there were no signs of a struggle and that the coat and stick were beside the body supported this theory. A post-mortem was arranged, but before it had taken place an appeal was issued to drivers of vehicles who had passed along the mid late on Friday night to come forward. A careful inspection was made of the scene of the occurrence and later the body was removed to Auchenfoyle Farm. It is understood that a cartridge wad and two pieces of cartridge-paper were picked by the Police."

Dundee Telegraph, 27th July 1931

"... Later came the discovery at the mortuary at Port-Glasgow, where Professor Glaister carried out a post-mortem examination, that Black had been shot through the right breast. The discovery set the police on a new line of inquiry and they soon received information which fixed the time of the shooting at about midnight."

POACHER'S EVIDENCE

Fife Free Press, & Kirkcaldy Guardian - Saturday 01 August 1931

"From a statement made to the police by two poachers, he seems have been shot about midnight, at which hour the poachers state they heard shots fired. They did not place any importance the matter the time, and only came forward when Black was found dead the morning." (Fife Free Press, & Kirkcaldy Guardian - Saturday 01 August 1931)

ARREST OF FARM WORKER, COLIN McMILLAN

Port Glasgow Express, 29th July 1931

"News of the new development quickly spread, and the affair was the sole topic of discussion in the district. The police redoubled their efforts to clear up the mystery, and a wide investigation was made on Saturday night, under Detective-Inspector William Gray, of County Police Headquarters, Paisley.

The arrest was made that night by Detective-Inspector Gray and Detective-Sergeant Coull, Port-Glasgow, of a young man named Colin McMilian, an 18 year old farm servant employed at Mathernock Farm."

Dundee Courier, 28th July 1931

"in the meantime McMillan will be detained in Gateside Prison, Greenock." (Dundee Courier, 28th July 1931)

Port Glasgow Express, 29th July 1931

"On Monday large crowds assembled in the vicinity of Bank Street Hall where the young man apprehended in connection with the death of Black, appeared before Justices R. J. Gourlay and A. R. Stewart. McMillan walked calmly into the Court and stood erect in the dock while the formal proceedings, which only lasted a few minutes, were carried through. He betrayed no signs of mental strain. Mr George Armitage, Fiscal, stated that that Court had no jurisdiction in this case, and he would ask their honours to remit accused to the Sheriff of Greenock. McMillan, a tall, manly-looking youth, was brought to Court in a closed motor accompanied by Detective-Inspector Gray and other officers of Renfrewshire Constabulary.

The crowds in court made their way back to the street, after the proceedings had terminated and watched with evident interest the departure of McMillan and his police escort to the county buildings in Nelson Street." (Port Glasgow Express, 29th July 1931).

MURDER CHARGE

Dundee Evening Telegraph - Friday 31 July 1931

"SCOTS SHOOTING TRAGEDY
FARM SERVANT CHARGED WITH MURDER
Body Found by Roadside

"Colin McMillan, a farm servant, aged 18, appeared private at Greenock Sheriff Court to-day on petition by the Procurator-Fiscal charging him with the murder of Donald Black (23), farmer, of Auchenfoil Farm, Kilmacolm, Renfrewshire, and was committed to prison for further examination."

The Scotsman - Monday 31 August 1931

GLASGOW MURDER CHARGE

"... The capital charge is preferred against Colin McMillan, the indictment alleging that on June 24 or 25 on a public highway between Kilmacolm and Greenock known as the High Greenock Road at a point near to the south entrance of Auchenfoil Farm, he did assault Donald Black, residing at Auchenfoil Farm, and discharged a gun loaded with cartridges containing powder and pellets, and did murder him."

The Port Glasgow Express, Friday July 31st, 1931

"Discussing the tragic affair a brother of the dead man said: "Donald was in the habit of visiting Mathernock farm and it was nothing unusual for the family to retire to bed before he returned home no one thought of going to his bedroom to see if he was there and it was not until my mother went to waken him in the morning that she discovered the room unoccupied. I went to where the body was lying and saw it was covered with blood. Donald appeared to have been terribly injured about the chest; and it was awful to think that he had lain there all night so near his own home. "One side of his jacket was stained green where he had fallen against the telegraph pole; and there was a mark on his forehead where it rested on the walking stick. I helped detectives to search the ground and was with them when they picked up the cartridge wad and two bits of paper from a cartridge.

A cousin of the victim said: "Donald was the eldest of a family of five sons and three daughters. Eighteen months ago his father died and his uncle was in charge of the farm for about six weeks when he, too, died suddenly. Since then Donald had managed the farm for his mother. He was a hard worker and extremely popular with everyone.

"I would not have believed that he had a single enemy. He was a good living chap and neither drank nor smoked. He must have been attacked in such a way that he had not a dog's chance of fighting for his life. He was about six feet in height, powerfully built, and had amazing strength."

THE FUNERAL

The Port Glasgow Express, Friday July 31st, 1931

THE KILMACOLM TRAGEDY
Funeral of the Victim.
Attended by Large Numbers.

"As briefly indicated in "The Express on Wednesday, the funeral of Mr Donald Black, the victim of the Kilmacolm shooting tragedy of last week, took place to Kilmacolm Cemetery on Tuesday afternoon. Over 200 people were present at the farm, and it was found necessary to hold the service in the open air. Impressive scenes were witnessed during the funeral, and practically every farm in the district was represented amongst the mourners. There were also present many of the brethren from the Church of God at Greenock, to which denomination the Black family belong. Rain fell throughout the service in the farmyard, which was conducted by Mr John Miller, Ayr, and Mr Norman Miller, Rothesay. When the motor hearse moved off from the farm it was followed about 40 motor cars, and the cortege was one of the largest ever seen in the district. At every farm on the four-mile route to Kilmacolm cemetery, work was suspended for the funeral, and the workers stood bare-headed in small groups by the roadside to pay their last tribute of respect to the popular young farmer, whose tragic end has caused widespread sorrow. The cortege passed through the village of Kilmacolm, and at the cemetery was joined by another large company of mourners. A touching scene was witnessed at the graveside, when Mrs Black, the widowed mother, headed the pallbearers, and, along with her four sons and three daughters, lowered the coffin into the grave. The service at the cemetery was also conducted by Messrs John and Norman Miller, and at the close a large number of the mourners filed past the open grave.

Numerous beautiful wreaths were placed on the grave, including one from Mathernock Farm."

THE FOUR-DAY TRIAL
TUESDAY 15 – FRIDAY 19 SEPTEMBER, 1931

<u>Dundee Evening Telegraph - Tuesday 15 September 1931</u>

GLASGOW MURDER CHARGE
FARM SERVANT'S ALLEGED ASSAULT
Guns Produced in Court

A young Kilmalcolm farm servant, Colin McMillan, was the accused in a murder charge which was heard before Lord Blackburn in the High Court, Glasgow, to-day. "

<u>Port Glasgow Express, 16th September 1931</u>

"Accused was simply dressed in the blue suit and was quite composed when he entered the dock. He looked round with interest at the jury."

<u>Dundee Evening Telegraph - Tuesday 15 September 1931</u>

McMillan was charged with having on July 24 and 25, 1931, on the public highway between Kilmalcolm and Greenock, known as the Greenock Road, and the entrance to Auchenfoil Farm, assaulted Donald Black, then residing at the farm, and discharged at him a gun loaded with cartridges containing powder and pellets and murdered him.

Accused pleaded not guilty.

Mr J. Cameron, advocate-depute, and Mr A. M. M. Williamson, advocate, prosecuted, and M'Millan was defended by Mr R. M'Gregor Mitchell, K.C., and Mr M'lnnes, advocate.

The case is expected to continue till tomorrow.

GUNS AND CARTRIDGES.

There were 45 witnesses for the prosecution, the majority of them from Greenock, Gourock, Port-Glasgow, and among the productions were a single-barrelled gun and a double-barrelled gun. cartridge cases and cartridges.

First witness, James William Robertson, a Greenock photographer, explained various photographs taken by him of Auchenfoil farm steading, of the scene of the crime, and of Mathernock Farm, at which the accused was employed.

In reply to Mr M'Gregor Mitchell, witness said in the area within a mile or two of the two farms there was a number of other farms. Both Auchenfoil and Mathernock farms occupied the bottom of valley, and the ground between them was slightly undulating.

MOTHER'S EVIDENCE.

Mrs Mary Spiers Black said that she was the mother of the dead man. She was a widow and lived at Auchenfoil Farm, where her son, Donald, who was unmarried, helped in the work.

Donald was in the habit, she said of visiting Mathernock farm, where he went to see Mary Duff and latterly was going there once a fortnight. Her son had another farm, the farm of East

Green for about two years, but he was not intending going to it for some time. He was almost 23 years of age.

On Friday, 24th July, Donald had his supper about six o'clock Auchenfoil and then dressed himself to go to Mathernock Farm. Witness brushed his boots for him..."

The Scotsman, 16 Sept 1931

"...When she went to bed about nine o'clock her son had not returned, but she did not expect him to be in until much later. When witness arose about five o'clock in the morning she discovered that Donald had not been home, as his bed had not been slept in. She roused the rest of the family, and dispatched John, another son, to Mathernock to find out if Donald had stayed there overnight. John returned a little before half-past six, and said that he had found Donald lying on the roadside. She went out herself and saw the body. She did not, however, touch it.

Replying to Mr McGregor Mitchell, witness said that her son Donald had never indicated that there was any ill will between him and the accused. There was a distant relationship between the Duffs and the Blacks, Mrs Duff was a cousin of the witness's husband.

Mr McGregor Mitchell – am I right in saying that there was some family squabble about the succession to your husband of an uncle's estate? – Yes.

Was it pretty bitter? – Not too bad.

Was it not so bad as this, that anonymous letters were sent? – Not to us.

But to the other side? – Yes.

Did one of these letters threatened to burn them out? – I heard something like that was in it.

The letter said witness, was handed to the police who called at her house in an endeavour to find out the writer.

The Advocate-Depute, in re-examination—was the name of the other party in this family difference Laird? – Yes.

What was the name of the Laird who was principally concerned with in it? – Donald.

Witness added that the dispute occurred about a year ago. But that since then Donald Laird and her son had become quite friendly. She had not heard her son speak of the matter for a long time.

BODY ON ROADSIDE

John Black, 13 years of age, described how he discovered the body of his brother. Witness said that on his mother's instructions he went to Mathernock to obtain news of Donald. When he reached Horsecraigs Road he saw his brothers footprints which he could easily recognise, leading from Mathernock and he came to the conclusion that Donald had started to walk home. After he had seen the Duffs he returned, and shortly before he reached Auchenfoil he came across the body of his brother lying on the grass at the side of the road. There was blood round about his face, and Donald was lying on his right side. His walking stick lay beneath his head, and his overcoat still hung over his left arm. After advising his mother of the tragedy, witness cycled to Kilmacolm to inform the police.

In reply to the Advocate-Depute, witness said that he had heard his brother speak of McMillan as a quiet, decent young fellow. Black said that he and his brothers used to shoot over the farm lands. Witness explained that the reason why he and the other members of his family affirmed, instead of taking the oath in the ordinary manner, was because they were associated with the

Plymouth Brethren, one of whose principles was not to take the oath.

Mrs Margaret Duff, of Mathernock, stated that the accused had been in her appointment for about two years, and was a quiet, steady and hard-working lad. She did not think he was particularly friendly with anyone member of her family, and they all treated him alike. McMillan's people lived in Paisley, and it was a usual thing for him to visit them and return to the farmhouse late in the evening. On the night of the tragedy he dressed himself to go out, and she presumed that he was going to Paisley. Next morning she was in the kitchen shortly after four o'clock when she heard someone go to the sink in the scullery. She thought it was the accused. McMillan then returned to the bothy which adjoined the scullery, and remained there until he was called at five o'clock by her daughter Agnes. The family learned of the tragedy later in the morning. McMillan did not look too well and he was given a dose of medicines shortly after seven o'clock. Witness suggested that if he was feeling unwell he should go to bed for a few hours, and accused went to bed until just before midday.

NIGHT OF THE TRAGEDY

Evidence as to the relations between Donald Black and herself was given by Mary Duff (25), who also affirmed. She admitted that Black came over to the farm specially to see her, and she did not discourage him in anyway, as they were friendly, but she denied that there was ever any lovemaking. Their discussions while they were alone in the kitchen after the rest of the family had retired were confined to "casual affairs." It was customary, explained Miss Duff, for the family to retire about 10:30 P.M., and for about an hour after that she and Black would remain alone in the kitchen. This practice was observed on the evening of the tragedy, and when Black rose to go he happened to look at his watch, and her recollection was that he remarked it was 11:20 P.M. She accompanied him to the door, and they eventually parted about ten minutes later. Black donned his raincoat as he was leaving her. Continuing in a halting voice, witness recalled how she went upstairs to her room and kneeled down by a chair to say her prayers. In doing so she fell asleep, and was wakened some minutes later by the sound of a dog barking in the farmyard. The room was dark, as she had not lit the lamp, but she was able to see the courtyard fairly clearly. She heard the dog bark again, and the sound of footsteps and then a figure which she recognised to be McMillan came up the yard towards the scullery door. Just as he was reaching the door the clock downstairs struck 1 o'clock, and as it was usually about 40 minutes fast, the correct time would be roughly 12:20 A.M.

When she went downstairs in the morning about 5 o'clock McMillan was already in the kitchen, and she said that he was unusually early, a remark which brought the reply from him that he could rise better after a late night. Nothing was said at the time about his movements earlier in the evening, but later when it was known that Black had been found dead, she went into the bothy where he slept and found him in bed. "

Daily Record, 16 Sept 1931

She said she wanted to clean the place, and he said it wouldn't disturb him as he would not sleep anyway.

Witness spoke to him about Black's death, but she did not remember Colin making any reply. Later on she spoke to Colin again and told him Black had been shot, whereupon Colin replied, "It is worse than ever."

Discussing the affair with the accused, witness told him that a police officer had said it might be the result of jealousy, and witness remarked to Colin: "Who would be jealous of me?"

She did not remember Colin having said anything after this, and when she told him he would likely be questioned, seeing he went to the meetings with her, the advice she gave was to tell nothing but the truth.

SOUND OF A CAR.

In cross-examination Miss Duff said shortly before she and Donald were standing at the door before he went away, she heard the sound of a motor car approaching. It came near the farm, then, judging by the noise, it turned and went back the way it came. It was unusual for a car to be there at that time.

Agnes Duff a sister of the previous witness, spoke to having heard that the accused, a week or so before the tragedy, was rabbit-shooting on the farm. The spent cartridge she had found after Black's death was found at the place where McMillan was said to have been shooting.

The trial will be resumed to-day."

The Scotsman, 16 Sept 1931

"Did you say anything to Colin McMillan about his attending the meetings of the Plymouth Brethren with you? – I told him they might question him, and advised him to tell nothing but the truth.

Mr Cameron asked witness if she had any special interest in McMillan and was told that she spoke to him often about his Bible. They went together on occasions to the meetings of the Plymouth Brethren in Greenock, and her interest in him was more of a religious nature.

Had you another kind of interest in him? – No.

Had he any other kind of interest in you? – No. Did you prefer him to Donald Black? – No.

Did you prefer Donald to him? – No.

What were Colin's feelings towards you? – He never said anything about it.

Did he ever try to indicate in any way? – He has teased me.

In what way? – He has tickled me.

Has he ever kissed you? – No."

Dundee Courier, Wednesday 16 September 1931

"Do you know why Donald Black was coming to see you so often," asked Mr Cameron.

He never said anything to me," replied witness.

Had you any idea why he was coming? – I suppose he must have liked me."

Daily Record, 17 Sept 1931

SHOTS HEARD IN THE NIGHT.
POACHERS' STORY IN KILMACOLM MURDER TRIAL.
COUNSEL OBJECTS TO EVIDENCE.

FOOTPRINT'S and shots in the night were mentioned frequently in evidence at the resumed trial in Glasgow High Court yesterday of a young farm servant, Colin McMillan, who is charged with having murdered Dunald Black, a Kilmacolm farmer, with a shot-gun on July 24 or 25 last. Black was found shot dead by the roadside on the Greenock-Kilmacolm highway. The most graphic points of evidence were accounts by two poachers of how they heard gunshots late at night and of seeing a motor car travelling towards Greenock some time before the shots were fired. Unusual interest was also created in Court by defending counsel's searching cross-examination of police witnesses regarding footprints in the vicinity of the place where Black's body was found. It was stated that footmarks which were examined at various points were found to correspond closely with the size and shape of shoes belonging to the accused.

Counsel for the defence, however, placed particular emphasis on a police admission that no one thought of taking photographs of the prints. It was impossible to make plaster casts, several witnesses said, owing to the crumbly nature of the ground where footprints were visible.

Samuel Easdon, 4 Chalmers Street, Greenock, told how he and John Burrows, another witness, went out about eleven o'clock on the Friday night to poach in the vicinity of Auchenfoil. Farm, where Donald Black lived.

Six or seven hundred yards from Auchenfoil on the High Greenock Road the two men turned into another road and some distance along sat down to eat food they had brought with them. Neither of them had a gun. They were going to use a net. Before they turned off the main road a motor car passed them travelling towards Greenock.

HEARD TWO SHOTS

"While we we are sitting by the roadside," Easdon said, "we heard two shots being fired in quick succession. The shots must have been fired from a double barrelled gun." The sound of the shots came from a point between where the two men were sitting and Auchenfoil farm.

"I remarked to Burrows," Easton continued, "that it was an unusual thing to hear shots at that time of night. Burrows looked at his watch and saw that the time was 12.13."

They heard a dog barking before the shots were fired and again a few minutes after the shots, but they did not connect the barking with the firing.

In subsequent cross-examination, Easdon said that while he and Burrows were sitting by the roadside they heard footsteps. Easdon rose and moved along the road to see who was about. He saw two men and asked them for a match. They were on the main road walking from Greenock direction towards Auchenfoil. Witness asking for a match was a ruse to find out if the men were gamekeepers, but he saw that they were not.

Asked if he thought it strange that the people in Auehenfoil farm did not hear the shots, Easdon replied that he thought it was impossible for them not to have heard.

On Saturday witness saw a newspaper report of Black's death, which suggested that he might have been killed by a motor accident.

Speaking to Burrows, he asked if the latter remembered the motor car which had passed them travelling to Greenock. Burrows said he did not, but recalled the sound of shots.

Ea;don thought he had better get in touch with the police, and on Sunday he and Burrows went with several officers to the place where they had been sitting on Friday night. Witness and Burrows were stationed at the spot to listen for shots being fired.

First they heard a single shot being fired, then two in rapid succession. The interval between the two shots fired in succession was just the same as that between the shots they heard on Friday night. The shots seemed, however, to be further away.

COULD NOT SLEEP.

Easdon caused some amusement when being cross-examined by remarking to Counsel who questioned him regarding his poaching activities—"In these days when there are so many unemployed you have to have a go at something, sir."

Questioned about the two men he had met, witness said he asked them if they had heard shots about fifteen minutes previously. They replied that they not. The men were walking in the direction of the place where the shots must have been fired.

Burrows in his evidence, which was largely corroborative, said it was well over an hour after the shots were fired that the two men approached. The men had explained that there was a party on somewhere and they had gone for a walk as they could not sleep.

Charles Beagley and Angus McKay, who were fishing at Gryffe Dam from late on the Friday night till about four' o'clock on Saturday morning, also spoke to having heard shots quite distinctly in the early hours.

BLOOD ON ROADWAY

Robert Patrick, North Priestside farm, Kilmacolm, who is employed on a farm at Houston, said he was returning from Priestside on Friday night, and on his way met Colin McMillan. McMillan nodded, but did not speak.

The first police witness was Sergeant Gray, of Renfrewshire Constabulary, who spoke of John Black calling at Kilmacolm police station on Saturday morning early and saying that his brother was lying dead on high Greenock Road.

Along with a doctor, Sergeant Gray went to the spot where Black was found face downwards near a telegraph pole. There was blood on the roadway. When the body was taken to Auchenfoil Farm it was found there was a gunshot wound. Witness thereupon telephoned to the Procurator-Fiscal.

SUSPECTED NO ONE.

Witness at that time suspected no one in particular with regard to Black's death, and he went to Mathernock Farm to see the doctor with an open mind. On his way there he met the accused, who was with a horse and cart in a field spreading manure.

He thought McMillan was one of the Duffs, but, on going over to him, had William and John Duff pointed out to him by the accused. Both the Duffs and also McMillan were questioned by him as to their movements the night before.

At this stage in the trial Mr McGregor Mitchell, K. C., counsel for the defence, objected twice to the line the evidence was taking. When Sergeant Gray started to say that he had asked McMillan where he had been the previous night, Mr McGregor Mitchell intervened, and while the point was debated, the jury left the courtroom.

Lord Blackburn said he could not sustain the objection at this stage, but indicated that objection might be made later.

CONTRARY TO JUSTICE.

Later on, defending Counsel interposed when Counsel for the Crown asked Sergeant Gray if he had asked the accused about hearing shots.

"It is contrary to the administration of justice but there should have been continued interrogation of this lad," he said to Lord Blackburn. The Judge replied that be could not see that the smallest injustice was done, he would allow the question.

Sergeant Gray went on to say that McMillan told him he had been to Paisley to see his parents, that he had returned by the last 'bus, which reached Kilmacolm at 11.25, and that he had got back to Mathernock some time after midnight. When the Sergeant asked if he had beard gunshots, McMillan shook his head. He also shook his head when asked if he had met a motor car or anyone on the road to Mathernock.

GUNS IN FARMHOUSE.

Questions were also put by witness to the accused regarding Donald Black's visits to Mathernock. Describing subsequent police movements, Sergeant Gray spoke to finding guns, live cartridges and one spent cartridge in the farmhouse at Mathernock.

On Sunday, witness went over the fields between Mathernock and Auchenfoil, and found footprints in a cornfield and a potato field. The marks were ill-defined, and made by a plain-soled boot.

Detective Sergeant Coull, describing a visit to the farm on Saturday, July 25. said that in the bothy Inspector Gray cautioned Colin McMillan, and told him he would be detained on suspicion of having caused Black's death. The accused did not reply at once. He hesitated, then said--"I came on the last 'bus, to Kilmacolm. It was a little late." The clothes worn by McMillan on the previous night were then taken by the police, including a pair of shoes. These shoes were very wet, and the soles had been bleached white. Particles of straw or hay were adhering to them.

WHO POLISHED SHOES?

On Sunday morning witness and others went to the place where Black's body had been found, and in a field across the road from the spot a wad from a cartridge was found. In a potato field and a cornfield steps were found which pointed in certain directions. One line of footprints pointed towards Auchenfoil, the other towards Mathernock. The prints were made by plain-soled shoes.

At this point Mr McGregor Mitchell cross-examined witness in considerable detail about the shoes. Taking them up and showing them to detective Coull counsel pointed out that although according to witness's evidence they had been soaking wet they were now well polished. Had they been cleaned or done up in any way? Witness said they had gone out of his possession, but he was sure the police had not cleaned them.

By anybody else? He was asked, and caused amusement by replying, "I don't know if Professor Glaister or someone else might have done it."

Counsel suggested that the shoes were not wet as he had said, but witness stuck to his evidence in spite of the conditions the shoes were now in. When he saw the shoes after the week had passed they were still damp.

FITTED THE PRINTS.

Detective constable Allan Armour was questioned by both Counsels regarding the footprints. These he said, compared closely with the shoes.

"Was the result of your examination that the shoes fitted the prints found in the fields? Crown Counsel asked him.

"Quite well" witness replied. But that was not sufficient for counsel, who said, "This is a murder trial not a poaching offence. A man's life may depend on this. 'Quite well' is not enough. Did the shoes fit the marks well?"

Witness replied briefly "Yes."

Witness measured the footprints and also the shoes and they corresponded closely.

No photograph taken.

In cross-examination Armour said the marks were well-defined in the potato field, but not so in the cornfield, where there was grass which did not take a firm impression. It was heelmarks which showed most clearly in the cornfield.

Detective Armour and Inspector Gray who was called afterwards, admitted that the shoes had not actually been laid in the prints. They were held over the prints as closely as possible, and both witnesses were satisfied that the sizes corresponded.

"Did it ever occur to you to take photographs of the footprints?" Defending counsel asked Inspector Gray, who replied "No." And said in answer to another question that the nature of the ground made the taking of plaster casts impossible.

The hearing of the case will be continued to-day."

Daily Record, 18 Sept 1931

DOCTORS DIFFER OVER BLOODSTAINS
DRAMATIC APPEAL IN KILMACOLM MURDER TRIAL
WOMEN JURORS IN TEARS

A jury of eight women and seven men will give their verdict today in the Glasgow High Court trial of Colin McMillan a 19-year-old farm servant, who is charged with having murdered Donald Black, a Kilmacolm farmer, with a shotgun on July 24 or 25 last. The trial has lasted since the court opened on Tuesday, and all that remains now is for the Judge, Lord Blackburn, to address the jury and for the jury to say whether they consider the charge against McMillan proved or not.

CONSIDERED FROM WRONG ANGLE.
JEALOUSY NOT THE MOTIVE

Two aspects of yesterdays proceedings stood out from everything else. one was a disagreement between two famous pathologists regarding the presence of blood traces on shoes belonging to the accused. Professor John Glaister said he found definite traces of blood. Professor Sydney Smith said he had found no traces whatever.

The other striking feature was a dramatic address to the jury by Mr. McGregor Mitchell on behalf of the accused. While counsel was speaking one, if not more, of the women jurors seemed to be greatly affected and there was a suggestion of tears in their eyes. "This case has been considered by the police from an entirely wrong angle," Mr McGregor Mitchell alleged. "They jumped to a hasty and ill considered supposition that jealousy was the motive."

INNOCENCE OF THAT BOY.

"I submit that the fabric which theories and suppositions have built up has been demolished by the evidence, and instead has been erected a structure which completely proves the innocence of that boy."

The Advocate-Depute, on the other hand, submitted that the person who committed the murder of assault was the accused.

"This was a deliberate, callous, cunningly-planned and cunningly-executed murder." he declared. "The murderer must have been someone who knew Donald Black's movements and knew he would pass along that road that night." Apart from addresses to the jury, only medical evidence was given yesterday.

22 PELLETS IN BODY.

Describing the injury from which he judged Donald Black had died, Professor Glaister said that close to the breastbone there was a roundish ragged wound with charred edges. Around the upper part of the wound and on the otherwise unbroken skin were 16 small punctured wounds, and around the lower half 11 puncture wounds, such as might be produced by gun pellets. Pellets, or small shot, 22 number, were removed from the body.

Professor Glaister, photograph by T&R Annan.

Judging by the evidence of burning at the edges of the wound, Professor Glaister inferred that the muzzle of the gun was at a comparatively short distance from the body, and that the gun was fired from a distance of from nine to twelve feet. The wound sloped slightly toward the left side, and in his view, the gun muzzle was pointing downwards."

The Scotsman, 18 Sept 1931

"Evidence was given by Mr A. A. Bryson, a gunsmith's salesman, who spoke of carrying out firing tests with tho double-barrelled gun. He explained that the extractor, of the gun made special and distinctive markings on the brass of the cartridge case. The marks on the tested cases corresponded with those on the cases which were produced by the police. This concluded the case for the Crown."

18th September, 1931 - Daily Record

"Professor Glaister also spoke to having examined certain articles of clothing: then, when both the witness and Advocate Depute had referred to a pair of shoes which he had examined, the proceedings were unexpectedly held up owing to an objection by counsel for the defence, which was discussed after the jury and Professor Glaister had been asked to retire.

HEARSAY EVIDENCE.

Mr McGregor Mitchell said certain scrapings have been taken from the shoes worn by the accused, and this had been examined under a microscope. Blood corpuscles had been discovered, and he contended that the slides showing these corpuscles should have been produced in court so that the defence might have had an opportunity of examining them.

They could not rely on the hearsay evidence of Professor Glaister in a case of this kind, Mr. McGregor Mitchell declared. He pressed this objection with great seriousness as it was a matter of vital importance on a general principle. Lord Blackburn repelled the objection and said it was something novel to him and very surprising that a scientific witness who made an examination with a view to discovering how a crime has been committed or how the death of a man had resulted should be called upon to produce the whole of the paraphernalia he had employed. Such a witness, of course, was subject to cross-examination.

BLOOD ON SHOE.

It seemed to his Lordship ridiculous that a scientific witness should require to produce the whole of the material he had used. Professor Glaister could go on with his evidence.

Returning to the witness box, Professor Glaister said that on the toe-cap of the right shoe he found a small area of reddish brown material. This was found to be negative blood, after being microscopically examined.

EXPERT DISAGREES.

This view was contested by Professor Sydney Smith, who was the only witness produced by the defence. Professor Smith said he had been asked by an agent for the poor, who was preparing Mitchell's case to examine some of the productions. He felt that it was his duty in the public interest to do so. This week therefore, along with the Clerk of the Court, he made certain experiments. He went over the soles and heels of the shoes thoroughly.

"As a result of your tests did you find any trace of blood?" Mr McGregor Mitchell asked.

Not the slightest trace whatever, Professor Smith replied.

NO TRACE OF BLOOD.

He had scraped generally round the place on the soles and heels where he had presumed Professor Glaister had scraped. A point of interest was that, from the part which Professor Glaister had examined, he (the witness) got a faint pinkish solution. He could, however, get that from any sort of leather.

In none of the tests could he find any trace of blood, although the tests were of the most delicate and reliable kind which would have revealed the slightest touch of blood. He first saw the shoes on Monday, and there was no trace of blood on them then or now.

In cross-examination, Professor Smith said that if stains were allowed to dry normally without being put on a wet surface they might get them for a long period of time, for months or weeks.

DOUBLE BARREL GUN.

Professor Smith was examined closely by both counsel regarding the marks of pellets or a walking stick found beside Donald Black's body and what he deduced from them as to the distance at which the shots were fired.

When the first shot was fired he said the gun might have been pointing downwards, but at the firing of the second and fatal shot, the gun appeared to have been raised higher. From the "spread" of the pellets indicated by the marks he judged that the first shot was fired from a distance of three to four yards and the second from about six yards.

In his opinion a double-barrelled gun was used and the shots would be fired in quick succession. Lord Blackburn asked that the stick should be handed up to him so that he might examine it. When his Lordship had done so he remarked that there seemed to him to be only one mark which might have been made by a pellet.

In reply to the Advocate Depute, Professor Smith said he had not probed for a bullet, and agreed that he would do so if required.

At this stage the Judge intervened and said the Court would adjourn for lunch. "The professor can amuse himself probing the stick," he observed amid laughter. When the court resumed

Professor Smith said he had found a pellet in the stick after probing one of the marks.

In his addressed to the jury the Advocate Depute, after submitting that Donald Black was killed as a result of a murderous attack and that the accused was the man who committed the assault, said it was a significant fact that the only routes by which the dead man could have approached his home converged at a certain point 200 yards from Auchenfoil Farm.

The murderer therefore lay in wait for him, knowing that it was deceased's only possible way of returning. It was also the farthest point from the farm at which he could be sure of meeting Black.

THE ACCUSED'S LIE.

Advocate Depute laid strong emphasis on the fact that the accused had told a falsehood in saying that he had got the last 'bus to Kilmacolm and that it had arrived late. The evidence showed that he travelled from Paisley by a 'bus which reached Kilmacolm at 10:45, and it had also been proved that the last 'bus was not late on Friday, July 24.

"We have the footprints, the blood, and the lie," the Advocate Depute reminded the jury, and also recalled to them the existence of what he described as the "mysterious triangle."

Mr McGregor Mitchell open his address on a dramatic note.

"That boy," he said softly, "is as innocent as you or I. He does not lose one shred of his innocence by being put in the dock and accused of a grave crime until they prove by clear and consistent evidence that his was the hand which killed Donald Black."

It was at this point that one of the jurywoman seemed to be in tears.

NO COURTSHIP.

Mr McGregor Mitchell went on to argue that the Crown case was built up on theories and suppositions which, he said, counted for nothing. The Crown had got to establish and put facts before the jury.

Regarding the supposed "triangle," there was no evidence that there had been any courtship, tristes, lovemaking of any kind between the girl Mary Duff and either Donald Black or Colin McMillan. With regard to McMillan it was obvious that the girl had simply taken a religious interest in him.

Regarding the night of the crime itself, Mr McGregor Mitchell asked did you find the accused skulking back to the farm concealing his movements and slipping in quietly? On the contrary, Mary Duff saw him return at 12:20, and, according to those who heard the shots, these were fired at 12:13, leaving an interval of seven minutes."

Could the accused, he asked, have travelled a mile across rough country, over barbed wire fences and hedges, carrying a gun in that short time? That, to put it mildly, was very far-fetched.

The Scotsman - Saturday 19 September 1931

NOT GUILTY
Closing Scenes of Farm Tragedy Trial
A MAJORITY VERDICT

"The trial of Colin McMillan, the 18-year-old farm labourer, on a charge of murdering Donald Black (23), a Kilmacolm farmer, concluded yesterday at Glasgow High Court with the acquittal of the accused. He was found not guilty by a majority verdict of the jury on a charge of shooting Black some distance from his farm at Auchenfoil, Kilmacolm, on July 24 or 25.

The jury, which was composed of eight women and seven men, were absent for almost half an hour. When their verdict was announced someone at the back of the Court exclaimed, "Hear hear," but otherwise there was no demonstration.

Tense silence reigned when Lord Blackburn addressed the accused and told him that he was now discharged. McMillan, a lightly-built young man above the medium height, appeared to be slightly dazed, and hesitated for a few seconds in the dock before stepping out into the well of the Court. Then he stopped momentarily behind the defending counsel, slowly turned, and, walking past the jury, proceeded to the back of the Court where he was escorted out by a police officer. His friends joined him in the lobby, and together they left the building. Throughout the entire proceedings McMillan appeared to be quite unperturbed by the ordeal through which he was passing.

For three-quarters of an hour Lord Blackburn addressed the jury in summing up the case, and both at the beginning and end of his speech he emphasised the importance of not allowing themselves to be influenced by the youth of the accused. Although the evidence had been very detailed, he thought there were only three or four matters which required their close attention. Murder was sometimes erroneously thought to mean that someone intentionally and deliberately killed a fellow-creature. It did not matter whether intention to kill was present in the mind of the assailant; it did not matter whether the person who fired the shot meant to kill, to injure, or to give him a fright.

QUESTION OF SYMPATHY

An eloquent appeal, he said, had been made to their sympathy that the boy was only 19 years of age. From one point of view his age was of no importance whatever. When they came to consider the facts of the case in a very careful light he asked them to put out of their mind the question of sympathy for the boy. If any sympathy was property due, it was to the mother of the unfortunate lad and to his young brother who were left to find him lying at the side of the road. From the evidence they knew that Black left the farm about 11.30 P.M., and there were two or three routes he could take to go home, and they all met very close to the point where he was assaulted and killed. The first point in the case was strongly in favour of the accused. When a crime like murder was committed, the first question one naturally asked — who had any motive to commit the crime? So far as the Crown was concerned they had failed completely to show there was any motive on the part of the accused. The next point was strongly against the accused. He had stated that he had been to Paisley, and had returned by the last bus, but they had the evidence of the bus owner and conductor that he returned home by an earlier bus, and arrived back at Kilmacolm at 10.45 P.M. He reached the cross-roads three minutes later. Why did he say he came back by the later bus? It was a singularly unfortunate statement for him to have made. It was clear that if he had come by the later bus it would have been difficult for him to get to the farm, get the gun, and be down to the place where Donald Black was shot. It was unfortunate he came by that bus, as the Court was left entirely uninformed as to what he had been doing between ten minutes to 11 P.M. and 12.30 A.M., when ho was seen coming into the farm.

MYSTERY OF THE SHOES

A feature in his favour was that if he had gone up to Mathernock Farm, got the gun and cartridges, he must have done so extremely quietly and cunningly, because nobody saw nor heard him, and Mary Duff and Donald Black were in the kitchen the whole time. There was not a particle of evidence to suggest he did so, but he might have done so, and it was a matter for the jury to consider whether he did so, and if so committed the crime. The evidence did not come to more than that he had the opportunity. Another point which would have to be carefully considered was wrapped in mystery. That was the evidence relating to the boy's shoes. When they were discovered by the police in his room they were said to be sodden wet, and with bits of corn and grass on them. When produced they were perfectly clean and polished. Whether McMillan committed the murder or not the shoes could not have been in the condition in which they were produced, considering he had been wearing them for several hours in a wet countryside. He had to advise them, however, that they could only accept the shoes as evidence as they had been submitted in Court. Dealing with the evidence of the experts as to the alleged bloodstains on the soles of the shoes, his Lordship said the evidence of Professor Glaister had been countered by Professor Sydney Smith.

MODERN YOUTH CRITICISED

In conclusion, Lord Blackburn impressed on the jury not to be influenced in any way by the age of the accused. The youth of the present generation, he said, was rather different to what it was years ago, and instead of settling their differences with one another with the instruments provided by Nature—their fists— they used knives, razors, and explosive weapons. It would be a serious matter if it went out that such courses could be followed with impunity because juries would acquit the accused persons on account of their youth.

At the close of the Court proceedings, his Lordship, in a brief speech, congratulated the Corporation on the light nature of the calendar, and one which did not contain a disgusting case in which small children were involved. Bailie Armstrong, replying for the Corporation, said he thought the moral tone of the city was higher now than it had ever been."

GRANNY ORR'S VERDICT

Granny Orr gave her own verdict on the outcome of the case. Her diary entry on 22 September 1931 reads:

"The trial of Colin McMillan for murder lasted 4 days. He got off, not guilty although it could have been proved he was guilty. Witnesses were never asked. Mitchel and Smith who spoke for him were unscrupulous rascals, all to win their case."

Eternity will reveal the truth.

Wee Willie

The short life of William Orr Johnson

"Wee Willie's" death certificate records the bald facts underlying this family tragedy. Born 25th June 1915, he died on 2nd March, 1919 at 4 am. Age 3 yrs 8 months. Cause of death, Influenza and Meningitis.

John Holmes Johnson (the editor's father), was born on 22nd May 1918. He was 11 months old when his brother William died.

Granny Orr recorded this entry in March 1919:

"End of March – Robert myself and father all had the flu for 5 weeks. Getting better. Jean Manson came one day when I was ill. Mary came two weeks to nurse then Janet 3 weeks."

So, three of the family at Gateside, had flu for five weeks, from the last week in February until the end of March 1919. It is therefore a possibility, although there is no evidence of this, that someone who visited the Orrs at Gateside also visited or came into contact with one of the Johnsons in Greenock around the end of February, and passed on the flu infection to 'Wee Willie'.

Even if there had been no contact between Gateside and Baxter Street Greenock, anyone in Greenock who was infected with the 'flu, might have passed it on. At this time, according to Granny Orr's diary entry in February 1918, his father Joe Johnson was working at Harland and Wolf's in Glasgow (Wee Willie's death certificate lists his father's occupation as Shipwright). Joe must have mixed with many people in the course of his work. He could easily have carried the virus home with him. Perhaps the absence of any mention of 'Wee Willie's' death in Granny Orr's diary, suggests that the depth of grief she shared with her daughter was so great, that the only way she could cope with the loss of her much loved grandson, was to block it out.

Granny Orr's diary entries about Wee Willie:

<u>25th June 1915</u> I went to Rothesay. Janet had a son that night to be called William Orr.

<u>13th May 1916</u> Janet came with wee Willie. He's now a year old.

<u>15th August 1916</u> Our Janet and baby came stayed 3 nights. Ria went to Rothesay with her. Came back that night.

<u>14th October 1916</u> Janet came to stay a while. Joe working in Greenock and stayoing with his sister. Wee Willie 17 months old, very tall & is just walking about a chair.

<u>1st January 1917</u> A quiet New Year. Wee Willie took ill the day before. He soon got better.

<u>31st August 1917</u> Wee Willie just commencing to say "Ta"

<u>22nd March 1918</u> Janet and Joe & wee Willie came. Went home at night. Joe a good lot better.

<u>21st May 1918</u> Janet had her second son. called John Holmes.

<u>20th September 1918</u> Janet and her two boys drove to Auchenfoil with James in gig.

'Wee Willie' was 3 years and 3 months old in September 1918. There is no mention of him after that. He died just five months later, on 2nd March, 1919.

The anonymous, handwritten poem entitled 'Mt Gathered Lily' on the next two pages, was found by Wee Willie's brother John, after his mother Janet died in 1956. The paper and the handwriting appear to be of an older generation, so it may have been written or copied by one of her maternal forbears. Whatever the circumstances, it poignantly sums up the feelings of a mother who has lost a child.

My Gathered Lily

My lovely little Lily, thou wert gathered very soon,
In the fresh and dewy morning, not in the glare of noon;
The Saviour sent His angels, to bear thee hence, my own,
And they'll plant thee in that garden, where decay is never known.

How peacefully, how sweetly, ebbed thy little life away,
Oh blessed for ever be the God, who heard thy mother pray;
She did not wish to keep thee in this world of sin and strife,
But she wished that thou without a pang might yield thy little life.
She watched thee, how she watched thee,
  thro' that anxious night and day,
And only turned her eyes from thee, to look to heaven and pray!
"Deal gently with my darling!" Was still her fervent cry,
And--"Trust me with thy little one", seemed still the Lord's reply.

My Lily, Oh! My lily! I saw thee hour by hour,
Still drooping nearer to the earth, my pale and precious flower!
And as I marked the glazing eye and felt the cheek grow cold--
The mingled thoughts that filled my heart, they never can be told.

'Twas in thy mother's arms, my own, thou didst resign thy breath,
And she will bless her God for that, till she too smiles in death!
Oh! tenderly indeed, my babe the Saviour dealt with us,
When He in pitying love disarmed, the king of terrors thus.
One long drawn sigh thy mother heard,
from thy unconscious breast,
And then she saw thy eyelids close, and knew thou wert at rest;
She pressed her lips upon thy cheek, how icy cold it felt!
And turning from thy chamber then, she went apart and knelt.

And often, often, ere it came, that last, sad, solemn day,
Beside thy cradle coffin she would sit, and gaze and pray;
And never, never from her heart, can thy sweet image fade,
So pure, so white, so still, so cold as if of marble made.

And when at length the day was come,-the solemn parting day,
That saw thee from thy earthly home, my loved one, borne away,
Still, still, my God was with me, and I was not seen to weep,
When they laid thee in the quiet tomb,
where thy father's kindred sleep.

And years have passed away since then, and many a joy and care,
Have filled by turns thy mother's heart,
in which thou had'st no share;
But still within that heart she keeps one sacred spot for thee,
And thine my Lily, thine alone, that spot shall ever be.

And often when I kneel in prayer, I thank my Saviour yet,
For all his tender love to thee which I can ne'er forget;
And when I pray for those I love, still left on earth with me,
I ask my God to deal with them as gently as with thee.

My Gathered Lily

My lovely little Lily, thou wert gathered very soon,
In the fresh & dewy morning, not in the glare of noon;
The Saviour sent His angels, to bear thee hence, my own,
And they'll plant thee in that garden, where decay is never known.

How peacefully & how sweetly ebbed thy little life away.
Oh blest for ever be the God, who heard thy mother pray;
She did not wish to keep thee in this world of sin & strife,
But she wished that thou without a pang, might yield thy little life.

She watched thee, how she watched thee, thro' that anxious night & day,
And only turned her eyes from thee, to look to Heaven & pray!
"Deal gently with my darling!" was still her fervent cry,
And—"Trust Me with thy little one", seemed still the Lord's reply.

My Lily! oh! my Lily! I saw thee hour by hour,
Still drooping nearer to the earth, my pale & precious flower!
And as I marked the glazing eye & felt the cheek grow cold—
The mingled thoughts that filled my heart, they never can be told.

'Twas in thy mother's arms, my own, thou didst resign thy breath,
And she will bless her God for that, till she too sinks in death!
Oh! tenderly indeed, my babe, the Saviour dealt with us,
When He in pitying love, disarmed the king of terrors thus.

"My Gathered Lily" page 1

One long-drawn sigh thy mother heard, from thy unconscious breast,
And then she saw thy eyelids close, & knew they were at rest;
She pressed her lips upon thy cheek, how icy cold it felt!
And turning from thy chamber then, she went apart & knelt—

And often, often, ere it came, that last, sad, solemn day,
Beside thy cradle coffin she would sit, & gaze & pray,
And never, never from her heart, can thy sweet image fade,
So pure, so white, so still, so cold, as if of marble made.

And when at length the day was come,—the solemn parting day
That saw thee from thy earthly home, my loved one, borne away;
Still, still, my God was with me, & I was not seen to weep,
When they laid thee in the quiet tomb, where thy father's kindred sleep.

And years have passed away since then, & many a joy & care,
Have filled by turns thy mother's heart, in which thou hadst no share;
But still within that heart she keeps one sacred spot for thee,
And there, my Lily, thine alone, that spot shall ever be—

And often when I kneel in prayer, I thank my Saviour yet,
For all His tender love to thee, which I can ne'er forget;
And when I pray for those I love, still left on earth with me,
I ask my God to deal with them as gently as with thee.

"My Gathered Lily" page 2

Mr Norman D.W. Miller

On 29th May 1938, Granny Orr went to hear Mr Norman Miller preaching at the Church of God in Greenock. Below, is an extract from a letter written by 98 year-old Hannah Morgan, who shared her memory of Mr Norman D. W. Miller, who preached at the Church of God in Peckham, London in the 1920s.

"Mr Norman Miller [1878-1940] was a great teacher and full of love for the Lord, as he unfolded to us the prophecies in the Bible night after night for 4 weeks. They were addresses one could not miss they were such a wonderful revealing of the things to come. I took a number of notes, so I have not forgotten and Mr Miller's stirring ministry remained with me."

In the following pages I have reproduced the text of a booklet written by N.D.W. Miller, which hints at the kind of preaching Granny Orr would have heard. It was originally published as a booklet by the Needed Truth Publishing Office, now known as Hayes Press—the publishing arm of The Churches of God.[1] (N.D.W. Miller = Norman Daniel William Miller - b. 1878 d. 1940).

27 YEARS WASTED
by N.D.W. Miller.

SALVATION is not of works (Ephesians 2. 9). It is "to him that worketh not" (Romans 4. 5): "Not by works done in righteousness, which we did ourselves" (Titus 3. 5).

These are among the many scriptures which attest this fact. Salvation is of Grace. "By grace have ye been saved through faith" (Ephesians 2. 8). And, says the Apostle, "I do not make void the grace of God: for if righteousness is through the law, then Christ died for nought" (Galatians 2. 21). "We reckon therefore that a man is justified by faith apart from the works of the law" (Romans 8. 28).

Twenty-seven years wasted! These words, forming the heading of this brief testimony, are associated with an incident which occurred in Scotland, where I was preaching Christ.

I noticed a man in the audience who seemed to be paying little or no attention, until, well on toward the end of the address, I happened to quote, "Upon this Rock I will build My Church." Instantly I had his ear, so much so, that at the end of the meeting, after others had gone, he waited behind and asked me for an explanation of the words, and if I would kindly jot down any kindred passages and let him have them the following night. As it happened, he was absent for about a week through illness, but as soon as he was better he came again. That night I was speaking about Law and Grace, and I could not help noticing that the man became more and more disturbed—so much was this so, that when everybody else had gone, he kept his seat. Then rising, and coming up to the front, he said, addressing me, "I must unburden my heart before I leave this place." So, assuring him of a patient hearing, he unburdened his heart for about half an hour. The gist of what he said was—"For twenty-seven years I have been a member of the Church of England. I'm a High-churchman, I love my church and I love my priest. A fortnight ago my priest gave me absolution. I confess I felt no better after what he said, but I had implicit confidence in him. I assure you I have strenuously endeavoured to the utmost of my ability to merit the favour of Almighty God. For twenty-seven years I have conscientiously attended my church, and have sought to be guided by my priest. And now, I come here, to a place like this, and I listen to you. If what you say is true, my twenty-seven years of strenuous endeavour all goes for nothing: you say it has been wasted time." This is the gist of what he told me; but no words of mine can convey to the reader the intense earnestness of the man, nor yet the evident distress of his soul. Having thus unburdened his heart, I asked him if he would now listen—not to me—but to what God had to say; for he had assured me that he believed the Bible to be the word of God from Genesis to the Revelation. So I quietly read to him from many parts of the Scriptures about Christ and His finished work; such as, that God "laid on Him the iniquity of us all" (Isaiah 53.); and how that "Christ died for our sins according to the Scriptures" (1 Corinthians 15.); how that He was "delivered up for our trespasses, and was raised for our justification" (Romans 4. 25), and how that God says, "By Him every one that believeth is justified from all things, from which ye could not be justified by the law of Moses" (Acts 13. 39). I shall never forget the effect it had upon him when I last of all quoted Galatians 2. 21—"If righteousness is through the law, then Christ died for nought." "If," said I, "your twenty-seven years of strenuous endeavour could have gained you entrance into the Courts above, there was no need for Christ to have come down here and to have suffered the dread agonies of the Cross. If you, or any other one, could possibly get righteousness by good works or law-keeping—THEN CHRIST DIED FOR NOUGHT." He shook with emotion, and, putting his elbows on his knees, and his head in his hands, he sobbed like a child.

Then, as we waited, the silence was broken by his slowly repeating from a full heart:—

> *"Just as I am, without one plea,*
> *But that Thy blood was shed for me,*
> *And that Thou bidd'st me come to Thee,*
> *O Lamb of God, I come!*
>
> *Just as I am, poor, wretched, blind;*
> *Sight, riches, healing of the mind,*
> *Yea, all I need, in Thee to find,*
> *O Lamb of God, I come!*
>
> *Just as I am, Thou wilt receive,*
> *Wilt welcome, pardon, cleanse, relieve;*
> *Because Thy promise I believe,*
> *O Lamb of God, I come!*
>
> *Just as I am — Thy love unknown-*
> *Has broken every barrier down-*
> *Now to be Thine, yea, Thine alone,*
> *O Lamb of God, I come!"*

"Ah," said he, "I learned that hymn when I was a little boy at my mother's knee, and many a time I have sung it since, but never as I can sing it now." (We had been singing that well-known hymn at the close of the meeting.)

The man had found Christ and had let Him in. He had let the Saviour into a heart formerly filled with so-called good works and strenuous endeavour, but that heart of his had been a Christless heart. Great was now his peace, and very evident his joy; but I cannot forget his face as he seemed to scan the past and to repeat—as if more to himself than to me—"twenty-seven years wasted!"

In rejoicing with him, I could only impress upon him it was a cause for thankfulness, that even after these many years his blind eyes had now been opened by Him Who said, "He that followeth Me shall not walk in the darkness, but shall have the light of life" (John 8. 12).

He might have gone on, as, alas, so many choose to do, blindly following "blind leaders of the blind."

Ere I put down my pen, may I ask, What about the reader? Are you safe in Christ, and the happy possessor of eternal life—God's gift? If not, then, whatever your age, and however your years may have been spent, I tell you plainly—yours are wasted years.

> *"O the years of sinning wasted,*
> *Could I but recall them now;*
> *I would give them to the Saviour*
> *To His will I'd gladly bow."*

Is that it? Then Come to Him now! Make your decision now! CHOOSE CHRIST! "He that believeth on the Son hath eternal life: and he that believeth not the Son shall not see life; but the wrath of God abideth on him" (John 8. 36).

N. D. W. MILLER.

Note: The other evangelist, Mr John Miller, was unrelated to Norman Miller. His prolific writings can be found in the online archives of the magazines published by the Churches of God.

---

1. **The Churches of God website:** https://churchesofgod.info/

Glossary of old Scots words used in the Granny's Diaries

brae: A steep hill.

Clecken: *v.* To hatch

Delve: to dig over a garden.

Gey: (the 'ey' is pronounced like the 'i' in bike or like). Meaning very, extremely, or, to a great extent—e.g., 'it's gey wet' = 'it is very wet'.

Howking: Digging up.

Jade: A term of abuse applied to a woman.

Kye: cattle

Midden: The dung heap. Kitchen waste e.g., potato peelings, eggshells and other scraps of food waste were also dumped there.

Ne'erday; Nerdy: New Year's Day

Quay: A young cow up to three years old which has not calved; a heifer.

Roup: an agricultural auction sale

Shifts: possibly, a change of clothes; or items made from fabric.

Snell: biting, keen, piercing, bitter, severe.

Wean/Weans - a contraction of 'wee' and 'ones' - as in 'wee-anes' - which then became 'weans' or as some spell it, 'wains'. A colloquial Scottish term for a child or children.

Acknowledgments

The map of Renfrewshire and Kilmacolm area is reproduced by kind permission of the National Library of Scotland. The various adverts for Greenock businesses which appear at the end of selected chapters, are also taken from the border surrounding this old map, which I found among documents belonging to my father.

The photographs of the Motorcade at the Glasgow International Exhibition, 1901 (p. vi), the Opening Parade at the 1901 Glasgow International Exhibition, (p. 81) and Professor Glaister, (p. 436), are reproduced by kind permission of Douglas Annan, (T & R Annan & Sons Ltd). Douglas is the custodian of a treasure-trove of early photographic images taken in Scotland by Thomas Annan and company before and around the turn of the 19th Century. This unique archive can be found online here: http://www.annanphotographs.co.uk. Prints are available from Douglas Annan, who represents the fifth generation of that illustrious family.

Carriage & Pair illustration (p. 56): Public Domain image, https://www.oldbookillustrations.com/illustrations/upon-top/

Photo Potato Howking, (p. 89), courtesy Museum of Hartlepool, https://www.flickr.com/photos/hartlepool_museum/6004547671

Photo of Black and White Collie (p. 94), by Chung Nguyen on Unsplash [https://unsplash.com/photos/kJlk-jW2nLI]

Photo of Emmy Souter of South Cave with bicycle c.1900s, (p. 153) courtesy East Riding Archives, https://www.flickr.com/photos/erarchives/25970739593/

Photo of horn gramophone (p. 204), by alerkiv (Alexander, Kiev) on Unsplash [https://unsplash.com/photos/agbFkAlsu48]

Photo of milk churns, (p. 227), by Kevin Woblick on Unsplash [https://unsplash.com/photos/C12Li0ws590]

Sideboard image (p. 231), Courtesy, British Library / Flikr Commons — [https://www.flickr.com/photos/britishlibrary/11082372354/]

Image of Clyde Steamers at Greenock (p. 243), courtesy British Library / Flikr Commons — [https://www.flickr.com/photos/britishlibrary/11189474646]

Photo of Kilmacolm Cemetery (p. 298) by wfmiller - https://www.geograph.org.uk/photo/1525418 (© wfmillar (cc-by-sa/2.0)

Photo Silver Jubilee 1935, (p. 336) public domain, Wikepdia: https://en.wikipedia.org/wiki/Silver_Jubilee_of_George_V

Photo Annie S. Swan (p. 383), public domain, Wikipedia: [https://en.wikipedia.org/wiki/Annie_S._Swan]

Photo of pigs (p. 375), by Daniel Kirsch, Pixabay: https://pixabay.com/photos/pig-piglet-happiness-suckle-drink-4453303/

Other photographs from the estate of John and Jean Johnson.

About the Editor

Jo Johnson, lives in Fife, Scotland, half an hour's drive from St Andrews. With his wife Norma, he divides his time between church, family, writing, tending his allotment and painting.

Photographs of the original diary pages from the three notebooks kept by the two grannies, can be found on:

jojohnson.uk

Send Jo an email:
jojohnsonart@gmail.com

Other stuff:
https://sleek.bio/jojohnson